THE COMPLETE
Gone With the Wind
SOURCEBOOK

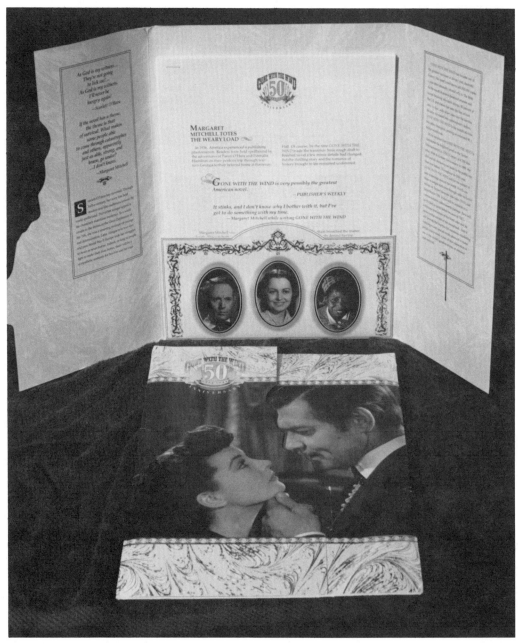

The *Gone With the Wind* 50th anniversary media kit.

THE COMPLETE
GONE WITH THE WIND
SOURCEBOOK

Pauline Bartel

Taylor Publishing Company
Dallas, Texas

Also by Pauline Bartel
The Complete GONE WITH THE WIND Trivia Book

Published by Taylor Publishing Company
    1550 West Mockingbird Lane
    Dallas, Texas 75235

Designed by Barbara Whitehead

**Library of Congress
Cataloging-in-Publication Data**

Bartel, Pauline C.
    The complete gone with the wind sourcebook / by Pauline Bartel.
       p.   cm.
    ISBN 0-87833-817-9 (sc)
    1. Gone with the wind (Motion picture).   2. Motion pictures-
-Collectibles.   I. Title.
PN1997.G59B365   1993
791.43—dc20   92–35649
                                                    CIP

Printed in the United States of America

10 9 8 7 6 5 4 3 2 1

To Janet Nardolillo *and to* David Lee Drotar
for their wise counsel and special friendship

A rare signed first edition of *Gone With the Wind*.
(The collection of John Wiley Jr.)

Contents

Scarlett coasters. *(The Turner Store)*

Acknowledgments   ix
Introduction   xi

I   Starting a Collection   1
   1   How to Begin
   4   Abbreviations Used in This Book

II   GWTW Collectibles of Today   5
   5   Audio
   6   Autographs
   7   Books
  11   Ceramics
  16   Clocks
  17   Clothing
  22   Dolls
  30   Edibles
  30   Film and Video
  42   Games, Puzzles, and Toys
  45   Jewelry
  46   Linens
  47   Music Boxes
  49   Needlecrafts
  50   Paper
  55   Plates
  58   Posters, Prints, and Photographs
  64   Scripts
  65   Stationery
  66   This and That
  69   Tote Bags

III   Acquiring Vintage GWTW Collectibles   71
  71   How to Judge Authenticity
  73   Assessing the Condition of a Collectible
  75   Finding and Buying Collectibles
  79   The Action at Auctions
  81   Locating Opportunities to Buy
  83   How to Get Connected to a Collector's Network
  86   Bargaining at Collectible Shows
  86   Trading

IV   GWTW Collectibles from Yesterday   89
   89   Auctions
   92   Autographs
   97   Books
  103   Ceramics
  103   Clothing
  105   Dolls
  111   Jewelry
  113   Paper
  121   Posters
  128   Records
  131   This and That

V   Searching for GWTW Collectibles   133
  133   What a Search Service Can Offer to the Collector
  133   Directory of Search Services
  135   A Glossary of Book Terms

VI   Caring for Your GWTW Collection   139
  139   How to Display Your Collection
  141   Caring for Your Collectibles
  144   Preparing an Inventory
  145   Insuring Your Collection
  146   Restoration
  147   Storing a Collection
  149   Selling Your Collectibles
  153   Estate Disposal of Collectibles

VII   Resources for GWTW Collectors   154
  154   Books
  156   Periodicals
  158   Organizations
  158   Suppliers
  161   Sample Inventory Sheet

VIII   The Ins and Outs of Buying by Mail   162
  162   Catalogs—Frequency and Cost
  162   Getting a Price Quote
  163   Comparison Shopping
  163   Ways to Pay
  163   Shipping
  163   Return Policies
  163   Tips for Successful Buying
  164   Second Choices and Substitutions
  164   How to Resolve Problems

Bibliography   166

The *Gone With the Wind* movie tie-in edition in hardcover.

Acknowledgments

I AM indebted to the following individuals for their assistance, support, and encouragement during the preparation of this book: Arline Alfieri of World Doll; my mother, Mary F. Bartel; Terry Brown; Kevin Callahan of Bob Callahan Agency, Inc.; Debbie Casale; Shelly Charles of The Turner Store; Mary Dee of Mary D's Dolls & Bears & Such; Karen DeMartino; my editor, Jim Donovan; my photographer, James Goolsby; Pamela Hatchfield of the American Institute for Conservation of Historic and Artistic Works; Jennifer Jones; Jan Lebow; Sheila Levine; members of The Arnold Madison Writers Group (Jackie Craven, David Lee Drotar, Joyce Hunt, Kate Kunz, Peg Lewis, Marie Musgrove, Jane Streiff, Donna Tomb); Carol and Alice Michon; Janet Nardolillo; James Nehring; Julia Payne; Jacquelyn Peake; Doreen Shea; Carole Stallone; Sean Sullivan of The Waterford Public Library; Lynne Van Derhoof; John Wiley, Jr.; Alyson Wyckoff; and most especially, George.

The author's first *Gone With the Wind* collectible.

Introduction

"I'LL go home, and I'll think of some way to get him back. After all, tomorrow is another day."

Almost as soon as a tearful Scarlett O'Hara spoke those never-to-be-forgotten words, I dried my own tears and thought about tomorrow, too. Tomorrow I would begin collecting anything and everything I could find related to *Gone With the Wind*. That was more than twenty-five years ago, but I still remember the joy of discovering the first piece of memorabilia that began my GWTW collection.

The small shop just off Main Street in my hometown of Poughkeepsie, New York, featured tie-dyed clothing, leather belts, incense, and dubious smoking paraphernalia. But there in the window was a poster of W. C. Fields. I thought well . . . maybe, and walked in the door.

"Do you have any other movie posters?" I asked the long-haired clerk behind the counter. He directed me to the back of the shop where posters of Humphrey Bogart, Marilyn Monroe, and Steve McQueen hung on the wall. On the floor, tucked into a corner was a large, round bin stuffed with rolled-up posters. I hunted eagerly through the posters having no idea what I would uncover. After a few minutes of searching, I finally struck gold. One of the posters I unrolled showed Clark Gable as Rhett Butler playing cards in the Yankee jail. He looked so handsome with his dashing cape and glowing cigar that I purchased the poster immediately.

Since that long-ago afternoon when I bought my first *GWTW* collectible, my acquisitions have included other posters, commemorative plates, autographs, dolls, books, newspapers and magazines, buttons, fans, and other items that truly make a collection eclectic. Most of the pieces were gathered serendipitously.

There's a thrill in stumbling upon a little-expected treasure. Yet there's a frustration, too, in wanting a particular item and not knowing when, or if, it will be found. For example, I once encountered a woman wearing a crystal *GWTW* initial pin and asked her where she had bought it. She replied that it had been a gift. It took me more than a year to find the same pin through a movie-memorabilia specialty store.

Are you looking for the latest *GWTW* collector plate or perhaps for a reproduction of the flaming-embrace poster? No matter what you're searching for, you'll find hundreds of items listed in *The Complete GONE WITH THE WIND Sourcebook*. The items are arranged by category—for example, Autographs, Dolls, Edibles, and Tote Bags. Within each category are listed the mail-order sources for the items, descriptions of each source's specialties, and complete ordering information.

The *Sourcebook* includes collectibles from today—tee-shirts, music boxes, mugs, for example; and memorabilia from yesterday—premiere programs, lobby cards, out-of-print books on *GWTW*, and so forth. There's even information on finding *GWTW* items through collectible shows, auctions and trades, plus valuable tips on caring for, storing, and insuring your collection, and much more. If you're starting your collection or adding to an existing one, *The Complete GONE WITH THE WIND Sourcebook* is your source for the collectibles and memorabilia you want.

Attention Readers!

With periodic updating, The *Complete GONE WITH THE WIND Sourcebook* will become the definitive reference for *Gone With the Wind* collectors. And that's where you can help.

If you know of a mail-order source that should be included in the next edition, please let me know. Also, tell me if you are unhappy with any response you receive from one of the listed companies. I will take all of your recommendations into consideration for the next edition.

I also call upon merchants or manufacturers of *Gone With the Wind* collectibles to respond as well. If you would like to be listed in the next edition or if your mailing address or telephone number has changed since this book went to press, please contact me and send a copy of your latest catalog.

I sincerely thank all those individuals and companies who participated in this edition and look forward to future editions of *The Complete GONE WITH THE WIND Sourcebook*.

Pauline Bartel
Post Office Box 491
Waterford, NY 12188–0491

THE COMPLETE

Gone With the Wind

SOURCEBOOK

Starting a Collection

How to Begin

AFTER I saw *Gone With the Wind* for the first time, I decided to begin collecting anything and everything I could find related to this magnificent movie. I soon learned that this was a noble yet impossible goal. There are simply too many items of *GWTW* memorabilia to collect, and the highly desired collectibles have big-ticket price tags.

Pursuing this goal, I realized, would force me either to fill every nook and cranny of my house with all the items I uncovered or to haul the more-prized collectibles along with me to the poor house. So I worked out a compromise by focusing on a specific area of collecting and determining how much money I wanted to spend on my hobby.

Focus the Collection. Since I adored the movie, I decided to focus my collection on memorabilia from the film. If you love the book, you may choose to focus your collection on the memorabilia honoring Mitchell's epic.

Within each area of focus, there are countless areas of specialization. For example, I collect *GWTW* film memorabilia that features Clark Gable tie-ins, including posters, photographs, books, and maga-

A *GWTW* collector might specialize in Scarlett tie-ins like this doll. *(World Doll)*

zines. Other film aficionados may choose to specialize in memorabilia of Vivien Leigh, Hattie McDaniel, any of the other *GWTW* players, costume designer Walter Plunkett, or producer David O. Selznick, for instance.

A collector with an affinity for the book might have a specific interest in Margaret Mitchell memorabilia and may acquire signed first editions, Mitchell letters, and biographies. Another bibliophile may want to collect only foreign editions of *GWTW*. By focusing your collection, you'll pursue acquisition realistically, build a more cohesive collection, and have more money for the expensive collectibles you really want.

Determine How Much Money To Spend. When I began my collection, I was a sophomore in high school, working part-time as a file clerk. I earmarked half of my meager salary for collecting, opened a savings account, and made weekly deposits. In this way, I had funds available whenever I found a *GWTW* item that I wanted to buy. Since then my savings priorities have changed. But there's still a small amount I tuck away into a savings account dedicated to my growing *GWTW* collection.

Determine how much money you can afford to spend for collectibles and work that figure into your budget. The amount you budget will not only depend on your other obligations but on the kind of collectibles you want to acquire. New collectibles such as plates are fairly affordable while vintage items such as signed first editions are more costly. Begin a systematic method of saving, and you'll have ready, guilt-free money to spend on the collectibles you love. And think of the collectibles in that way— as things you love. Many collectors who approach collecting as an investment are often sorely disappointed. But if you approach collecting as something you do for the joy of it, your riches will be unending.

Here are some other suggestions to help you start your collection:

• Become a student of your collecting area. Read and study price guides, books, and magazines about the collectibles in which you are interested; attend collecting forums; talk to dealers and other collectors; view the collections of others, especially those collections on display in museums or historical centers. Only by becoming immersed in your special collecting area will you be able to rely on your own judgment to determine which items are worth adding to your collection, whether an item is an original or a reproduction, or if the price quoted by the seller is a fair one.

• Buy what you like. If you couldn't care less about posters, don't buy them. If you'd love to have a room full of *GWTW* dolls, go for it. The important aspect of collecting is buying those items that appeal to you rather than purchasing items you think *should* be in a collection.

• Make a list of your "most wanted" items. This is a fun way to set collecting goals. Make the list reasonable yet challenging enough to keep the pursuit of items interesting.

• Be a savvy mail-order buyer. Read the section in this book called "The Ins and Outs of Buying by Mail" if you have limited experience making purchases through the mail.

• Always purchase the finest example of a collectible in the best possible condition. Collectibles are generally graded from poor (damaged or incomplete), fair (noticeable signs of wear), good (in average condition), fine (only a few signs of wear) to mint (excellent condition, with no defects). Therefore, you should strive to purchase a signed first edition of *Scarlett* with dust jacket in mint condition rather than an unsigned, unjacketed first edition in fine condition.

• Buy a wanted item when you see it. You may regret passing up a Scarlett perfume decanter, especially if you never find another one.

• Spend your collecting dollars wisely. A good rule of thumb is that the amount of money you spend on an item should equal the amount of pleasure you will get from it.

• Have a business card printed. On the card have your name, address, and telephone number listed as well as a notation that you are a *GWTW* collector. Give a card to anyone who might provide leads to collectibles, including dealers at collecting

This Rhett and Scarlett figurine tableaux has been retired and sold out. *(Dave Grossman Creations. © 1939 Turner Entertainment Co. All rights reserved. "Gone With the Wind" and Scarlett, Rhett, Ashley, and Tara are trademarks of Turner Ent. Co. and the Stephens Mitchell Trusts.)*

forums, antique shows, and flea markets. Place your card on community or supermarket bulletin boards, and enclose a card when you purchase *GWTW* items through the mail. You never know when someone may have just the collectible you are looking for.

• Tap other collectors as the best source for collectibles. Make friends at collecting shows and exchange those business cards. Check the buy and sell ads placed by collectors in publications such as *The GONE WITH THE WIND Collector's Newsletter*. Place your own ads in appropriate periodicals.

• Know your collection. By cataloging your collection, you'll avoid buying duplicate items. But sometimes purchasing another copy of a particular item at a good price can help to upgrade or to expand your collection. The duplicate might be in better condition than the one in your collection, or you could use the duplicate to trade with another collector.

• Realize you'll make mistakes. Sometimes you'll pay too much for a collectible, and sometimes you'll sell an item for much less than it's worth. Just remember that it happens to everyone, and everything usually averages out.

• Enjoy your collection, but continue to look for new pieces of memorabilia. The true collector never stops searching for collectibles, and half of the fun is the pursuit. You'll never know what will surface, so keep your eyes peeled for any and all collecting opportunities.

Abbreviations Used in This Book

AE – American Express
AEO – American Express/Optima
C – check
CB – Carte Blanche
CC – cashier's check/certified check
COD – cash on delivery
D – Discover
DC – Diner's Club
MC – Mastercard
MIB – mint in box
MO – money order
SASE – self-addressed, stamped envelope
UPS – United Parcel Service
USPS – United States Postal Service
V – Visa

II

GWTW Collectibles of Today

Audio

Have you heard the news? You can now get *Gone With the Wind* to go. *Scarlett* as well as the sound track to *Gone With the Wind* are available on audio tape. Imagine enjoying Scarlett's new adventures on your walk-about stereo or car stereo. Or slip in the tape of GWTW's music to rekindle the memories of Margaret Mitchell's novel. Whether you're headed to work, to the mall or wherever, you now can be gone with *the Wind*.

Audio Diversions
306 Commerce Street
Occoquan, VA 22125
Phone: 703-490-5466
800-628-6145 (orders)
FAX: 703–442-9344
Specialties: Audio books for purchase and rental, including *Scarlett* by Alexandra Ripley, read by Dixie Carter; #H2437.
Catalog: Free with $2.00 in postage. Stock is subject to change. Collectors should contact Audio Diversions to check the current availability of GWTW-related items.
Payment: C, MO, V, MC
Delivery: UPS, USPS, Federal Express, Express Mail

Returns: Defective tapes are replaced free of charge.

Audio Editions Books-on-Cassette
PO Box 6930
Auburn, CA 95604
Phone: 916–888-7801
Specialties: Audio books for purchase, including *Scarlett* by Alexandra Ripley, read by Dixie Carter; #M4P966.
Catalog: Free. Stock is subject to change. Collectors should contact Audio Editions to check the current availability of *GWTW*-related items.
Payment: C, V, MC, D, AE
Delivery: UPS, USPS
Returns: Defective tapes are replaced free of charge, and postage is refunded.

The Turner Store
One CNN Center
Box 105366
Atlanta, GA 30348–5366
Phone: 404–827-4406
FAX: 404–827-3696
Specialties: Gone With the Wind soundtrack, cassette #GW 83; CD #GW 82.
Catalog: Free (call 404-827-2500 to order). Stock is subject to change. Collectors should contact The Turner Store to check the current availability of *GWTW*-related items.
Payment: C, MO, V, MC

Delivery: UPS, USPS, Federal Express
Returns: Return item within 30 days in
   original packaging with sales receipt.

Autographs

THERE is magic and joy in collecting
   autographs. Possessing the signature of
a member of *Gone With the Wind*'s family
links you to that celebrity. You can touch
the paper that he or she touched. Your
finger can trace the loops and curves of the
letters in the star's name. If the celebrity
included an inscription, you can have the
feeling of being close to that person.

Autographs are the magic carpets of collectibles, sheets of paper which allow the
collector to soar to heights unattainable
through other memorabilia. With an autograph, you have a part of the celebrity.
What, after all, is more personal than an
individual's signature?

Obtaining autographs from the remaining
Gone With the Wind family members can
be done either through the mail or in person. Collecting through the mail is the sim-
plest way to begin.

You can locate the addresses of celebrities
by looking through library reference books
such as *Who's Who* or telephone directories
if you know where the star resides. Networking with other autograph collectors
can also be useful in obtaining addresses.

Approach the celebrity with a brief, po-
lite letter, explaining that you are a fan and
requesting an autograph. Be sure to enclose
material for the star to sign (an index card
or a photograph) and include a self-
addressed stamped envelope so that the
celebrity can return the autograph to you.

If you are hoping to receive more than
just a signature, include a question in your
letter. A thought-provoking query combined
with evidence of your respect and admiration for the star may result in a handwritten
letter.

Be aware, though, that no matter how
flattering your request, there are some
celebrities—Alicia Rhett (India Wilkes), for

example—who just refuse to provide autographs.

One of the problems with soliciting autographs through the mail is the likelihood of
receiving a nonauthentic autograph. Some
celebrities send facsimile signatures, those
written by a secretary, and signatures produced by Autopen machines.

The best way to guarantee the authenticity of an autograph is to obtain the signature in person. But how do you meet *Gone
With the Wind* celebrities?

Collectible shows and forums often fea-
ture special appearances by *Gone With the
Wind* stars. The Clark Gable Foundation
has hosted a series of birthday parties and
barbecues attended by Butterfly McQueen
(Prissy), Ann Rutherford (Carreen O'Hara),
Fred Crane (Brent Tarleton), Rand Brooks
(Charles Hamilton), Cammie King Conlon
(Bonnie Blue Butler), Patrick Curtis (baby
Beau), Daniel Mayer Selznick (son of direc-
tor David O. Selznick), and John Clark
Gable (son of Clark Gable).

If you plan to attend an event at which a
Gone With the Wind celebrity will be appearing, follow the Scouting motto and be
prepared. Bring with you items that the star
can autograph, including books, index
cards, or photographs. Sometimes an event
will offer a souvenir program, and this is
ideal for celebrities to sign. Stars who make
public appearances expect to provide autographs and will probably be happy to sign
both the book you've brought and the commemorative booklet from the event.

If the book you've brought happens to be
a first edition of *Gone with the Wind,* you
need to be especially careful about whom
you ask to autograph the volume. Avoid
mixing and matching Mitchell's novel and
Selznick's film. For example, you could ask
a cousin of Margaret Mitchell to autograph
the first edition. Having Butterfly McQueen
sign the novel may actually reduce the value
of the book since the star has no connection to Mitchell's masterpiece. On the other
hand, McQueen's autograph on a Motion
Picture Edition of *Gone with the Wind*

would be appropriate and could add to the volume's value.

Celebrities pen more than just simple signatures. They can also provide inscriptions. A personal inscription such as *To . . ., with all good wishes* that is signed by the celebrity will create that special link with the star. But autograph experts advise against having every item inscribed. If you later decide to offer the inscription for sale to a dealer or another collector, you may receive a lower price than if the item contained only a simple signature. Why?

If the autograph is fairly common and inexpensive to obtain, a purchaser is more likely to prefer the signature alone. Most collectors do not want to add to their collection items originally intended for someone else.

Experts recommend having a celebrity inscribe one item that you can display or frame. If you seek further autographs, request only a signature. Asking the individual to date the signature or inscription is good, especially if the date is significant. For example, Darden Asbury Pyron autographed and dated for me a copy of his book *Southern Daughter: The Life of Margaret Mitchell* which he signed on November 8, 1991—the anniversary of Mitchell's birth.

Discover the joy of collecting *Gone With the Wind* autographs, and capture the glamour of the golden age of Hollywood. The magic awaits you.

Scarlett's Sales
PO Box 6351
3401 Gentian Boulevard
Columbus, GA 31907
Phone: 706-569-7316
Specialties: Autographed books about *Gone With the Wind,* cachets, postcards.
Catalog: $1.00. Cost of catalog may be deducted from first order. Stock is subject to prior sale. Collectors should contact Scarlett's Sales to check the current availability of *GWTW*–related items.
Payment: C, MO, V, MC
Delivery: UPS, USPS

Returns: Items in salable condition may be returned within fourteen days of receipt for refund, less the cost of shipping and handling.

Books

W HEN *Scarlett: The Sequel to Margaret Mitchell's GONE WITH THE WIND* was published in September 1991 by Warner Books, collectors scrambled to purchase first editions.

First edition copies are those produced during the first press run. The characteristics that identify a first edition are known as "points." The points that identify a volume of *Scarlett* as a first edition include on the copyright page the words "First printing: September 1991" and a series of numbers from one to ten, running from right to left.

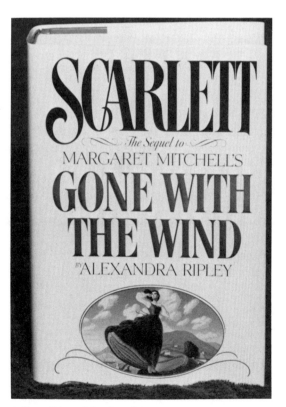

A first edition of *Scarlett,* the sequel to *Gone With the Wind.*

Publishers use this numeric series to indicate printings. If the numeral "1" appears, the volume is a first edition. For the second printing, the publisher deletes the "1" so that the series begins with "2".

First editions of *Scarlett* as well as editions of other books in your collection deserve to be treated well. You risk being accused of bibliocide if you engage in any of these bad book behaviors:

• *Crime:* packing books too tightly on shelves. *Punishment:* the cover can tear when a book is removed.

• *Crime:* packing books too loosely on shelves. *Punishment:* the covers can warp.

• *Crime:* cracking the book open, laying the book face down, and placing other books on top. *Punishment:* the back can break.

• *Crime:* using bulky objects as place holders. *Punishment:* the back can split.

• *Crime:* using paper clips or rubber bands as place holders. *Punishment:* the pages can be marked or torn.

• *Crime:* folding the corner as a place holder. *Punishment:* the creased corner can break off.

• *Crime:* turning pages violently. *Punishment:* pages can tear.

• *Crime:* using the book as a coaster. *Punishment:* the cover can be damaged by moisture; pages can be damaged by spills.

• *Crime:* reading the book while smoking. *Punishment:* a hot ash can burn a hole.

• *Crime:* reading the book while eating. *Punishment:* dropped crumbs can attract rodents, which might take a few bites out of your book.

• *Crime:* leaving the book outside in the hot sun, or near a sunny window. *Punishment:* the colors of the dust jacket can fade, and the book can warp.

Abbeville Press
488 Madison Avenue
New York, NY 10022
Phone: 212-888-1969
800-227-7210 (orders)
Specialties: GONE WITH THE WIND Cookbook.

Catalog: Free. Stock is subject to change. Collectors should contact Abbeville Press to check the current availability of *GWTW*–related items.
Payment: V, MC, AE
Delivery: UPS, USPS
Returns: If item arrives damaged, contact Abbeville Press for return.

Avon Books
PO Box 767
Dresden, TN 38225
Phone: 800-223-0690 (main number)
901-364-5742 (main number in Tennessee)
800-238-0658 (for orders paid by check)
800-762-0779 (for orders paid by credit card) [Minimum order by credit card is $6.00 or two books.]
Specialties: Gone with the Wind by Margaret Mitchell, paperback.
Catalog: Free. Stock is subject to change. Collectors should contact Avon Books to check the current availability of *GWTW*–related items.
Payment: C, MO, V, MC
Delivery: UPS, USPS
Returns: If item arrives damaged, contact Avon Books for return.

Cinemonde
1932 Polk Street
San Francisco, CA 94109
Phone: 415-776-9988
415-776-5270
Specialties: Lobby Cards: The Classic Films (1987), quality reproductions of 80 exceptional pieces (1919–1943) from the Michael Hawks collection. Hardcover, 176 pages, including advice on how to acquire well. #3736.
Hollywood Souvenirs (1986), 136-page hardcover book showing Belgian posters (165 in color) for American movies, 1925–1950. Imported. #3939.
Cinemonde Movie Poster Collection, Fall 1985 catalog, with over 300 photos (54 in full color), of highly desirable posters/lobby cards from 1929 to 1985. Features the *Gone With the*

Wind French poster on the cover. Very limited copies. #3735.

The Movie Poster Book (1979), 100-page book showing rare US and foreign posters (119 in full color), 1896 to 1965, 14 pages on the history of film posters and collecting. Out of print. #1855.

Catalog: $8.50. Stock is subject to prior sale. Collectors should contact Cinemonde to check the current availability of *GWTW*–related items.

Payment: MO, V, MC, AE, DC, CB

Delivery: UPS, Federal Express

Returns: Any item may be returned within seven days.

Collectors Book Store
1708 North Vine Street
Hollywood, CA 90028
Phone: 213-467-3296
FAX: 213-467-4536
Specialties: Books on *Gone With the Wind.*
Catalog: None. Stock is subject to change. Collectors should contact Collectors Book Store to check the current availability of GWTW–related items.
Payment: C, MO, V, MC, D, AE
Delivery: UPS, USPS
Returns: Any item may be returned for full refund or credit if returned in good condition within fourteen days.

Critics' Choice Video
PO Box 549
Elk Grove Village, IL 60009-0549
Phone: 800-367-7765 (orders)
800-544-9852 (customer service)
FAX: 708-437-7298
Specialties: The Complete Films of Clark Gable; oversized, 225-paged paperback that includes listings of each film's cast and credits, synopses of the plots, production notes, reviews, biographical and critical commentary; #CDCFB000985.
Catalog: Free
Payment: C, MO, V, MC, AEO, D
Delivery: UPS, Federal Express
Returns: Any item may be returned with original invoice within thirty days of purchase for refund, credit, or exchange.

Eugenia's Place
1574 Cave Road NW
Atlanta, GA 30327
Phone: 404-261-0394 (weekdays)
404-458-0682 (weekends)
Specialties: Books on *Gone With the Wind.*
Catalog: None. Stock is subject to change. Collectors should notify Eugenia's Place of particular wants by sending a letter of inquiry with a SASE.
Payment: C, MO, V, MC
Delivery: UPS, USPS
Returns: Any item may be returned for store credit only.

Jan Lebow
504 South Independence Boulevard
Virginia Beach, VA 23452
Phone: 804-497-4338
804-486-1992
Specialties: The Fashion History of Alexander Scarlett O'Hara Dolls, 1937–1992, Volume 2, a comprehensive reference book on Alexander Scarlett dolls, fully illustrated with 4 ″ by 6 ″ color photographs.
Catalog: None. Write or call to order.
Payment: C, MO
Delivery: UPS
Returns: No returns.

The Lighter Side Gift Catalog
4514 19th Street Court East
Box 25600
Bradenton, FL 34206-5600
Phone: 813-747-2356
FAX: 813-746-7896
Specialties: GONE WITH THE WIND Cookbook, #2447.
Catalog: Free. Stock is subject to change. Collectors should contact The Lighter Side to check the current availability of *GWTW*–related items.
Payment: C, MO, V, MC, AE, DC, D ($15.00 minimum credit card charge)
Delivery: UPS, USPS, Air Express delivery option
Returns: Return item in original condition and in original packaging for refund or item exchange.

Michael Motes
282 Kennesaw Avenue NW
Marietta, GA 30060-1636
Phone: 404-429-8262
Specialties: Foreign editions of *Gone with the Wind, Scarlett,* biographies of Margaret Mitchell, and books about the making of *Gone With the Wind.*
Catalog: None. Flyers are available for a SASE. Stock is subject to change. Collectors should contact Michael Motes to check the current availability of GWTW-related items.
Payment: C, MO
Delivery: UPS
Returns: Any item may be returned for full refund or credit if returned in good condition within thirty days.

Rainbow Connection I
3333 Coulter Drive
Amarillo, TX 79106
Phone: 806-352-2088
800-TOY-DOLL (orders)
Specialties: *Gone With the Wind*–related books.
Catalog: None. Stock is subject to change. Collectors should notify Rainbow Connection I of particular wants by telephoning or sending a letter of inquiry with a SASE.
Payment: C, MO, V, MC, D
Delivery: UPS, USPS
Returns: Any item may be returned within ten days for exchange or store credit.

Rainbow Connection II
7657 West 88th Avenue
Arvada, CO 80005
Phone: 303-424-3988
800-TOY-DOLL (orders)
Specialties: *Gone With the Wind*–related books.
Catalog: None. Stock is subject to change. Collectors should notify Rainbow Connection II of particular wants by telephoning or sending a letter of inquiry with a SASE.
Payment: C, MO, V, MC, D
Delivery: UPS, USPS

Returns: Any item may be returned within ten days for exchange or store credit.

Scarlett's
247 East Main Street
Ashland, OR 97520
Phone: 503-488-2745
Specialties: Books about *Gone With the Wind.*
Catalog: None. Scarlett's has a large inventory of books. Write or telephone with specific wants for a price quote.
Payment: C, MO, V, MC, D, AE
Delivery: UPS
Returns: Items may be returned for exchange or refund within thirty days of receipt.

Scarlett's Sales
PO Box 6351
3401 Gentian Boulevard
Columbus, GA 31907
Phone: 706-569-7316
Specialties: *Gone with the Wind,* Literary Guild Edition.
Memo From David O. Selznick, edited by Rudy Behlmer.
Scarlett by Alexandra Ripley, first edition copies.
Hollywood Be Thy Name by William Bakewell; random recollections of a movie veteran from the silents to the talkies to television. Author was the mounted soldier in *Gone With the Wind* who advised Scarlett to refugee south.
I Could Have Written GWTW, but Cousin Margaret Beat Me to It by Sara Spano; includes information about growing up in the Fitzgerald family.
Catalog: $1.00. Cost of catalog may be deducted from first order. Stock is subject to prior sale. Collectors should contact Scarlett's Sales to check the current availability of *GWTW*–related items.
Payment: C, MO, V, MC
Delivery: UPS, USPS
Returns: Items in salable condition may be returned within fourteen days of receipt

for refund, less the cost of shipping and handling.

Taylor Publishing Company
1550 West Mockingbird Lane
Dallas, TX 75235
Phone: 214-819-8100
800-275-8188 (orders)
Specialties: The Complete GONE WITH THE WIND Trivia Book by Pauline Bartel.
Catalog: Free.
Payment: C, MO, V, MC
Delivery: UPS
Returns: If item arrives damaged, contact Taylor Publishing Company for return.

The Turner Store
One CNN Center
Box 105366
Atlanta, GA 30348-5366
Phone: 404-827-4406
FAX: 404-827-3696
Specialties: The Art of GONE WITH THE WIND: The Making of a Legend by Judy Cameron and Paul J. Christman, paperback; #GW 53.
GWTW: Definitive Illustrated History of the Book, the Movie and the Legend by Herb Bridges, paperback; #GW 59.
The Complete GONE WITH THE WIND Trivia Book by Pauline Bartel, paperback; #GW 61.
GONE WITH THE WIND Cook Book, paperback reprint of the 1939 original; #GW 62.
GONE WITH THE WIND: A Pictorial History by Gerald Gardner and Harriet Modell Gardner, hardback; #GW 63.
Other books are available. Call for a complete listing.
Catalog: Free (call 404-827-2500 to order). Stock is subject to change. Collectors should contact The Turner Store to check the current availability of *GWTW*–related items.
Payment: C, MO, V, MC
Delivery: UPS, USPS, Federal Express
Returns: Return item within thirty days in original packaging with sales receipt.

A few of the many popular books about *GWTW* that are still in print. *(The Turner Store)*

CERAMICS

In honor of *Gone With the Wind*'s fiftieth anniversary, MGM and Turner Entertainment authorized The Franklin Mint to create "The *Gone With the Wind* Portrait Sculpture Collection," a subscription series of fifteen portrait sculptures depicting the most important characters in *Gone With the Wind.*

Crafted of Tesori porcelain, a blend of powdered porcelain and resins, each hand-painted figure was created as an authentic likeness of the movie character. The figures included: Scarlett, Rhett, Melanie, Ashley, Ellen and Gerald O'Hara, Aunt Pittypat, Mammy, Prissy, Bonnie Blue, Frank Kennedy, Dr. Meade, Belle Watling, Charles Hamilton, and Tom the Yankee Captain. Accompanying the figures was a custom-designed, three-shelf, glass-and-brass display case with the facade of Tara etched into the mirror backing.

Scarlett (in red dress) figurine. *(Dave Grossman Creations. © 1939 Turner Entertainment Co. All rights reserved. "Gone With the Wind" and Scarlett, Rhett, Ashley, and Tara are trademarks of Turner Ent. Co. and the Stephens Mitchell Trusts.)*

Scarlett figurine (retired and sold out). *(Dave Grossman Creations. © 1939 Turner Entertainment Co. All rights reserved. "Gone With the Wind" and Scarlett, Rhett, Ashley, and Tara are trademarks of Turner Ent. Co. and the Stephens Mitchell Trusts.)*

In 1992 The Franklin Mint announced the creation of the "Scarlett O'Hara Portrait Sculpture Collection." This subscription set of miniature Tesori porcelain figurines depicted Vivien Leigh in fifteen of Scarlett's most famous *Gone With the Wind* costumes:

• the white ruffled gown from the opening scene
• the wedding gown
• the black mourning outfit with the green Paris hat
• the wartime calico dress and straw hat
• the green velvet drapery dress
• the tan-and-plaid "convict labor" dress
• the blue-and-black "Shantytown" ensemble
• the black-and-white New Orleans honeymoon ensemble
• the white-and-green "rebuilding Tara" dress
• the pink-and-brown "taking Bonnie for a stroll" ensemble
• the green-and-gold "no more babies" dressing gown
• the blue-and-white "mill" ensemble
• the burgundy velvet gown
• the red "rape and row" dressing gown
• the paisley "Bonnie's return" dressing gown.

As with the previous collection, a three-shelf, glass-and-brass Tara display case was included.

The Franklin Mint is known for fine-quality *Gone With the Wind*–related items. For information on currently-available collectibles, write **The Franklin Mint** at Franklin Center, PA 19091 or call 1-800-THE MINT.

Aunt Edye's Show Plates, Collectibles & Gifts
9832 Albemarle Road
Charlotte, NC 28227
Phone: 704-545-2658
Specialties: Gone With the Wind ceramic and bronze figurines.
Catalog: None. Stock is subject to change. A list of items offered by Aunt Edye's is available by sending a request and enclosing a SASE.
Payment: C, V, MC
Delivery: UPS
Returns: If an item should be unsatisfactory, telephone Aunt Edye's to discuss a return or exchange.

Bluff Park Rare Books
2535 East Broadway
Long Beach, CA 90803
Phone: 310-438-9830
Specialties: Gone With the Wind figurines.
Catalog: None. Stock is subject to change. Collectors should notify Bluff Park Rare Books of particular wants by sending a letter of inquiry with a SASE.
Payment: C
Delivery: UPS, USPS, Federal Express
Returns: Any item may be returned within ten days for refund if not as described.

Ceramica Gift Gallery, Inc.
1009 Sixth Avenue
New York, NY 10018
Phone: 212-354-9216
800-666-9956 (orders)
Specialties: Gone With the Wind figurines.
Catalog: None. Stock is subject to change. Collectors should contact Ceramica Gift Gallery to check the current availability of *GWTW*–related items.
Payment: C, MO, V, MC
Delivery: UPS, USPS
Returns: Any item may be returned with receipt within fourteen days for refund.

Clark Gable Foundation
PO Box 65
Cadiz, OH 43907
Phone: 614-942-GWTW
Specialties: Marble plaque, 3″ by 3″, featuring the birthplace of Clark Gable. Commemorative mugs marking the 1989 Clark Gable Foundation barbecue.
Catalog: None. Stock is subject to change. Collectors should contact the Clark Gable Foundation to check the current availability of items.
Payment: C, MO, V, MC
Delivery: UPS, USPS
Returns: Any item may be returned for refund.

Gifts & Accents
9611 Metcalf Avenue
Overland Park, KS 66212
Phone: 913-381-8856
800-822-8856 (orders)
Specialties: Gone With the Wind figurines.
Catalog: None. Stock is subject to change. Collectors should contact Gifts & Accents to check the current availability of *GWTW*–related items.
Payment: C, MO, V, MC, D
Delivery: UPS
Returns: Any item may be returned within thirty days for refund.

Hawthorne Architectural Register
9210 North Maryland Avenue
Niles, IL 60714
Phone: 800-772-4277
Specialties: "Tara . . . Scarlett's Pride," a limited-edition sculpture, 3³/₄″ high, 5⁵/₈″ long, 4³/₄″ deep. This handpainted sculpture is a portrayal of the opening scene of *Gone With the Wind*. A pewter figurine depicts Scarlett storming away from her home after learning of Ashley's engagement, and another figurine portrays Mammy from an upstairs window, calling for Scarlett to return.
Catalog: None. Stock is subject to change. Collectors should contact Hawthorne Architectural Register to check the current availability of GWTW-related items.
Payment: V, MC, D

Delivery: UPS, USPS

Returns: Each new issue purchased from Hawthorne Architectural Register is protected by an unconditional 365-day guarantee. Within one full year after receipt of a sculpture, it may be returned for any reason if customer is not satisfied.

The Lighter Side Gift Catalog
4514 19th Street Court East
Box 25600
Bradenton, FL 34206-5600
Phone: 813-747-2356
FAX: 813-746-7896
Specialties: Rhett Mug, 12-ounce ceramic, green background with portrait of Rhett; #3743.

Scarlett Mug, 12-ounce ceramic, green background with portrait of Scarlett; #3744

Gone With the Wind limited-edition ornaments by Dave Grossman, including Scarlett in the green dress, #3974.

Catalog: Free. Stock is subject to change. Collectors should contact The Lighter Side to check the current availability of *GWTW*–related items.

Payment: C, MO, V, MC, AE, DC, D ($15.00 minimum credit card charge)

Delivery: UPS, USPS, Air Express delivery option

Returns: Return item in original condition and in original packaging for refund or item exchange.

Mary D's Dolls & Bears & Such
8407 West Broadway
Minneapolis, MN 55445-2266
Phone: 612-424-4375
Specialties: *Gone With the Wind* mugs.
Catalog: Free newsletter. Stock is subject to change. Collectors should contact Mary D's Dolls & Bears & Such to check the current availability of *GWTW*–related items.

Payment: C, MO, V, MC, D, layaways and collector club discounts

Delivery: UPS, USPS

Returns: Buyer must call Mary D's Dolls & Bears & Such within ten days of receiv-

ing order to arrange return. Returned items must be in the same condition as shipped and must be accompanied by receipt. No returns on layaways or sale items.

Painting the Town, Inc.
530 Park Avenue, 7G
New York, NY 10021
Phone: 212-888-0281
Specialties: *Gone With the Wind* ceramic magnets, 2″ by 2″.

Gone With the Wind ceramic trivets, 6″ by 6″.

Catalog: None. Stock is subject to change. A list of items offered by Painting the Town is available by sending a request and enclosing a SASE.

Payment: C, MO, COD

Delivery: UPS

Returns: Returns are not accepted unless item is damaged in shipping. Contact Painting the Town before returning damaged item.

Rainbow Connection I
3333 Coulter Drive
Amarillo, TX 79106
Phone: 806-352-2088
800-TOY-DOLL (orders)
Specialties: *Gone With the Wind* porcelain figurines.
Catalog: None. Stock is subject to change. Collectors should notify Rainbow Connection I of particular wants by telephoning or sending a letter of inquiry with a SASE.

Payment: C, MO, V, MC, D

Delivery: UPS, USPS

Returns: Any item may be returned within ten days for exchange or store credit.

Rainbow Connection II
7657 West 88th Avenue
Arvada, CO 80005
Phone: 303-424-3988
800-TOY-DOLL (orders)
Specialties: *Gone With the Wind* porcelain figurines.
Catalog: None. Stock is subject to change. Collectors should notify Rainbow Con-

nection II of particular wants by telephoning or sending a letter of inquiry with a SASE.

Payment: C, MO, V, MC, D
Delivery: UPS, USPS
Returns: Any item may be returned within ten days for exchange or store credit.

Scarlett's
247 East Main Street
Ashland, OR 97520
Phone: 503-488-2745
Specialties: Gone With the Wind mugs, showing various poses and scenes.
Catalog: None. Scarlett's has a large inventory of items. Write or telephone with specific wants for a price quote.
Payment: C, MO, V, MC, D, AE
Delivery: UPS
Returns: Items may be returned for exchange or refund within thirty days of receipt.

Scarlett's Sales
PO Box 6351
3401 Gentian Boulevard
Columbus, GA 31907
Phone: 706-569-7316
Specialties: Gone With the Wind mugs.
Gone With the Wind marble paper weights.
Mammy Teapot, 7¹/₂″ H by 7¹/₂″ W, finely crafted ceramic of a kerchiefed Mammy wearing a white apron over a black dress—the red silk petticoat peeks out from underneath. Her left hand is on her hip to form the handle; her right arm is extended to form the spout; #H4118.
Dave Grossman figurine of Ashley, approximately 8¹/₂″ high.
Dave Grossman figurine of Mammy, approximately 8″ high.
Catalog: $1.00. Cost of catalog may be deducted from first order. Stock is subject to change. Collectors should contact Scarlett's Sales to check the current availability of *GWTW*–related items.

Mammy figurine. *(Dave Grossman Creations. ©
1939 Turner Entertainment Co. All rights reserved.
"Gone With the Wind" and Scarlett, Rhett, Ashley,
and Tara are trademarks of Turner Ent. Co. and
the Stephens Mitchell Trusts.)*

Payment: C, MO, V, MC
Delivery: UPS, USPS
Returns: Items in salable condition may be returned within fourteen days of receipt for refund, less the cost of shipping and handling.

The Turner Store
One CNN Center
Box 105366
Atlanta, GA 30348-5366
Phone: 404-827-4406
FAX: 404-827-3696
Specialties: Dave Grossman miniature bronze collection, including Gerald and Ellen O'Hara, Scarlett, Mammy, and Pork, all less than 1¹/₂″ in height. Complete set; #GW 55.

Gone With the Wind mugs. (The Turner Store)

An 8″ Scarlett figurine. *(The Turner Store)*

Musical Scarlett, limited-edition coldcast figurine, plays "Tara's Theme," 8¹/₂″ high; #GW 105.

Scarlett ornament, limited-edition hand-painted coldcast porcelain, 3¹/₂″ high; #GW 103.

Scarlett figurine, 8″ high; #GW 104.

Scarlett mug, 11-ounce ceramic; #GW 15.

Rhett mug, 10-ounce ceramic; #GW 29.

Embrace mug, 10-ounce ceramic; #GW 30.

Scarlett mug, 10-ounce ceramic; #GW 31.

Tara mug, 10-ounce ceramic; #GW 32.

Catalog: Free (call 404-827-2500 to order). Stock is subject to change. Collectors should contact The Turner Store to check the current availability of *GWTW*–related items.

Payment: C, MO, V, MC

Delivery: UPS, USPS, Federal Express

Returns: Return item within thirty days in original packaging with sales receipt.

Worldwide Collectibles & Gifts

2 Lakeside Avenue

Berwyn, PA 19312-0158

Phone: 215-644-2442

800-222-1613 (orders)

Specialties: Gone With the Wind Dave Grossman figurines and ornaments, including the miniature bronze collection.

Catalog: Free. Stock is subject to change. Collectors should contact Worldwide Collectibles & Gifts to check the current availability of *GWTW*–related items.

Payment: C, MO, V, MC, D, AE

Delivery: UPS, USPS

Returns: Any item may be returned within thirty days for refund.

Clocks

"**D**O not squander time. That is the stuff life is made of." That was the adage on the sundial at Twelve Oaks.

Time pieces have advanced since sundial days; today we have clocks with quartz movements. Since, like Scarlett, you still need to make the most of every moment, now you can do so beautifully with *Gone With the Wind* wall clocks.

Scarlett's Sales
PO Box 6351
3401 Gentian Boulevard
Columbus, GA 31907
Phone: 706-569-7316
Specialties: Gone With the Wind clocks.
Catalog: $1.00. Cost of catalog may be deducted from first order. Stock is subject to change. Collectors should contact Scarlett's Sales to check the current availability of *GWTW*–related items.
Payment: C, MO, V, MC
Delivery: UPS, USPS
Returns: Items in salable condition may be returned within fourteen days of receipt for refund, less the cost of shipping and handling.

Tomkin & Rodney Ventures
PO Box 641219
Los Angeles, CA 90064
Phone: 310-841-0514
Specialties: The Fred A. Parrish Collection of Photographs titled "Behind the Scenes . . . *Gone With the Wind.*"
Products include:
Rhett and Scarlett quartz wall clock, sweep second hand, runs on one "AA" battery.
Scarlett quartz wall clock, sweep second hand, runs on one "AA" battery.
Hattie McDaniel wall clock, sweep second hand, runs on one "AA" battery.
Catalog: None. Stock is subject to change. Descriptive flyers are available by sending a request and enclosing a SASE.
Payment: C, MO
Delivery: UPS, USPS
Returns: Any item may be returned within thirty days for an exchange or refund. Clocks have a one-year warranty.

Clothing

THOSE involved in Civil War reenactments need authentic reproduction CSA and US military uniforms and accou-

Miniature Tara set. *(The Turner Store)*

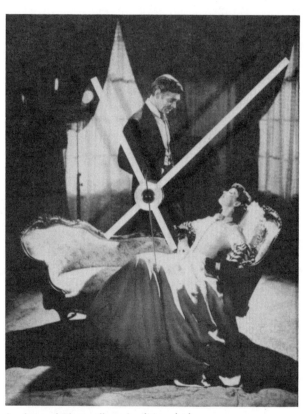

Scarlett and Rhett collector's edition clock. *(Tomkin & Rodney. Photograph © 1981 The Fred A. Parrish Collection. © 1939 Turner Entertainment Co. "Gone With the Wind" is a trademark of Turner Ent. Co. and the Stephens Mitchell Trusts.)*

terments. Ladies wishing to emulate the fashion styles of the 1860s require bonnets, hoop-skirt dresses, corsets, petticoats, slippers, and other accessories. Happily, custom-made, Civil–War era clothing is available from a number of companies.

The term "custom-made" means that the company will make the garments to your measurements. They will not make nonregulation garments. In fact, companies that stitch uniforms and civilian clothing have conducted extensive research in museums and archives to guarantee the authenticity of the garments they produce. Many also serve as consultants for museums, historic sites, television, and motion picture studios.

Frequently, custom-made clothing is not returnable. You must be certain, therefore, that the measurements you provide are accurate. If you goof, most companies will offer alterations, but you will incur added expense plus lost time. Here are suggestions to make sure you are delighted with the custom-made garments you order:

• request the company's catalog, which includes information on available styles, materials, and accessories. Catalogs also provide detailed directions on taking key measurements.

• have a friend help with the measurements. Stand naturally and wear your usual type of undergarments. Use an easy-to-read tape measure.

• take measurements carefully and honestly then recheck them. Some catalogs point out that authentic garments are cut to fit quite snugly. Provide measurements with this in mind.

Careful, realistic measurements are vital, so don't fudge them. If you do, when your garment arrives and you try it on, you'll mutter in true Mammy fashion, "It ain' fittin'. It just ain' fittin'. It ain' fittin'."

Dixie Fashions
PO Box 9203
Richmond, VA 23227
Phone: 804-262-7995
Specialties: Authentic, custom-made reproduction Confederate and Union uniforms and accouterments, including hats, belts, cap boxes, cartridge boxes, sashes, gauntlets, spurs, bayonets and sabers, saddle holsters, chevrons and service stripes, socks, haversacks, gaiters, canteens. Dixie Fashions also offers custom-made civilian clothing including vests, tailcoats, sackcoats, trousers, greatcoats and shirts. No clothing for children.
Catalog: $3.00
Payment: C, CC, MO
Delivery: UPS
Returns: Custom-made clothing is not returnable. If customer measured incorrectly and requests an alteration, changes will be made at a price of $15.00 per hour, plus shipping. If company made an error in a custom-made garment, Dixie Fashions will make corrections at no charge, provided customer returns the garment within four days of receipt.

Harriet's Tailoring and Custom Sewing
PO Box 1363
Winchester, VA 22601
Phone: 703-667-2541
Specialties: Authentic, custom-made reproductions of historical civilian clothing and accessories for men, women and children; authentic, custom-made reproductions of historical military uniforms and accessories; authentic reproduction patterns for civilian clothing and military uniforms. Rentals of period fashions and military uniforms.
Catalog: $3.50 for men's catalog; $3.50 for women's catalog; $3.00 for children's catalog; $10.00 for the set of three.
Payment: C, MO, V, MC, D, AE
Delivery: UPS, USPS, Federal Express
Returns: Patterns may be returned or exchanged if uncut and unused. No returns on clothing, but all work is guaranteed.

Heidi's Pages & Petticoats
810 El Caminito
Livermore, CA 94550
Phone: No phone orders.
Specialties: Authentic patterns for Civil

War–era style uniforms and civilian clothing for men, women, and children. Other items include uniform fabrics, fans, reproduction jewelry, buttons, insignia, and belt buckles.
Catalog: $3.00
Payment: C, CC, MO
Delivery: UPS, USPS
Returns: Unused patterns may be returned. Fabric can be returned only with authorization from company.

Laidacker Historical Garments
RD#2, Box 313A
Watsontown, PA 17777
Phone: 717-538-9490
Specialties: Authentic, custom-made reproductions of historical civilian clothing and accessories for men, women, and children. Accessories include hats, petticoats and undergarments, parasols, gloves, walking sticks, and more.
Catalog: $3.00
Payment: C, CC, MO, V, MC
Delivery: UPS, USPS
Returns: Unworn items may be returned within thirty days for refund or exchange if accompanied by receipt.

The Lighter Side Gift Catalog
4514 19th Street Court East
Box 25600
Bradenton, FL 34206-5600
Phone: 813-747-2356
FAX: 813-746-7896
Specialties: Tee-shirt, features the flaming embrace against a white background; 100 percent preshrunk cotton; machine wash and dry; adult sizes in M, L, XL; #99281.
Oversized tee-shirt, belt-screen process, features the flaming embrace; scarlet color, adult sizes in L, XL only; #99381.
Catalog: Free. Stock is subject to change. Collectors should contact The Lighter Side to check the current availability of *GWTW*–related items.
Payment: C, MO, V, MC, AE, DC, D ($15.00 minimum credit card charge)

Delivery: UPS, USPS, Air Express delivery option
Returns: Return item in original condition and in original packaging for refund or item exchange.

Mary Ellen & Co.
29400 Rankert Road, Department G
North Liberty, IN 46554
Phone: 219-656-3000
800-669-1860 (orders)
Specialties: Authentic patterns for Civil War–era style civilian clothing for men and women. Other items include undergarments, aprons, parasols, gloves and mitts, hats and bonnets, snoods, high-top shoes, and more.
Catalog: $3.00
Payment: C, MO, V, MC, COD
Delivery: UPS, USPS
Returns: Patterns may not be returned or exchanged. All other items may be returned for refund or exchange within thirty days of receipt.
NOTE: Wholesale available for quantity discounts.

New Columbia
PO Box 327
Brandon, VT 05733
Phone: 800-383-5927
Specialties: Authentic reproductions of Confederate and Union officer uniforms.
Catalog: $4.50
Payment: C, MO, V, MC
Delivery: UPS, USPS
Returns: Items may be returned within ten days.

Patti Marsh Productions, Inc.
118 Greenfield Avenue
San Anselmo, CA 94960
Phone: 415-459-3792
800-359-9417 (orders)
Specialties: Color-Me Tees, features the flaming embrace; white, 50/50 cotton/polyester blend; comes with 4 nontoxic, waterbased markers for coloring the tee-shirt. Colors wash out during laundering

so that the shirt can be recolored. Youth sizes include S (6 to 8), M (10 to 12), L (14 to 16); one adult size is available, called "oversize," which is equivalent to Large.

Catalog: Free. Stock is subject to change. Collectors should contact Patti Marsh Productions, Inc. to check the current availability of *GWTW*–related items.

Payment: C, MO

Delivery: UPS, USPS

Returns: Any item may be returned for refund or exchange.

Salt Lake Costume Company
1701 South 11th East
Salt Lake City, UT 84105

Phone: 801-467-9494

FAX: 801-467-9047

Specialties: Authentic Civil War–era style uniforms and civilian costumes for men and women for purchase or rental. Custom-made flags and banners.

Catalog: $16.00

Payment: C, MO, V, MC

Delivery: UPS, USPS, Federal Express, via bus

Returns: Defective clothing may be returned accompanied by a return authorization number and a copy of the invoice from which the merchandise was purchased.

Scarlett's
247 East Main Street
Ashland, OR 97520

Phone: 503-488-2745

Specialties: Gone With the Wind tee-shirts.

Catalog: None. Scarlett's has a large inventory of items. Write or telephone with specific wants for a price quote.

Payment: C, MO, V, MC, D, AE

Delivery: UPS

Returns: Items may be returned for exchange or refund within thirty days of receipt.

Scarlett's Sales
PO Box 6351
3401 Gentian Boulevard
Columbus, GA 31907

Phone: 706-569-7316

Specialties: "Frankly My Dear" tee-shirt, features photograph of Clark Gable in brown suit with fiftieth-anniversary logo on the left sleeve; white, 50/50 cotton/ polyester blend; adult sizes L or XL.

Catalog: $1.00. Cost of catalog may be deducted from first order. Stock is subject to change. Collectors should contact Scarlett's Sales to check the current availability of *GWTW*–related items.

Payment: C, MO, V, MC

Delivery: UPS, USPS

Returns: Items in salable condition may be returned within fourteen days of receipt for refund, less the cost of shipping and handling.

Tomkin & Rodney Ventures
PO Box 641219
Los Angeles, CA 90064

Phone: 310-841-0514

Specialties: The Fred A. Parrish Collection of Photographs titled "Behind the Scenes . . . *Gone With the Wind.*" Products include:

Rhett and Scarlett tee-shirt, adult sizes L and XL.

Scarlett tee-shirt, adult sizes L and XL.

Rhett and Scarlett sweatshirt, adult sizes L and XL.

Scarlett sweatshirt, adult sizes L and XL.

Hattie McDaniel tee-shirt, adult sizes L, XL and XXL.

Hattie McDaniel sweatshirt, adult sizes L, XL, XXL.

Catalog: None. Stock is subject to change. Descriptive flyers are available by sending a request and enclosing a SASE.

Payment: C, MO

Delivery: UPS, USPS

Returns: Any item may be returned within thirty days for an exchange or refund.

The Turner Store
One CNN Center
Box 105366
Atlanta, GA 30348-5366

Phone: 404-827-4406

FAX: 404-827-3696

Specialties: Flaming embrace tee-shirt,

Hattie McDaniel sweatshirt. *(Tomkin & Rodney/© 1992 E. Goff)*

"Looking behind the scenes" with a Scarlett T-shirt. *(Tomkin & Rodney. Photograph © 1981 The Fred A. Parrish Collection. © 1939 Turner Entertainment Co. "Gone With the Wind" is a trademark of Turner Ent. Co. and the Stephens Mitchell Trusts.)*

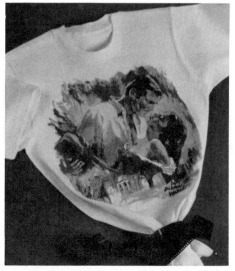

Flaming-embrace T-shirt. *(The Turner Store)*

Scarlett T-shirt. *(The Turner Store)*

screenprinted from a hand-painted original; 100 percent cotton; adult sizes S, M, L, XL; #GW 68.

Flaming embrace sweatshirt, screenprinted from a hand-painted original; 50/50 cotton/polyester blend; adult sizes S, M, L, XL; #GW 108.

Scarlett tee-shirt, features Scarlett in the barbecue dress; adult sizes M, L, XL; #GW 008.

Scarlett sweatshirt, features Scarlett in the barbecue dress; adult sizes S, M, L, XL; #GW 009.

All-over-print tee-shirt, dramatic sepia print design covers the entire shirt; 100 percent cotton; adult sizes M, L, XL; #GW 05.

Catalog: Free (call 404-827-2500 to order). Stock is subject to change. Collectors should contact The Turner Store to check the current availability of *GWTW*–related items.

Payment: C, MO, V, MC

Delivery: UPS, USPS, Federal Express

Returns: Return item within thirty days in original packaging with sales receipt.

The Winchester Sutler, Inc.
4145 Hunting Ridge Road
Winchester, VA 22603
Phone: 703-888-3595
Specialties: Authentic, custom-made reproduction Confederate and Union uniforms and accouterments including rank insignia, boots and brogans, hats and hat insignia, belts and buckles, leather gear, haversacks, longarms, revolvers, edged weapons and accessories. The Winchester Sutler also offers patterns for civilian clothing for men, women, and children.
Catalog: $3.00
Payment: C, MO, V, MC
Delivery: UPS, USPS
Returns: Any item may be returned for a refund if shipped back to company within three working days of receipt. Customer pays shipping both ways. After three working days, item may be returned on an exchange-only basis. Defective items

will be repaired or replaced on a no-charge basis.

Dolls

WORLD Doll offers a series of lovely, limited-edition *Gone With the Wind* dolls. Several dolls from the first "Movie Greats Mini Collection" proved so popular that in 1992 the company brought back a few that collectors had missed:

• Scarlett in the green-and-white barbecue dress
• Scarlett in the green velvet drapery dress
• Mammy in the black dress with white apron and the red petticoat
• Rhett in white tie and tails
• Rhett in the black suit with burgundy cravat

World Doll certainly proved that *Gone With the Wind* dolls are just as sweet—and just as collectible—the second time around.

Alwais Toy Box
PO Box 17566
San Antonio, TX 78217
Phone: 512-654-7677
Specialties: Dolls from Alexander Doll Company and World Doll.
Catalog: None. Stock is subject to change. Collectors should contact Alwais Toy Box to check the current availability of *GWTW*–related items.
Payment: C, MO, V, MC, AE
Delivery: UPS
Returns: Any item may be returned in original condition within ten days for refund.

Anything Goes, Inc.
PO Box 92
Anna Maria, FL 34216
Phone: 813-778-4456
Specialties: Dolls from Alexander Doll Company.
Catalog: $2.00. Stock is subject to change. Collectors should contact Anything Goes, Inc. to check the current availability of *GWTW*–related items.

Rhett, Scarlett, Melanie, and Ashley. *(World Doll)*

Payment: C, MO, V, MC, D, AE
Delivery: UPS
Returns: Any item may be returned with
receipt within five days for refund.

Celia's Dolls & Collectibles
800 East Hallandale Beach Boulevard
Hallandale, FL 33009
Phone: 305-458-0661
800-762-7994 (orders)
FAX: 305-458-5609
Specialties: Dolls from Alexander Doll
Company.
Catalog: Free. Stock is subject to change.
Collectors should contact Celia's Dolls to
check the current availability of *GWTW–*
related items.
Payment: C, V, MC, AE, layaways
Delivery: UPS, USPS
Returns: Any item may be returned within
seven days for refund.

Doll House
5022 North May
Oklahoma City, OK 73112
Phone: 405-943-1498
800-735-4811 (orders)
Specialties: Dolls from World Doll.
Catalog: Free. Stock is subject to change.
Collectors should contact Doll House to

check the current availability of *GWTW–*
related items.
Payment: C, MO, V, MC, D, AE
Delivery: UPS
Returns: Exchange only.

Dollsville Dolls & Bearsville Bears
461 North Palm Canyon Drive
Palm Springs, CA 92262
Phone: 619-325-2241
800-225-2327 (orders)
FAX: 619-322-1691
Specialties: Dolls from Alexander Doll
Company and Robin Woods.
Catalog: $1.00. Stock is subject to change.
Collectors should contact Dollsville Dolls
to check the current availability of
*GWTW–*related items.
Payment: V, AE, layaways
Delivery: UPS
Returns: Items may be returned within three
days for in-store credit only.

Dolly's Hideaway
14637 200th Avenue SE
Renton, WA 98059
Phone: 206-255-8295
Specialties: Dolls from World Doll.
Catalog: None. Stock is subject to change.
A list of items offered by Dolly's Hide-

Mammy. *(World Doll)*

Rhett and Scarlett. *(World Doll)*

Left. Prissy. *(World Doll)*

Above. Gerald O'Hara and Aunt Pittypat. *(World Doll)*

away is available by sending a request and enclosing a SASE.
Payment: C, MO
Delivery: UPS
Returns: Any item may be returned within ten days for refund.

Empress Doll Boutique
Route 3, Box 152-I
Laurel, DE 19956
Phone: 302-875-9700
Specialties: Dolls from World Doll.
Catalog: None. A list of items offered by Empress Doll Boutique is available by sending a request and enclosing a SASE.
Payment: C, V, MC
Delivery: UPS
Returns: Any item may be returned for exchange or in-store credit.

The Enchanted Doll House
Operations Center
PO Box 1617
Manchester, CT 06045-1617
Phone: 203-646-5008
800-243-9110 (orders)
FAX: 203-645-0504
Specialties: Dolls from Alexander Doll Company and World Doll and doll accessories.
Catalog: Free (call 203-646-5008 to order). Stock is subject to change. Collectors should contact The Enchanted Doll House to check the current availability of *GWTW*–related items.
Payment: C, MO, V, MC, D, AE, layaways
Delivery: UPS, USPS, Federal Express
Returns: Items may be returned within thirty days for refund or exchange.

Gifts & Accents
9611 Metcalf Avenue
Overland Park, KS 66212
Phone: 913-381-8856
800-822-8856 (orders)
Specialties: Dolls from World Doll.
Catalog: None. Stock is subject to change. Collectors should contact Gifts & Accents to check the current availability of *GWTW*–related items.
Payment: C, MO, V, MC, D

Belle Watling. *(World Doll)*

Mrs. O'Hara. *(World Doll)*

Delivery: UPS

Returns: Any item may be returned within thirty days for refund.

Gifts Now & Then

1408 Washington Avenue

Racine, WI 53403

Phone: 414-634-8883

Specialties: Dolls from World Doll.

Catalog: None. Stock is subject to change. Collectors should contact Gifts Now & Then to check the current availability of *GWTW*–related items.

Payment: C, MO, V, MC

Delivery: UPS

Returns: Any item may be returned within seven days for refund.

Green's / Collectors United

PO Box 1160

Chatsworth, GA 30705

Phone: 706-695-8242

Specialties: Dolls from World Doll.

Catalog: None. Stock is subject to change. Collectors should notify Green's/Collectors United of particular wants by sending a letter of inquiry with a SASE.

Payment: C, MO, V, MC, D, AE

Delivery: UPS

Returns: Any item may be returned within five days for refund.

LeAllala's Doll Shop

16060 Street Route 28

Chillicothe, OH 45601

Phone: 614-775-5960

Specialties: Dolls from Alexander Doll Company, Robin Woods, and World Doll.

Catalog: $2.00 (free with order). Stock is subject to change. Collectors should contact LeAllala's Doll Shop to check the current availability of *GWTW*–related items.

Payment: C, MO, V, MC. Layaways welcome (thirty days for purchases up to $100; sixty days for purchases over $100)

Delivery: UPS or as requested by customer

Returns: If item is defective, LeAllala's will replace. Otherwise the item will be accepted for exchange.

Jan Lebow

504 South Independence Boulevard

Virginia Beach, VA 23452

Phone: 804-497-4338

804-486-1992

Specialties: The Fashion History of Alexander Scarlett O'Hara Dolls, 1937–1992, Volume 2, a comprehensive reference book on Alexander Scarlett dolls, fully illustrated with 4″ by 6″ color photographs.

Catalog: None. Write or call to order.

Payment: C, MO

Delivery: UPS

Returns: No returns.

The Lighter Side Gift Catalog

4514 19th Street Court East

Box 25600

Bradenton, FL 34206-5600

Phone: 813-747-2356

FAX: 813-746-7896

Specialties: Dolls from World Doll.

Catalog: Free. Stock is subject to change. Collectors should contact The Lighter Side to check the current availability of *GWTW*–related items.

Payment: C, MO, V, MC, AE, DC, D ($15.00 minimum credit card charge)

Delivery: UPS, USPS, Air Express delivery option

Returns: Return item in original condition and in original packaging for refund or item exchange.

Mary D's Dolls & Bears & Such

8407 West Broadway

Minneapolis, MN 55445-2266

Phone: 612-424-4375

Specialties: Dolls from Alexander Doll Company, Royal House of Dolls, and World Doll.

Catalog: Free newsletter. Stock is subject to change. Collectors should contact Mary D's Dolls & Bears & Such to check the current availability of *GWTW*–related items.

Payment: C, MO, V, MC, D, layaways, and collector club discounts

Delivery: UPS, USPS

Returns: Buyer must call Mary D's Dolls & Bears & Such within ten days of receiving order to arrange return. Returned items must be in the same condition as shipped and must be accompanied by receipt. No returns on layaways or sale items.

J and L Meyers
595 Route 18
East Brunswick, NJ 08816
Phone: 908-257-1720
800-332-0176 (orders)
Specialties: Dolls from Alexander Doll Company, Royal House of Dolls, Robin Woods and World Doll.
Catalog: None. Stock is subject to change. A list of items offered by J and L Meyers is available by sending a request and enclosing a SASE.
Payment: C, MO, V, MC, D, AE. Free layaways on orders over $100
Delivery: UPS. Orders over $100 are shipped free; for orders under $100 there is a $3.00 charge
Returns: If not happy with an item, call within ten days to arrange a return. J and L Meyers will replace item or issue refund.

Monarch Collectibles
2012 Northwest Military Highway
San Antonio, TX 78213
Phone: 512-341-3655
800-648-3655 (orders)
Specialties: Dolls from Alexander Doll Company and World Doll.
Catalog: None. Stock is subject to change. Collectors should contact Monarch Collectibles to check the current availability of *GWTW*–related items.
Payment: C, V, MC, D, layaways
Delivery: UPS
Returns: Any item may be returned along with receipt for exchange or in-store credit.

My Doll House of Hilltop, Inc.
1860 Laskin Road
Virginia Beach, VA 23454
Phone: 804-425-6900
FAX: 804-461-4669
Specialties: Dolls from Alexander Doll Company.

Bonnie. *(World Doll)*

Catalog: Free. Stock is subject to change. Collectors should contact My Doll House to check the current availability of *GWTW*–related items.
Payment: C, MO, V, MC, D, AE, layaways
Delivery: UPS, USPS, Federal Express
Returns: Defective items may be returned for refund within seven days of purchase if accompanied by receipt.

Rainbow Connection I
3333 Coulter Drive
Amarillo, TX 79106
Phone: 806-352-2088
800-TOY-DOLL (orders)
Specialties: Gone With the Wind dolls and bears.
Catalog: None. Stock is subject to change. Collectors should notify Rainbow Connection I of particular wants by telephoning or sending a letter of inquiry with a SASE.
Payment: C, MO, V, MC, D
Delivery: UPS, USPS

Returns: Any item may be returned within ten days for exchange or store credit.

Rainbow Connection II
7657 West 88th Avenue
Arvada, CO 80005
Phone: 303-424-3988
800-TOY-DOLL (orders)
Specialties: Gone With the Wind dolls and bears.
Catalog: None. Stock is subject to change. Collectors should notify Rainbow Connection II of particular wants by telephoning or sending a letter of inquiry with a SASE.
Payment: C, MO, V, MC, D
Delivery: UPS, USPS
Returns: Any item may be returned within ten days for exchange or store credit.

Rug Rats & Ruffles
309 Romero, NW
Albuquerque, NM 87104
Phone: 505-243-9691
Specialties: Dolls from World Doll.
Catalog: Free. Stock is subject to change. Collectors should contact Rug Rats & Ruffles to check the current availability of *GWTW*–related items.
Payment: C, MO, V, MC, D, AE
Delivery: UPS
Returns: No cash refunds. Rug Rats & Ruffles will gladly exchange item for other store merchandise or issue an in-store credit.

Scarlett's
247 East Main Street
Ashland, OR 97520
Phone: 503-488-2745
Specialties: Dolls and bears.
Catalog: None. Scarlett's has a large inventory of items. Write or telephone with specific wants for a price quote.
Payment: C, MO, V, MC, D, AE
Delivery: UPS
Returns: Items may be returned for exchange or refund within thirty days of receipt.

Scarlett's Sales
PO Box 6351
3401 Gentian Boulevard
Columbus, GA 31907
Phone: 706-569-7316
Specialties: Dolls from World Doll.
Catalog: $1.00. Cost of catalog may be deducted from first order. Stock is subject to change. Collectors should contact Scarlett's Sales to check the current availability of *GWTW*–related items.
Payment: C, MO, V, MC
Delivery: UPS, USPS
Returns: Items in salable condition may be returned within fourteen days of receipt for refund, less the cost of shipping and handling.

Shirley's Dollhouse
20509 North Highway 21
PO Box 99A
Wheeling, IL 60090
Phone: 708-537-1632
Specialties: Dolls from Alexander Doll Company and World Doll.
Catalog: None. Stock is subject to change. Descriptive flyers are available by sending a request and enclosing a SASE.
Payment: C, MO, V, MC
Delivery: UPS
Returns: Items may be returned within ten days for in-store credit.

Simply Lovely
572 New Brunswick Avenue
Fords, NJ 08863
Phone: 908-738-4181
800-235-4181 (orders)
Specialties: Dolls from Alexander Doll Company.
Catalog: Free. Stock is subject to change. Collectors should contact Simply Lovely to check the current availability of *GWTW*–related items.
Payment: C, MO, V, MC, AE, layaways
Delivery: UPS, USPS
Returns: Items may be returned within seven days for in-store credit.

Sirocco Productions, Inc.
Suite 103
5660 East Virginia Beach Boulevard
Norfolk, VA 23502
Phone: 804-461-8987
FAX: 804-461-4669
Specialties: video, *Scarlett Dolls: An Alexander Tradition 1937–1991,* VHS format. This 72-minute video features more than 85 Scarlett dolls, and includes footage of rare composition Scarletts and the only "official" *GWTW* Scarlett O'Hara Doll released during the film's 1939 Atlanta premiere.
Catalog: Free. Stock is subject to change. Collectors should contact Sirocco Productions, Inc. to check the current availability of *GWTW*–related items.
Payment: C, MO, V, MC, D, AE
Delivery: UPS, USPS, Federal Express
Returns: Defective tapes may be returned for refund within seven days of purchase if accompanied by receipt.

The Turner Store
One CNN Center
Box 105366
Atlanta, GA 30348-5366
Phone: 404-827-4406
FAX: 404-827-3696
Specialties: Dolls from World Doll.
Catalog: Free (call 404-827-2500 to order). Stock is subject to change. Collectors should contact The Turner Store to check the current availability of *GWTW*–related items.
Payment: C, MO, V, MC
Delivery: UPS, USPS, Federal Express
Returns: Return item within thirty days in original packaging with sales receipt.

Under the Lilac
10101 Balsamwood Drive
Laurel, MD 20708-3153
Phone: 301-725-3655
Specialties: Dolls from World Doll.
Catalog: Free. Stock is subject to change. Collectors should contact Under the Lilac to check the current availability of *GWTW*–related items.
Payment: C, MO, V, MC, layaways
Delivery: UPS, USPS

Scarlett and Belle. (*The Turner Store*)

Returns: Any item can be returned within ten days for a refund or exchange. Shipping charges are not refundable. Please notify Under The Lilac for a Return Authorization Number. All returns will be refused if Number is not on the face of the package.

Edibles

IF you're looking for incredible *Gone With the Wind* edibles, search no longer. You'll find popcorn, chocolates, plus famous Southern recipes for everything from soup to nuts, with nary a radish in sight.

Forget about having an eighteen-inch waistline and enjoy! As God is my witness, you'll never be . . . well, you know the rest.

Abbeville Press
488 Madison Avenue
New York, NY 10022
Phone: 212-888-1969
800-227-7210 (orders)
Specialties: GONE WITH THE WIND *Cookbook.*
Catalog: Free. Stock is subject to change. Collectors should contact Abbeville Press to check the current availability of *GWTW*–related items.
Payment: V, MC, AE
Delivery: UPS, USPS
Returns: If item arrives damaged, contact Abbeville Press for return.

The Lighter Side Gift Catalog
4514 19th Street Court East
Box 25600
Bradenton, FL 34206-5600
Phone: 813-747-2356
FAX: 813-746-7896
Specialties: GONE WITH THE WIND *Cookbook, #2447.*
Catalog: Free. Stock is subject to change. Collectors should contact The Lighter Side to check the current availability of *GWTW*–related items.
Payment: C, MO, V, MC, AE, DC, D ($15.00 minimum credit card charge)

Delivery: UPS, USPS, Air Express delivery option
Returns: Return item in original condition and in original packaging for refund or item exchange.

Scarlett's Sales
PO Box 6351
3401 Gentian Boulevard
Columbus, GA 31907
Phone: 706-569-7316
Specialties: Gone With the Wind popcorn tin, decorated with the flaming embrace and containing 3 kinds of popcorn.
Catalog: $1.00. Cost of catalog may be deducted from first order. Stock is subject to change. Collectors should contact Scarlett's Sales to check the current availability of *GWTW*–related items.
Payment: C, MO, V, MC
Delivery: UPS, USPS
Returns: Items in salable condition may be returned within fourteen days of receipt for refund, less the cost of shipping and handling.

The Turner Store
One CNN Center
Box 105366
Atlanta, GA 30348-5366
Phone: 404-827-4406
FAX: 404-827-3696
Specialties: Scarlett's Chocolates, 1/2-pound, shrink-wrapped, box features Scarlett's portrait from Rhett's bedroom, #GW 23.
Catalog: Free (call 404-827-2500 to order). Stock is subject to change. Collectors should contact The Turner Store to check the current availability of *GWTW*–related items.
Payment: C, MO, V, MC
Delivery: UPS, USPS, Federal Express
Returns: Return item within thirty days in original packaging with sales receipt.

Film and Video

WHEN *Gone With the Wind's* first run ended in June 1940, Metro-Goldwyn-Mayer and Selznick International

Gone With the Wind cd and video and audiocassettes. *(The Turner Store)*

took the film out of circulation. To whet the appetites of those who hadn't been able to afford the premium prices of the film's initial run, print ads promised that *GWTW* would return the following year at reduced admissions.

Moviegoers were ecstatic when *GWTW*'s general release began. Print ads shouted "Nothing cut but the price!" Twenty-four million people flocked to large cinemas in major cities as well as to small neighborhood theaters to see Scarlett O'Hara battle hunger and despair. At the end of the 1941 general release, MGM decided to withdraw *GWTW* again. The prints were battered, but the studio believed one final fling for *GWTW* was possible.

The film returned to movie theaters for the third time in the spring of 1942 and stayed in release until late 1943. Then MGM pulled the film from exhibition, destroyed all worn-out prints and declared that *GWTW* was at last out of circulation. But not for long.

Fans clamored to see *Gone With the Wind* again. They wrote letters to David O. Selznick, asking when the film would return. He passed all the mail on to MGM, which decided to bring *GWTW* back to the theaters in June 1947.

MGM splurged on the 1947 revival of *GWTW*. There were new Technicolor prints and a spanking-new ad campaign. Posters for the film for the first time showed Rhett holding Scarlett in his arms and boasted that "Everybody wants to see *Gone With the Wind*."

And everybody did. Crowds this time around rivaled those that had waited on line for tickets in 1939. Many who saw the film during its first release returned to see if the film was as good as they remembered it. They brought their children, too, to introduce a new generation to the story of Scarlett and Rhett until *GWTW*'s fourth reissue ended in late 1948.

Gone With the Wind returned with a flourish in 1954, and MGM celebrated the film's fifteenth anniversary with a "premiere" at the Loew's Grand Theatre in Atlanta. *GWTW* was now in CinemaScope. The film had been reprocessed for showing on the now-popular wide screen. The new process made the spectacular scenes more powerful, but the color was faded and grainy in certain parts of the film. MGM had made other alterations as well. *GWTW* had been transferred from volatile nitrate film to acetate safety film, and Perspecta stereophonic sound had been added.

Gone With the Wind's next reissue came in 1961, in honor of the one-hundredth anniversary of the Civil War. The film premiered in Atlanta, played other first-run engagements in the United States and Canada and then made the rounds of smaller neighborhood theaters. Audiences may have noticed that the film's color was darker than they remembered. This was because of a new technique called Metrocolor that was used to process new prints of the film and that replaced the more expensive Technicolor process. Fans didn't care. *GWTW* was back, and they flocked to see it.

When *Gone With the Wind* returned in 1967, the film was bigger than ever. *GWTW* was reissued in a 70-millimeter wide-screen version. In the process, each of *GWTW*'s 35-millimeter frames was stretched to fit the wide, 70-millimeter format. To achieve this, however, the tops of heads and the bottoms of legs were sacrificed, ruining the composition. The film's title lost its sweeping grandeur, too. The main title was replaced with four small words, stationary on the screen.

Another new feature was the addition of a stereophonic soundtrack, very different from the enhancement made in 1954. The new soundtrack amplified sounds such as the rustle of hoop skirts or the clop of horses' hooves, but often these extraneous sounds muffled essential dialogue.

Gone With the Wind's next move was from the big screen to the television screen. Under a deal MGM struck with Home Box Office, *GWTW* appeared on the commercial-free cable station fourteen times during the month of June 1976. *GWTW*'s network television debut took place five months later when NBC broadcast the film on two successive nights, November 7 and 8, l976.

Two years later, MGM and CBS concluded an unprecedented twenty-year deal for *GWTW*. CBS bought exclusive television rights to broadcast the film twenty times during the length of the agreement at a price tag of $35 million, the largest license fee ever paid for a single film in the history of television.

Fans were content to watch *Gone With the Wind* on television once a year, but in March 1985 it became possible to watch the story of Scarlett and Rhett anytime at all at the touch of the PLAY button. *GWTW* had debuted as a double videocassette, and fans rushed to add the deluxe edition to their collections.

In 1986 the Atlanta–based Turner Broadcasting System, Inc., bought the MGM library of films, including *GWTW*. A year later a separate deal between TBS and CBS brought the television rights to *Gone With the Wind* under the Turner umbrella as well.

Turner Entertainment Company (a subsidiary of Turner Broadcasting System, Inc.), which is responsible for managing the films, called *Gone With the Wind* "the brightest jewel" in its library of more than 6,700 features. But *GWTW* was showing its age. Prints made from second- and later-generation negatives had lost color. The soundtrack was plagued by noises and distortions and in some parts muffled dialogue. So in 1988 Turner Entertainment Company decided to polish its jewel back to its 1939 splendor in time for the film's fiftieth anniversary.

Using the original 1939 three-strip nitrate negative, technicians worked for about seven months creating a fully color-corrected print. Once the print was approved, the original nitrate negative was used again to make an interpositive, incorporating all the color and density corrections that had been made. From this, an internegative was produced that was used to manufacture identical prints for exhibition.

For the sound, technicians used the soundtrack negative produced for the 1954 reissue. Through modern technology, experts eliminated the clicks and pops that had accumulated over the years, incorporated soundtrack changes made by David O. Selznick for the film's 1961 reissue, and located sound elements that were missing from the original tracks.

The resulting clean, stereo-enhanced soundtrack was the perfect accompaniment for the restored color negative. Together they allowed a sparkling *Gone With the Wind* to dazzle theater, television, and

Ava Gardner, Clark Gable, and Grace Kelly in *Mogambo*.

Bette Davis, Leslie Howard, and Humphrey Bogart in *The Petrified Forest*.

video audiences for its fiftieth birthday in 1989. *GWTW*'s extraordinary magic was not only still there, it was better than ever.

Eddie Brandt's Saturday Matinee
6310 Colfax Avenue
North Hollywood, CA 91606
Phone: 818-506-4242
818-506-7722
Specialties: Videocassettes in VHS or Beta format for rental by mail. Eddie Brandt's Saturday Matinee has more than 25,000 titles, including *Gone With the Wind* and films by *GWTW*'s stars and supporting cast.
Catalog: Free. Stock is subject to change. Collectors should contact Eddie Brandt's Saturday Matinee to check the current availability of *GWTW*–related items.
Payment: C, MO, V, MC, AE
Delivery: UPS, Federal Express
Returns: Tapes are rented then returned. Company allows seven days to view the videos plus four days shipping (two each way).

Cable Films
PO Box 7171
Kansas City, MO 64113
Phone: 913-362-2804
Specialties: Videocassettes of Hollywood classics in VHS or Beta formats, including:
The Painted Desert, 1931, featuring Clark Gable, William Boyd, Helen Twelvetrees; VHS or Beta format.
Fire Over England, 1937, featuring Vivien Leigh, Laurence Olivier, Flora Robson; VHS or Beta format.
The Scarlet Pimpernel, 1935, featuring Leslie Howard, Merle Oberon, Nigel Bruce; sepia tone color-tinted; VHS or Beta format.
Catalog: Free. Stock is subject to change. Collectors should contact Cable Films to check the current availability of *GWTW*–related items.
Payment: C, CC, MO
Delivery: UPS, USPS
Returns: Contact company before returning defective items.

Critics' Choice Video
PO Box 549
Elk Grove Village, IL 60009-0549
Phone: 800-367-7765 (orders)
800-544-9852 (customer service)
FAX: 708-437-7298
Specialties: More than 2000 videocassette and laserdisc titles, including films by *Gone With the Wind*'s stars and supporting cast.

Video Search Line offers assistance in locating hard-to-find videos, 8-mm tapes and laserdiscs. Call Monday through Friday, 9:00 to 5:00 Central Time at 900-370-6500 ($1.95 for the first minute, $.95 for each additional minute). Film professionals will research over 35,000 movies on videocassette and call or write back with availability and pricing information. No obligation to buy.

Gone With the Wind, 1939, featuring Clark Gable, Vivien Leigh, Olivia de Havilland, Leslie Howard; VHS format, #CGMGM901678.

Gone With the Wind, 1939, special collector's edition laserdisc; #CGMLD102244.

The Making of a Legend: GONE WITH THE WIND, 1988, behind-the-scenes view of the real story; VHS format, #CGMGM301527.

A Free Soul, 1931, featuring Clark Gable, Norma Shearer, Lionel Barrymore; VHS format, #CGMGM302142.

Dance Fools Dance, 1931, featuring Clark Gable and Joan Crawford; VHS format, #CGMGM302075.

Night Nurse, 1931, featuring Clark Gable, Barbara Stanwyck, Joan Blondell; VHS format, #CGMGM302069.

Possessed, 1931, featuring Clark Gable and Joan Crawford; VHS format, #CGMGM300607.

Chained, 1934, featuring Clark Gable and Joan Crawford; VHS format, #CGMGM202368.

It Happened One Night, 1934, featuring Clark Gable and Claudette Colbert; VHS format, #CGRCA060382.

Manhattan Melodrama, 1934, featuring Clark Gable, William Powell, Myrna Loy; VHS format, #CGMGM202371.

Mutiny on the Bounty, 1935, featuring Clark Gable, Charles Laughton, Franchot Tone; VHS format, #CGMGM400450.

San Francisco, 1936, featuring Clark · Gable, Spencer Tracy, Jeanette Mac-Donald; VHS format, #CGMGM100474.

Wife Vs. Secretary, 1936, featuring Clark Gable, Jean Harlow, Myrna Loy; VHS format, #CGMGM202380.

Test Pilot, 1938, featuring Clark Gable, Spencer Tracy, Myrna Loy, Lionel Barrymore; VHS format, #CGMGM202372.

Idiot's Delight, 1939, featuring Clark Gable, Norma Shearer, Edward Arnold; VHS format, #CGMGM300610.

Boom Town, 1940, featuring Clark Gable, Spencer Tracy, Claudette Colbert, Hedy Lamarr; VHS format, #CGMGM201588.

Honky Tonk, 1941, featuring Clark Gable and Lana Turner; VHS format, #CGMGM202369.

Command Decision, 1948, featuring Clark Gable, Walter Pidgeon, Van Johnson; VHS format, #CGMGM202113.

Across the Wide Missouri, 1951, featuring Clark Gable, Ricardo Montalban, John Hodiak; VHS format, #CGMGM202366.

Mogambo, 1953, featuring Clark Gable, Ava Gardner, Grace Kelly; VHS format, #CGMGM600055.

Betrayed, 1954, featuring Clark Gable, Lana Turner, Victor Mature; VHS format, #CGMGM202367.

The King and Four Queens, 1956, featuring Clark Gable, Eleanor Parker, Barbara Nichols, Jo Van Fleet; VHS format, #CGMGM202370.

Run Silent, Run Deep, 1958, featuring Clark Gable, Burt Lancaster, Jack Warden; VHS format, #CGMGM202133.

But Not For Me, 1959, featuring Clark Gable, Carroll Baker, Lilli Palmer, Lee J. Cobb; VHS format, #CGPAR005903.

The Misfits, 1961, featuring Clark Gable, Marilyn Monroe, Montgomery Clift, Thelma Ritter, Eli Wallach; VHS format, #CGMGM201650.

Errol Flynn and Olivia de Havilland in *Captain Blood*.

Dear Mr. Gable, 1968. This 52-minute documentary looks at the career of "The King," and includes interviews with his friends and co-workers and clips from home movies and a number of his classic films. Narrated by Burgess Meredith; VHS format, #CGMGM202376.

Captain Blood, 1935, featuring Olivia de Havilland and Errol Flynn; VHS format, #CGMGM201470.

That Hamilton Woman, 1941, featuring Vivien Leigh and Laurence Olivier; VHS format, #CGEHE003107.

A Streetcar Named Desire, 1951, featuring Vivien Leigh and Marlon Brando; VHS format, #CGWHV034019.

The Roman Spring of Mrs. Stone, 1961, featuring Vivien Leigh and Warren Beatty; VHS format, #CGWHV011183.

Intermezzo, 1939, featuring Leslie Howard and Ingrid Bergman; VHS format, #CGFOX008036.

Anthony Adverse, 1936, featuring Olivia de Havilland and Fredric March; VHS format, #CGMGM300743.

The Charge of the Light Brigade, 1936, featuring Errol Flynn, Olivia de Havilland, David Niven; VHS format, #CGMGM201510.

The Adventures of Robin Hood, 1938, featuring Errol Flynn, Olivia de Havilland, Basil Rathbone, Claude Rains; VHS format, #CGMGM201377.

They Died With Their Boots On, 1941, featuring Errol Flynn and Olivia de Havilland; VHS format, #CGMGM201473.

The Heiress, 1949, featuring Olivia de Havilland and Montgomery Clift; VHS format, #CGMCA080153.

Catalog: Free. Stock is subject to change. Collectors should contact Critics' Choice Video to check the current availability of *GWTW*–related items.

Payment: C, MO, V, MC, AEO, D

Delivery: UPS, Federal Express

Returns: For defective items, call customer service at 800-544-9852 to arrange UPS pickup at company expense. Any item may be returned with original invoice within thirty days of purchase for refund, credit or exchange.

Home Film Festival
PO Box 2032
Scranton, PA 18501-2032

Phone: 800-258-3456

Specialties: Videocassettes for purchase and rental by mail (annual membership required). Home Film Festival has more than 1400 titles, including Hollywood classics by *Gone With the Wind*'s stars and supporting cast.

A Free Soul, 1931, featuring Clark Gable, Norma Shearer, Leslie Howard, Lionel Barrymore; VHS format.

Susan Lenox: Her Fall and Rise, 1931, featuring Clark Gable and Greta Garbo; VHS format.

Dancing Lady, 1933, featuring Clark Gable, Joan Crawford, Franchot Tone; VHS format.

Mutiny on the Bounty, 1935, featuring Clark Gable, Charles Laughton, Franchot Tone; VHS format.

A Streetcar Named Desire, 1951, featuring Vivien Leigh and Marlon Brando; VHS format.

Catalog: A 152-page program guide is included in the membership kit.

Payment: MC, V

Delivery: UPS, USPS

Returns: If dissatisfied after receiving membership packet and reviewing the program guide and other materials, return the packet within thirty days for a full refund of membership fee.

KVC Entertainment
12801 Schabarum Avenue
PO Box 7878
Irwindale, CA 91706-7878
Phone: 800-331-1387
Specialties: Videocassette titles, including films by *Gone With the Wind*'s stars and supporting cast.

No Man Of Her Own, 1932, featuring Clark Gable and Carole Lombard; VHS format, #HM01-94.

Dark Journey, 1937, featuring Vivien Leigh and Conrad Veidt; VHS format, #HM00-57.

Fire Over England, 1937, featuring Vivien Leigh, Laurence Olivier, Flora Robson; VHS format, #HM00-70.

Storm In A Teacup, 1937, featuring Vivien Leigh, Rex Harrison, Cecil Parker; VHS format, #HM01-65.

Of Human Bondage, 1934, featuring Leslie Howard and Bette Davis; VHS format, #110-29.

Flikbaks–1939, the pop-up video greeting card, contains 30 minutes of exciting original newsreel footage highlighting events from politics, world events, people in the news, sports, fashion, entertainment and more; VHS format, #HM04-50.

Catalog: Free. Stock is subject to change.

Collectors should contact KVC Entertainment to check the current availability of *GWTW*–related items.

Payment: C, MO, V, MC, AE, D

Delivery: UPS

Returns: Any video may be returned within sixty days for replacement or full refund.

The Lighter Side Gift Catalog
4514 19th Street Court East
Box 25600
Bradenton, FL 34206-5600
Phone: 813-747-2356
FAX: 813-746-7896
Specialties: The Making of a Legend: GONE WITH THE WIND, 1988, behind-the-scenes view of the real story, VHS format; #7628.

Catalog: Free. Stock is subject to change. Collectors should contact The Lighter Side to check the current availability of *GWTW*–related items.

Payment: C, MO, V, MC, AE, DC, D ($15 minimum credit card charge)

Delivery: UPS, USPS, Air Express delivery option

Returns: Return item for refund or item exchange.

The Margaret Mitchell House, Inc.
PO Box 77673
Atlanta, GA 30357
Phone: 404-780-2360
Specialties: It May Not Be Tara, a 17-minute video about Margaret Mitchell and the house and neighborhood in which she wrote *GWTW.*

Catalog: None. Stock is subject to change. Collectors should contact The Margaret Mitchell House, Inc. to check the current availability of *GWTW*–related items.

Payment: C, MO

Delivery: UPS

Returns: Defective tapes will be replaced. Payment refunded if not completely satisfied.

Moore Video
PO Box 5703
Richmond, VA 23220
Phone: 804-745-9785

FAX: 804-745-9785

Specialties: More than 2,000 videocassettes, including films by *Gone With the Wind*'s stars and supporting-cast members plus films about the Civil War era.

The Painted Desert, 1931, featuring Clark Gable, William Boyd, Helen Twelvetrees; VHS, Beta, other formats; #0218.

Hollywood Without Makeup, 1964 (TV), featuring Clark Gable, Cary Grant, Lucille Ball, others; VHS, Beta, other formats: #0743.

Dark Journey, 1937, featuring Vivien Leigh, Conrad Veidt; VHS, Beta, other formats; #0166.

Fire Over England, 1937, featuring Vivien Leigh, Laurence Olivier, Flora Robson; VHS, Beta, other formats; #0241.

Storm In A Teacup, 1937, featuring Vivien Leigh, Rex Harrison, Cecil Parker; VHS, Beta, other formats; #0512.

Sidewalks of London, 1938, featuring Vivien Leigh, Charles Laughton; VHS, Beta, other formats; #0343.

Anna Karenina, 1948, featuring Vivien Leigh, Kieron Moore; VHS, Beta, other formats; #1187.

Of Human Bondage, 1934, featuring Leslie Howard, Bette Davis; VHS, Beta, other formats; #0174.

The Scarlet Pimpernel, 1935, featuring Leslie Howard, Merle Oberon, Nigel Bruce; VHS, Beta, other formats; #0229.

Pygmalion, 1938, featuring Leslie Howard and Wendy Hiller; VHS, Beta, other formats; #0091.

49th Parallel, 1941, featuring Leslie Howard and Laurence Olivier; VHS, Beta, other formats; #1689.

Invaders, 1941, featuring Leslie Howard and Laurence Olivier; VHS, Beta, other formats; #1689.

Spitfire, 1942, featuring Leslie Howard and David Niven; VHS, Beta, other formats; #0326.

Santa Fe Trail, 1940, featuring Olivia de Havilland and Ronald Reagan; VHS, Beta, other formats; #0087.

Catalog: $5.00. Stock is subject to change. Collectors should contact Moore Video to check the current availability of *GWTW*–related items.

Payment: C, MO

Delivery: UPS, USPS

Returns: All videos have full same-title exchange for the life of the tape.

Movie Poster Place

PO Box 128

Lansdowne, PA 19050-0128

Phone: 215-622-6062

FAX: 215-622-6062

Specialties: Video trailer tape #9, featuring trailers of *Gone With the Wind* and 32 other films; 95 minutes, VHS format.

Catalog: $1.00 which can be deducted from first order. Stock is subject to change. Collectors should contact Movie Poster Place to check the current availability of *GWTW*–related items.

Payment: C, MO, V, MC

Delivery: UPS, USPS, Federal Express

Returns: Any item may be returned for refund or exchange for any reason.

Movies Unlimited

6736 Castor Avenue

Philadelphia, PA 19149

Phone: 215-722-8298

215-722-8398 (customer service)

800-523-0823 (orders)

FAX: 215-725-3683

Specialties: More than 25,000 videocassette titles, including films by *GWTW*'s stars and supporting cast members.

Gone With the Wind, 1939, featuring Clark Gable, Vivien Leigh, Olivia de Havilland, Leslie Howard; VHS format, #12-1381

The Making of a Legend: GONE WITH THE WIND, 1988, behind-the-scenes view of the real story; VHS format, #12-1889.

The Painted Desert, 1931, featuring Clark Gable, William Boyd, Helen Twelvetrees; VHS format, #10-2013.

Vivien Leigh and Marlon Brando in *A Streetcar Named Desire*.

A Free Soul, 1931, featuring Clark Gable, Norma Shearer, Leslie Howard, Lionel Barrymore; VHS format, #12-2149.

Susan Lenox: Her Fall and Rise, 1931, featuring Clark Gable and Greta Garbo; VHS format, #12-2102.

Possessed, 1931, featuring Clark Gable and Joan Crawford; VHS format, #12-1468.

Red Dust, 1932, featuring Clark Gable, Jean Harlow, Mary Astor; VHS format, #12-1441.

No Man of Her Own, 1932, featuring Clark Gable and Carole Lombard; VHS format, #10-3064.

Night Nurse, 1933, featuring Clark Gable, Barbara Stanwyck, Joan Blondell; VHS format, #12-2297.

It Happened One Night, 1934, featuring Clark Gable and Claudette Colbert; VHS format, #02-1363.

Mutiny on the Bounty, 1935, featuring Clark Gable, Charles Laughton, Franchot Tone; VHS format, #12-1350.

China Seas, 1935, featuring Clark Gable, Jean Harlow, Wallace Beery, Rosalind Russell, Hattie McDaniel; VHS format, #12-1436.

Chained, 1934, featuring Clark Gable and Joan Crawford; VHS format, #12-2329.

Manhattan Melodrama, 1934, featuring Clark Gable, William Powell, Myrna Loy; VHS format, #12-2332.

San Francisco, 1936, featuring Clark Gable, Spencer Tracy, Jeanette MacDonald; VHS format, #12-1444.

San Francisco (color version); VHS format, #12-2100.

Wife Vs. Secretary, 1936, featuring Clark Gable, Myrna Loy, Jean Harlow; VHS format, #12-2301.

Test Pilot, 1938, featuring Clark Gable,

Spencer Tracy, Myrna Loy, Lionel Barrymore; VHS format, #12-2333.

Too Hot to Handle, 1938, featuring Clark Gable, Walter Pidgeon, Myrna Loy; VHS format, #12-2098.

Idiot's Delight, 1939, featuring Clark Gable, Norma Shearer, Edward Arnold; VHS format, #12-1470.

Strange Cargo, 1940, featuring Joan Crawford, Clark Gable, Peter Lorre; VHS format, #12-2008.

Boom Town, 1940, featuring Clark Gable, Spencer Tracy, Claudette Colbert, Hedy Lamarr; VHS format, #12-2070.

Honky Tonk, 1941, featuring Clark Gable and Lana Turner; VHS format, #12-2330.

The Hucksters, 1947, featuring Clark Gable, Deborah Kerr, Sydney Greenstreet; VHS format, #12-2099.

Command Decision, 1948, featuring Clark Gable, Walter Pidgeon, Van Johnson; VHS format, #12-2115.

Across the Wide Missouri, 1951, featuring Clark Gable, Ricardo Montalban, John Hodiak; VHS format, #12-2327.

Mogambo, 1953, featuring Clark Gable, Grace Kelly, Ava Gardner; VHS format, #12-1050.

Betrayed, 1954, featuring Clark Gable, Lana Turner, Victor Mature; VHS format, #12-2328.

The Tall Men, 1955, featuring Clark Gable, Jane Russell, Robert Ryan; VHS format, #04-3146.

Soldier of Fortune, 1955, featuring Clark Gable, Susan Hayward, Gene Barry; VHS format, #04-2358.

The King and Four Queens, 1956, featuring Clark Gable, Eleanor Parker, Barbara Nichols, Jo Van Fleet; VHS format, #12-2331.

Run Silent, Run Deep, 1958, featuring Clark Gable, Burt Lancaster, Jack Warden; VHS format, #12-2114.

Teacher's Pet, 1958, featuring Clark Gable, Doris Day, Gig Young; VHS format, #06-1905.

But Not for Me, 1959, featuring Clark

Gable, Carroll Baker, Lilli Palmer, Lee J. Cobb; VHS format, #06-1845.

It Started in Naples, 1960, featuring Clark Gable and Sophia Loren; VHS format, #06-1857.

The Misfits, 1961, featuring Clark Gable, Marilyn Monroe, Montgomery Clift, Thelma Ritter, Eli Wallach; VHS format, #12-1117.

Dear Mr. Gable, 1968. This 52-minute documentary looks at the career of "The King" and includes interviews with his friends and co-workers, and clips from home movies and a number of his classic films. Narrated by Burgess Meredith; VHS format, #12-2326.

Fire Over England, 1937, featuring Vivien Leigh, Laurence Olivier, Flora Robson; VHS format, #10-4010.

Waterloo Bridge, 1940, featuring Vivien Leigh and Robert Taylor; VHS format, #12-1446.

That Hamilton Woman, 1941, featuring Laurence Olivier and Vivien Leigh; VHS format, #44-1842.

A Streetcar Named Desire, 1951, featuring Vivien Leigh and Marlon Brando; VHS format, #19-1403.

The Roman Spring of Mrs. Stone, 1961, featuring Vivien Leigh, Warren Beatty, Jill St. John, Lotte Lenya; VHS format, #19-1396.

Ship of Fools, 1965, featuring Vivien Leigh, Lee Marvin, Oskar Werner, Simone Signoret, Jose Ferrer; VHS format, #02-1523.

Vivien Leigh: Scarlett and Beyond. Hosted by Jessica Lange, this documentary traces Leigh's tumultuous life and work through interviews with co-stars and from film clips; VHS format, #18-7333.

Of Human Bondage, 1934, featuring Leslie Howard and Bette Davis; VHS format, #10-2007.

The Scarlet Pimpernel, 1935, featuring Leslie Howard, Merle Oberon, Nigel Bruce; VHS format, #10-2004.

The Petrified Forest, 1936, featuring

Humphrey Bogart, Bette Davis, Leslie Howard; VHS format, #12-2000.

Intermezzo, 1939, featuring Leslie Howard and Ingrid Bergman; VHS format, #04-1612.

Pimpernel Smith, 1941, directed and produced by and starring Leslie Howard; VHS format, #09-1573.

Captain Blood, 1935, featuring Olivia de Havilland, Errol Flynn, Basil Rathbone; VHS format, #12-2232.

Anthony Adverse, 1936, featuring Fredric March, Olivia de Havilland, Claude Rains; VHS format, #12-1484.

The Charge of the Light Brigade, 1936, featuring Errol Flynn, Olivia de Havilland, David Niven; VHS format, #12-2234.

The Adventures of Robin Hood, 1939, featuring Errol Flynn, Olivia de Havilland, Basil Rathbone, Claude Rains; VHS format, #12-1153.

Dodge City, 1939, featuring Errol Flynn, Olivia de Havilland, Bruce Cabot, Ann Sheridan; VHS format, #12-2168.

They Died With Their Boots On, 1941, featuring Errol Flynn, Olivia de Havilland, Anthony Quinn; VHS format, #12-2036.

They Died With Their Boots On, color version; VHS format, #12-2037.

Santa Fe Trail, 1941, featuring Errol Flynn, Olivia de Havilland, Ronald Reagan; VHS format, #10-2040.

The Strawberry Blonde, 1941, featuring James Cagney, Olivia de Havilland, Rita Hayworth, George Reeves; VHS format, #12-1557.

In This Our Life, 1942, featuring Bette Davis, Olivia de Havilland, George Brent, Hattie McDaniel; VHS format, #12-1957.

The Heiress, 1949, featuring Olivia de Havilland, Montgomery Clift, Ralph Richardson, Miriam Hopkins; VHS format, #07-1291.

Catalog: $7.95 plus $3.00 for postage and handling for a 650-page videocassette catalog. Stock is subject to change. Collectors should contact Movies Unlimited to check the current availability of *GWTW*–related items.

Payment: C, MO, V, MC, D, AE
Delivery: UPS, USPS
Returns: Defective items may be returned within ten days of purchase.

Postings
PO Box 8001
Hilliard, OH 43026-8001
Phone: 800-262-6604
FAX: 614–777-1470
Specialties: Gone With the Wind Special Fiftieth Anniversary Edition, 1939, featuring Clark Gable, Vivien Leigh, Olivia de Havilland, Leslie Howard; VHS format; #VHS 927861.

Manhattan Melodrama, 1934, featuring Clark Gable, William Powell, Myrna Loy; VHS format, #VHS V28061.

Chained, 1934, featuring Clark Gable and Joan Crawford; VHS format, #VHS V2810X.

Test Pilot, 1938, featuring Clark Gable, Spencer Tracy, Myrna Loy, Lionel Barrymore; VHS format, #VHS V28053.

Honky Tonk, 1941, featuring Clark Gable and Lana Turner; VHS format, #VHS V28088.

Run Silent, Run Deep, 1958, featuring Clark Gable, Burt Lancaster, Jack Warden; VHS format; #VHS V08834.

Command Decision, 1948, featuring Clark Gable, Walter Pidgeon, Van Johnson; VHS format; #VHS V08796.

Mogambo, 1953, featuring Clark Gable, Grace Kelly, Ava Gardner; VHS format; #VHS 885387.

Betrayed, 1954, featuring Clark Gable, Lana Turner, Victor Mature; VHS format: #VHS V27995.

The King and Four Queens, 1956, featuring Clark Gable, Eleanor Parker, Barbara Nichols, Jo Van Fleet; VHS format; #VHS V2807X.

It Started in Naples, 1960, featuring Clark Gable, Sophia Loren, Vittorio de Sica; VHS format; #VHS V24902.

Dear Mr. Gable, 1968. This 52–minute

documentary looks at the career of "The King," and includes interviews with his friends and co-workers, and clips from home movies and a number of his classic films. Narrated by Burgess Meredith; VHS format, #VHS V28118.

Intermezzo, 1939, featuring Leslie Howard, Ingrid Bergman; VHS format; #VHS V09792.

The Adventures of Robin Hood, 1938, featuring Errol Flynn, Olivia de Havilland, Basil Rathbone, Claude Rains; VHS format; #VHS 865475.

Captain Blood, 1935, featuring Olivia de Havilland, Errol Flynn, Basil Rathbone; VHS format; #VHS 728834.

The Charge of the Light Brigade, 1936, featuring Errol Flynn, Olivia de Havilland, David Niven; VHS format; #VHS 728850.

Dodge City, 1939, featuring Errol Flynn, Olivia de Havilland, Bruce Cabot, Ann Sheridan; VHS format; #VHS 75259X.

They Died With Their Boots On, 1941, featuring Errol Flynn, Olivia de Havilland, Arthur Kennedy; B&W and colorized versions, VHS format; #VHS 723964.

Catalog: Free. Stock is subject to change. Collectors should contact Postings to check the current availability of *GWTW*–related items.
Payment: C, MO, V, MC, AE, AEO, D
Delivery: UPS
Returns: For defects or damages in videocassettes, leave the tape at the point where the damage occurs and return for replacement of that tape. All returns must be made within ninety days. Original shipping charges not refundable.

Sem Video Products, Inc.
2147 East 17th Street
Brooklyn, NY 11229
Phone: 718-645-1663
800-247-6644 (orders)
FAX: 718-382-6056

Specialties: Gone With the Wind Special Fiftieth Anniversary Edition, 1939, featuring Clark Gable, Vivien Leigh, Olivia de Havilland, Leslie Howard; video laserdisc; #ML101678.
Gone With the Wind (full feature format), 1939, featuring Clark Gable, Vivien Leigh, Olivia de Havilland, Leslie Howard; video laserdisc; #ML102244.
Catalog: Free. Sem Video offers a "wish-list service." Call or write to let company know the titles you would like to purchase. Information is kept in an active database, and customer is notified when selection becomes available.
Payment: CC, MO, V, MC
Delivery: UPS
Returns: Defective laserdiscs may be exchanged for the same title. No refunds. No returns accepted without return authorization.

Sirocco Productions, Inc.
Suite 103
5660 East Virginia Beach Boulevard
Norfolk, VA 23502
Phone: 804-461-8987
FAX: 804-461-4669
Specialties: Scarlett Dolls: An Alexander Tradition 1937–1991, VHS format. This 72-minute video features more than 85 Scarlett dolls, and includes footage of rare composition Scarletts and the only "official" *GWTW* Scarlett O'Hara doll released during the film's 1939 Atlanta premiere.
Catalog: Free. Stock is subject to change. Collectors should contact Sirocco Productions, Inc., to check the current availability of *GWTW*–related items.
Payment: C, MO, V, MC, D, AE
Delivery: UPS, USPS, Federal Express
Returns: Defective tapes may be returned within seven days of purchase if accompanied by receipt.

Starship Audio–Industries
605 Utterback Store Road
Great Falls, VA 22066
Phone: 703-450-5780

703-430-8692

FAX: 703-430-6657

Specialties: Gone With the Wind, 1939,
featuring Clark Gable, Vivien Leigh,
Olivia de Havilland, Leslie Howard;
video laserdisc.

The Making of a Legend: GWTW, 1988,
behind-the-scenes view of the real
story; video laserdisc.

Dancing Lady, 1933, featuring Clark
Gable, Joan Crawford, Franchot Tone;
video laserdisc.

The Misfits, 1961, featuring Clark Gable, Marilyn Monroe, Montgomery
Clift, Thelma Ritter, Eli Wallach; video
laserdisc.

Waterloo Bridge, 1940, featuring Vivien
Leigh, Robert Taylor; video laserdisc.

Ship of Fools, 1965, featuring Vivien
Leigh, Lee Marvin, Simone Signoret,
Jose Ferrer; video laserdisc.

Catalog: Free. Stock is subject to change.
Collectors should contact Starship Audio-
Industries to check the current availability
of *GWTW*–related items.

Payment: C, MO, V, MC, COD

Delivery: UPS, USPS

Returns: Contact company before returning
defective items.

The Turner Store
One CNN Center
Box 105366
Atlanta, GA 30348-5366
Phone: 404-827-4406
FAX: 404-827-3696
Specialties: Gone With the Wind Deluxe
Edition, featuring Clark Gable, Vivien
Leigh, Olivia de Havilland, Leslie Ho-
ward; restored from the 1939 original,
with digital quality VHS video, has ex-
cerpts from *The Making of a Legend:
GWTW;* #GW 22.

*The Making of a Legend: GONE WITH
THE WIND,* 1988, behind-the-scenes view
of the real story, VHS format; #GW 21.

Catalog: Free (call 404-827-2500 to order).
Stock is subject to change. Collectors
should contact The Turner Store to check

the current availability of *GWTW*–related
items.

Payment: C, MO, V, MC

Delivery: UPS, USPS, Federal Express

Returns: Videos are nonrefundable. Re-
placements are made for defective videos
only.

Games, Puzzles, and Toys

IN the movie, Rhett Butler is shown in the
military jail playing cards with Yankee
officers. The Major's hand features "kings
and treys," which Rhett declares are too
good for him. He throws in his cards, and
the Major rakes in the chips.

The men were probably playing with an
ordinary deck, but you can play poker,
hearts, or even Go Fish with *Gone With the
Wind* playing cards. Each deck comes in a
specially decorated tin. Chips are available,
too.

If card games aren't your favorite form of
amusement, try a *Gone With the Wind*
puzzle, jack-in-the-box, or chess set. The
Metropolitan Guild offers the official *Gone
With the Wind* chess set with which you
can stage a battle between Tara and Twelve
Oaks. Check it out.

Bits & Pieces
1 Puzzle Place
B8016
Stevens Point, WI 54481-7199
Phone: 800-544-7297 (orders)
715-341-3521 (customer service)
FAX: 715-341-5958
Specialties: Gone With the Wind puzzle,
24 " by 15 ", 800 pieces, features the
flaming embrace; #01-H4067.
Catalog: Free. Stock is subject to change.
Collectors should contact Bits & Pieces
to check the current availability of
GWTW–related items.
Payment: C, MO, V, MC, AE, D ($20.00
minimum on credit card order).
Delivery: UPS, Rush Air delivery option
Returns: Return item within sixty days for
replacement or refund.

GWTW chess set. *(The Metropolitan Guild)*

The Lighter Side Gift Catalog
4514 19th Street Court East
Box 25600
Bradenton, FL 34206-5600
Phone: 813-747-2356
FAX: 813-746-7896
Specialties: Gone With the Wind puzzle,
24″ by 15″, 800 pieces, features the
flaming embrace. Puzzle Finish adhesive
included so that the puzzle can be hung
on a wall; #2537.
Catalog: Free. Stock is subject to change.
Collectors should contact The Lighter
Side to check the current availability of
GWTW–related items.
Payment: C, MO, V, MC, AE, DC, D
($15.00 minimum credit card charge)
Delivery: UPS, USPS, Air Express delivery
option
Returns: Return item in original condition
and in original packaging for refund or
item exchange.

Mary D's Dolls & Bears & Such
8407 West Broadway
Minneapolis, MN 55445-2266
Phone: 612-424-4375
Specialties: Gone With the Wind tins with
playing cards and tins with poker chips.
Catalog: Free newsletter. Stock is subject to
change. Collectors should contact Mary
D's Dolls & Bears & Such to check the
current availability of *GWTW*–related
items.
Payment: C, MO, V, MC, D, layaways and
collector club discounts
Delivery: UPS, USPS
Returns: Buyer must call Mary D's Dolls &
Bears & Such within ten days of receiving order to arrange return. Returned
items must be in the same condition as
shipped and must be accompanied by
receipt. No returns on layaways or sale
items.

The Metropolitan Guild
60 Madison Avenue
Department GWTW
New York, NY 10010
Phone: 212-481-6960
800-652-5544 (orders)
FAX: 212-481-4265
Specialties: Limited-edition *Gone With the
Wind* Fiftieth Anniversary Chess Set. The
custom-designed chess board is hand-
crafted in solid mahogany. The interior of

GWTW puzzle. *(The Turner Store)*

the playing board contains custom-molded, felt-lined storage compartments to protect and preserve each of the playing pieces when not on display. Each of the 32 playing pieces is hand-carved by world renowned Metropolitan Guild artists. The Tara side is layered in pure 24-karat antique gold, and the Twelve Oaks side is layered in pure antique sterling silver.

Catalog: Free. Stock is subject to change. Collectors should contact The Metropolitan Guild to check the current availability of *GWTW*–related items.

Payment: C, MO, V, MC, AE

Delivery: UPS

Returns: Items may be returned for full refund within four weeks after receipt.

Scarlett's
247 East Main Street
Ashland, OR 97520
Phone: 503-488-2745
Specialties: Puzzles, jack-in-the-boxes.
Catalog: None. Scarlett's has a large inventory of items. Write or telephone with specific wants for a price quote.

Payment: C, MO, V, MC, D, AE

Delivery: UPS

Returns: Items may be returned for exchange or refund within thirty days of receipt.

The Turner Store
One CNN Center
Box 105366
Atlanta, GA 30348-5366
Phone: 404-827-4406
FAX: 404-827-3696
Specialties: Gone With the Wind puzzle, approximately 24″ by 15″, 800 pieces, features the flaming embrace, comes with glue and finish for hanging; #GW 04.

Playing cards and tin, features a Scarlett deck and a Rhett deck enclosed in a decorated tin; #GW 56.

Catalog: Free (call 404-827-2500 to order). Stock is subject to change. Collectors should contact The Turner Store to check the current availability of *GWTW*–related items.

Payment: C, MO, V, MC

Delivery: UPS, USPS, Federal Express

Returns: Return item within thirty days in original packaging with sales receipt.

Jewelry

SHOW your love of Selznick's masterpiece by wearing a unique timepiece, a *Gone With the Wind* watch. Its arrival at your door will come not a moment too soon.

Atlanta Historical Society Museum Shop
3101 Andrews Drive, NW
Atlanta, GA 30305
Phone: 404-261-1837
Specialties: Rhett and Scarlett quartz watch with black leather band; one size fits men and women; from the Fred A. Parrish Collection of Photographs titled "Behind the Scenes . . . *Gone With the Wind.*"
  Scarlett quartz watch with black leather band; one size fits men and women; from the Fred A. Parrish Collection of Photographs titled "Behind the Scenes . . . *Gone With the Wind.*"
Catalog: None. Stock is subject to change. A list of items offered by the Museum Shop is available by sending a request and enclosing a SASE.
Payment: C, MO, V, MC
Delivery: UPS
Returns: Only items damaged in shipping may be returned.

Clark Gable Foundation
PO Box 65
Cadiz, OH 43907
Phone: 614-942-GWTW
Specialties: "Cadiz, OH, Birthplace of Clark Gable" watch; one size fits men and women; designed by William J. Tomkin Ltd.
Catalog: None. Stock is subject to change. Collectors should contact the Clark Gable Foundation to check the current availability of items.
Payment: C, MO, V, MC
Delivery: UPS, USPS

Scarlett and Rhett watch. *(The Turner Store)*

Returns: Any item may be returned for refund.

The Lighter Side Gift Catalog
4514 19th Street Court East
Box 25600
Bradenton, FL 34206-5600
Phone: 813-747-2356
FAX: 813-746-7896
Specialties: Gone With the Wind quartz watch, featuring the flaming embrace; one size fits men and women; #2774.
Catalog: Free. Stock is subject to change. Collectors should contact The Lighter Side to check the current availability of *GWTW*–related items.
Payment: C, MO, V, MC, AE, DC, D ($15.00 minimum credit card charge)
Delivery: UPS, USPS, Air Express delivery option
Returns: Return item in original condition and in original packaging for refund or item exchange.

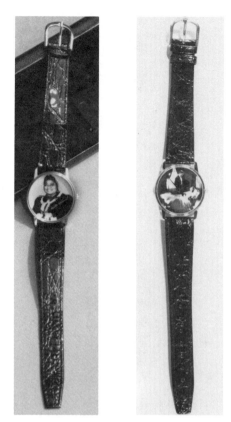

Above Left. Hattie McDaniel collector's watch.
*(Tomkin & Rodney/© 1992 E. Goff) Above
Right.* Scarlett and Rhett collector's edition
watch. *(Tomkin & Rodney/© 1992 E. Goff)*

R&R/Valdawn, Inc.
600 Sylvan Avenue
Englewood Cliffs, NJ 07632
Phone: 201-871-1616
Specialties: Scarlett and Rhett quartz watch
with genuine lizard-grain black leather
band, features the flaming embrace with
the words *Gone With the Wind* in gold
on a black bezel; one size fits men and
women, #5001.
Catalog: None. Stock is subject to change.
Descriptive flyers are available by sending
a request and enclosing a SASE.
Payment: C, MO
Delivery: UPS, USPS
Returns: Defective items will be replaced.

Tomkin & Rodney Ventures
PO Box 641219

Los Angeles, CA 90064
Phone: 310-841-0514
Specialties: The Fred A. Parrish Collection
of Photographs titled "Behind the
Scenes . . . *Gone With the Wind.*"
Products include:
Rhett and Scarlett quartz watch with
black leather band; one size fits men
and women.
Scarlett quartz watch with black leather
band; one size fits men and women.
Hattie McDaniel quartz watch with black
leather band; one size fits men and
women.
Catalog: None. Stock is subject to change.
Descriptive flyers are available by sending
a request and enclosing a SASE.
Payment: C, MO
Delivery: UPS, USPS
Returns: Any item may be returned within
thirty days for an exchange or refund.
Watches have a one-year warranty.

Linens

THE summer scene sizzles with a *Gone
With the Wind* beach towel. Choose
one or both: the torrid flaming embrace or
the smoldering proposal embrace. Each is
emblazoned on 100 percent cotton and just
might kindle the fires of romance for you.

The Turner Store
One CNN Center
Box 105366
Atlanta, GA 30348-5366
Phone: 404-827-4406
FAX: 404-827-3696
Specialties: Gone With the Wind beach
towel, 30 " by 60 ", features the flaming
embrace in 100 percent cotton terry
cloth; #GW 24.
Gone With the Wind beach towel, 30 " by
60 ", features Scarlett and Rhett em-
bracing in 100 percent cotton terry
cloth; #GW 28.
Catalog: Free (call 404-827-2500 to order).
Stock is subject to change. Collectors
should contact The Turner Store to check

the current availability of *GWTW*–related items.

Payment: C, MO, V, MC

Delivery: UPS, USPS, Federal Express

Returns: Return item within thirty days in original packaging with sales receipt.

Music Boxes

ARDLEIGH–ELLIOTT is dedicated to bringing new classics of music-box art to today's collector. This commitment is exquisitely expressed in The *Gone With the Wind* Music Box Collection. The collection contains the following boxes with melodies from *Gone With the Wind*'s musical score:

1. "Scarlett at Twelve Oaks" (plays "Tara's Theme")
2. "The Proposal" (plays "Scarlett O'Hara")
3. "The Burning of Atlanta" (plays "Fall of the South")
4. "Scarlett's Resolve" (plays "For He's a Jolly Good Fellow")
5. "The Charity Bazaar" (plays "The Ball")
6. "Scarlett & Rhett" (plays variations on "Tara's Theme")

The first issue in the series, "Scarlett at Twelve Oaks," was proclaimed 1992 Musical of the Year by the National Association of Limited Edition Dealers.

Ardleigh–Elliott

9204 Center for the Arts

Niles, IL 60714

Phone: 800-828-0118

708-966-0165 (in Illinois)

Specialties: The *Gone With the Wind* Music Box Collection.

Catalog: None. Flyers are available on recently issued music boxes. Stock is subject to change. Collectors should contact Ardleigh–Elliott to check the current availability of *GWTW*–related items.

Payment: C, MO, V, MC, D

Delivery: UPS, USPS

Returns: Each music box is protected by an unconditional 365-day guarantee. Within

GWTW music box. *(The Bradford Exchange)*

one full year after receipt of a box, it may be returned for any reason if a customer is not fully satisfied. Ardleigh–Elliott will issue a refund check (or credit for credit card purchase) for the entire cost of the music box, including postage.

J and L Meyers

595 Route 18

East Brunswick, NJ 08816

Phone: 908-257-1720

800-332-0176 (orders)

Specialties: Gone With the Wind music boxes.

Catalog: None. Stock is subject to change. A list of items offered by J and L Meyers is available by sending a request and enclosing a SASE.

Payment: C, MO, V, MC, D, AE (Free layaways on orders over $100)

Delivery: UPS. Orders over $100 are shipped free; for orders under $100 there is a $3.00 charge

Returns: If not happy with an item, call within ten days to arrange a return. J and L Meyers will replace item or issue refund.

Four *GWTW* music boxes. *(The Turner Store)*

Postings
PO Box 8001
Hilliard, OH 43026-8001
Phone: 800-262-6604
FAX: 614-777-1470
Specialties: "Embrace" music box, limited
   edition, wooden, lined, 6 " by 7 " by
   2¹/₂", comes with certificate of authen-
   ticity; #M0690X.
Catalog: Free. Stock is subject to change.
   Collectors should contact Postings to
   check the current availability of *GWTW*–
   related items.
Payment: C, MO, V, MC, AE, AEO, D
Delivery: UPS
Returns: Return item for full credit or re-
   fund. All returns must be made within
   ninety days. Original shipping charges
   not refundable.

Scarlett's Sales
PO Box 6351
3401 Gentian Boulevard
Columbus, GA 31907
Phone: 706-569-7316
Specialties: Gone With the Wind music
   boxes.

Dave Grossman *Gone With the Wind*
   animated, musical waterglobes.
Catalog: $1.00. Cost of catalog may be
   deducted from first order. Stock is subject
   to change. Collectors should contact
   Scarlett's Sales to check the current availability of *GWTW*–related items.
Payment: C, MO, V, MC
Delivery: UPS, USPS
Returns: Items in salable condition may be
   returned within fourteen days of receipt
   for refund, less the cost of shipping and
   handling.

Shirley's Dollhouse
20509 North Highway 21
PO Box 99A
Wheeling, IL 60090
Phone: 708-537-1632
Specialties: Gone With the Wind music
   boxes.
Catalog: None. Stock is subject to change.
   Descriptive flyers are available by sending
   a request and enclosing a SASE.
Payment: C, MO, V, MC
Delivery: UPS

Returns: Items may be returned within ten
days for in-store credit.

The Turner Store
One CNN Center
Box 105366
Atlanta, GA 30348-5366
Phone: 404-827-4406
FAX: 404-827-3696
Specialties: "Scarlett" music box, limited
edition, wooden, lined, 6^1/$_2$" by 9" by
2^1/$_2$", plays "Tara's Theme," comes with
certificate of authenticity; #GW 64.
Catalog: Free (call 404-827-2500 to order).
Stock is subject to change. Collectors
should contact The Turner Store to check
the current availability of *GWTW*–related
items.
Payment: C, MO, V, MC
Delivery: UPS, USPS, Federal Express
Returns: Return item within thirty days in
original packaging with sales receipt.

GWTW needlepoint pillow. *(The Turner Store)*

Needlecrafts

AFTER being attacked at Shantytown,
Scarlett spends the evening at Melanie's house while Frank, Ashley, and the
other men attend a political meeting. The
ladies of the sewing circle are on pins and
needles, not only because of their darning
and mending but because something is going on of which Scarlett is unaware. The
atmosphere crackles with tension. But the
sewing circle scene as written by Margaret
Mitchell differs from the scene as portrayed
on the silver screen.
• **Guests.** In Mitchell's version, the ladies
include Melanie, Scarlett, India Wilkes, and
Aunt Pittypat. Scarlett's driver and protec-
tor, Archie, whittles by the hearth. In
Selznick's version, the ladies include Melanie, Scarlett, India, and Mrs. Meade.
Mammy watches over the sewing circle.
• **Events.** In the novel, Archie hears
Rhett on the walk, and Melanie flings open
the door. After Rhett leaves, Archie tells
Scarlett that she will be responsible if the
men are caught or killed. He receives a
warning from Melanie that one more word

and "you go out of this house." He directs
the ladies to continue with their sewing.
In the movie, Mammy hears Rhett's foot-
steps and at Melanie's request admits him
to the parlor. India reads the riot act to
Scarlett and receives Melanie's warning
about saying another word against Scarlett.
Melanie urges the ladies to continue sewing.
• **Reading Material.** In the novel, Melanie reads from *Les Misérables* by Victor
Hugo. In the movie, her book of choice is
David Copperfield by Charles Dickens.
Selznick had brought this classic to the
screen while associated with MGM.
• **Rhett to the Rescue.** In both the novel
and movie, Rhett returns with a wounded
Ashley. However, Hugh Elsing is the com-
panion in the novel while Dr. Meade comes
along in the movie.
• **Resolution.** In the novel, Melanie faints
at the mention of Belle Watling's name.
Hugh Elsing leaves under the custody of
Tom Jaffery, the Yankee captain. Archie
helps Ashley into the bedroom, and Rhett
sends India for a doctor other than Dr.
Meade, who is implicated in the Shantytown raid. She brings back Dr. Dean.

Scarlett asks about Frank, and Rhett eventually tells her of the fate her husband suffered at the old Sullivan plantation. In the movie, Melanie appears stoic at the news that the gentlemen spent the evening at Belle's establishment. The Yankees withdraw, taking no prisoners. Rhett carries Ashley into the bedroom, and since Dr. Meade is already there, he begins looking for an implement to use as a probe. Deeply concerned about Ashley's condition, Scarlett gives no thought to Frank Kennedy's whereabouts. Rhett brings the shocking reality to her.

Postings
PO Box 8001
Hilliard, OH 43026-8001
Phone: 800-262-6604
FAX: 614-777-1470
Specialties: Needlepoint pillow, wool, with polyester filling, 9 ″ by 7 ″, red background with "Frankly, My Dear, I Don't Give A Damn!" in white with white border; #M04087.
Catalog: Free. Stock is subject to change. Collectors should contact Postings to check the current availability of *GWTW*–related items.
Payment: C, MO, V, MC, AE, AEO, D
Delivery: UPS
Returns: Return item for full credit or refund. All returns must be made within ninety days. Original shipping charges not refundable.

The Turner Store
One CNN Center
Box 105366
Atlanta, GA 30348-5366
Phone: 404-827-4406
FAX: 404-827-3696
Specialties: Needlepoint pillow, handstitched, front is 100-percent wool, back is velveteen, 14 ″ by 14 ″; #GW 51.
Counted cross-stitch kit, includes detailed graph, DMC floss, 16-count antique white aida and #24 needle. Design size is 9³/₄ ″ square. Frame not included; #GW 007.

GWTW counted cross-stitch kit. *(The Turner Store)*

Catalog: Free (call 404-827-2500 to order). Stock is subject to change. Collectors should contact The Turner Store to check the current availability of *GWTW*–related items.
Payment: C, MO, V, MC
Delivery: UPS, USPS, Federal Express
Returns: Return item within thirty days in original packaging with sales receipt.

Paper

Like shimmering jewels in a crown, extraordinary items of paper ephemera heralded *Gone With the Wind*'s fiftieth-anniversary celebration in 1989:

• **Media Kit.** An elaborate presentation folder graced the media materials prepared by Turner Broadcasting System, Inc. On the folder's cover was a color photograph of Scarlett and Rhett. The cover separated along Rhett's profile to reveal the contents within.

Inside the folder, a pocket—featuring oval photographs of Ashley, Melanie, and Prissy—held a black-and-white montage photograph and nine feature articles exploring *Gone With the Wind*'s history. The arti-

GWTW address book. *(The Turner Store)*

cles were entitled "Margaret Mitchell Totes the Weary Load," "The Man Who Built Tara: David O. Selznick," "Hollywood's Civil Wars," "Cast and Credits," "Fifty Years at Tara: The Continuing Popularity of *Gone With the Wind*," "Tara's Toughest Trivia Test," "The Glory of the South Restored," "Scarlett O'Hara Comes Home" and "The Making of a Legend: *Gone With the Wind*."

• **Ball Program.** Commissioned by the Clayton County Chamber of Commerce, the program marked the Fiftieth Anniversary Ball held on December 14, 1989, at the Georgia International Convention and Trade Center.

The glossy white cover featured the fiftieth-anniversary logo in gold on the front and the autographs of Clark Gable, Vivien Leigh, Ann Rutherford, Leslie Howard, Evelyn Keyes, Harry Davenport, Laura Hope Crews, Alicia Rhett, Barbara O'Neil, Ona Munson, Thomas Mitchell, and Olivia de Havilland in gold on the back. The inside pages included letters of welcome from Andrew Young, mayor of the city of Atlanta; Ted Turner, chairman of the board of Turner Broadcasting System, Inc.; stills from *Gone With the Wind* and photo-graphs of the 1939 premiere; and reproductions of pages from the original Junior League of Atlanta, Inc., 1939 World Premiere Ball program.

• **Poster of Scarlett.** One of the gifts given to each guest at the Fiftieth Anniversary Ball was a limited-edition, silk-screened poster of Scarlett O'Hara produced by Delta Airlines, which served as the official airline of the *Gone With the Wind* fiftieth-anniversary celebration. Executed by an Atlanta graphic artist, the poster was inspired by an original Delta destination poster, one of a series used by the airline from 1959 until the early 1970s.

• **Re-premiere Program.** The program for the re-creation of the world premiere of *Gone With the Wind* was a duplicate of the one issued at the 1939 premiere. Included in the program were portraits and brief biographies of the stars; photographs of David O. Selznick, Margaret Mitchell, Victor Fleming and Sidney Howard; a two-paged spread listing the cast and production crew; facts about production; and articles by Clark Gable and Vivien Leigh on their respective roles. The back of the program

GWTW 50th
anniversary programs
and button.

GWTW Delta Airlines poster.

featured the schedule of events for the December 15, 1989, re-premiere of *Gone With the Wind* at Atlanta's Fox Theater.

Atlanta Historical Society Museum Shop
3101 Andrews Drive, NW
Atlanta, GA 30305
Phone: 404-261-1837
Specialties: Catalog from the exhibit, "*Gone With the Wind:* The Facts about the Fiction," held December 1989 to June 1990.
Catalog: None. Stock is subject to change. A list of items offered by the Museum Shop is available by sending a request and a SASE.
Payment: C, MO, V, MC
Delivery: UPS
Returns: Only items damaged in shipping may be returned.

Atlanta Journal–Constitution
PO Box 2198
Atlanta, GA 30301
Phone: 404-222-2000
800-876-2076 (orders)
Specialties: "Her Byline Was Peggy Mitchell," 24-page commemorative reprint of 8 of Margaret Mitchell's articles published in *The Atlanta Journal Magazine* from 1922 to 1926.
Catalog: None. Stock is subject to change. Collectors should contact *Atlanta*

Journal–Constitution to check the current availability of *GWTW*–related items.
Payment: C, MO, V, MC
Delivery: UPS, USPS, local delivery by newspaper carriers
Returns: Items may be returned postpaid up to fourteen days after receipt.

Eugenia's Place
1574 Cave Road NW
Atlanta, GA 30327
Phone: 404-261-0394 (weekdays)
404-458-0682 (weekends)
Specialties: Gone With the Wind reproduction postcards; programs; *Atlanta Journal* December 15, 1939, special issue.
Catalog: None. Stock is subject to change. Collectors should notify Eugenia's Place of particular wants by sending a letter of inquiry with a SASE.
Payment: C, MO, V, MC
Delivery: UPS, USPS
Returns: Any item may be returned for store credit only.

Clark Gable Foundation
PO Box 65
Cadiz, OH 43907
Phone: 614-942-GWTW
Specialties: Commemorative cachets postmarked Cadiz, OH.
Programs from the 1989 Clark Gable Foundation barbecue.
Catalog: None. Stock is subject to change. Collectors should contact the Clark Gable Foundation to check the current availability of items.
Payment: C, MO, V, MC
Delivery: UPS, USPS
Returns: Any item may be returned for refund.

Hemetro
127 South Main Street
New Hope, PA 18938
Phone: 215-862-5629
800-362-5336 (orders)
Specialties: Gone With the Wind hand fans.
Catalog: None. Stock is subject to change. Collectors should notify Hemetro of particular wants by telephoning or sending a letter of inquiry with a SASE.
Payment: C, MO, V, MC, D, AE
Delivery: UPS
Returns: No returns.

The Lighter Side Gift Catalog
4514 19th Street Court East
Box 25600
Bradenton, FL 34206-5600
Phone: 813-747-2356
FAX: 813-746-7896
Specialties: Gable and Leigh paper dolls, set of two full-color books. Gable book has 3 dolls and 32 outfits (5 from *GWTW*); Leigh book has 1 doll with 28 costumes (8 from *GWTW*); #2597
Catalog: Free. Stock is subject to change. Collectors should contact The Lighter Side to check the current availability of *GWTW*–related items.
Payment: C, MO, V, MC, AE, DC, D ($15.00 minimum credit card charge)
Delivery: UPS, USPS, Air Express delivery option
Returns: Return item in original condition and in original packaging for refund or item exchange.

Mary D's Dolls & Bears & Such
8407 West Broadway
Minneapolis, MN 55445-2266
Phone: 612-424-4375
Specialties: Gone With the Wind paper dolls.
Catalog: Free newsletter. Stock is subject to change. Collectors should contact Mary D's Dolls & Bears & Such to check the current availability of *GWTW*–related items.
Payment: C, MO, V, MC, D, layaways. Collector club discounts available.
Delivery: UPS, USPS
Returns: Buyer must call Mary D's Dolls & Bears & Such within ten days of receiving order to arrange return. Returned items must be in the same condition as shipped and must be accompanied by receipt. No returns on layaways or sale items.

Mary Ellen & Co.
29400 Rankert Road, Department G
North Liberty, IN 46554
Phone: 219-656-3000
800-669-1860 (orders)
Specialties: Vivien Leigh paper dolls has 1
    doll and 28 color costumes (8 from
    GWTW); #24207-2
    Clark Gable paper dolls has 3 dolls and
    32 costumes (5 from *GWTW*);
    #25234-5
Catalog: $3.00. Stock is subject to change.
    Collectors should contact Mary Ellen &
    Co. to check the current availability of
    GWTW–related items.
Payment: C, MO, V, MC, COD.
Delivery: UPS, USPS
Returns: Books may not be returned or
    exchanged.

Scarlett's
247 East Main Street
Ashland, OR 97520
Phone: 503-488-2745
Specialties: Gone With the Wind commemo-
    rative postage stamps.
Catalog: None. Scarlett's has a large inven-
    tory of items. Write or telephone with
    specific wants for a price quote.
Payment: C, MO, V, MC, D, AE
Delivery: UPS
Returns: Items may be returned for ex-
    change or refund within thirty days of
    receipt.

Scarlett's Sales
PO Box 6351
3401 Gentian Boulevard
Columbus, GA 31907
Phone: 706-569-7316
Specialties: Postcards (b&w and color),
    cardboard stand-ups, pop-up greeting
    cards, programs, and periodicals, in-
    cluding:
    Cosmopolitan, January 1992; contains
    excerpt from *Scarlett.*
    Georgia Living, September/October
    1991; includes article about collectors
    of *Gone With the Wind* memorabilia.
    Bookland, September l991; published by

Clark Gable paperdoll book.

    Oxford Book Store in Atlanta, GA,
    and includes full-page article about
    Scarlett.
    Ladies' Home Journal, November 1991;
    includes excerpts from *Scarlett.*
    Life magazine, September 1991; contains
    first publication of excerpt from
    Scarlett.
    Sky magazine, December 1989; includes
    a five-page article about *Gone With the
    Wind*'s fiftieth anniversary.
    Time magazine, October 7, 1991; con-
    tains a review of *Scarlett.*
    Atlanta newspaper, December 15, 1939;
    replica of the souvenir edition covering
    the premiere of *Gone With the Wind.*
    Souvenir programs from the Clark Gable
    Foundation's annual celebration of his
    birthday.
Catalog: $1.00. Cost of catalog may be
    deducted from first order. Stock is subject
    to change. Collectors should contact
    Scarlett's Sales to check the current avail-
    ability of *GWTW*–related items.
Payment: C, MO, V, MC

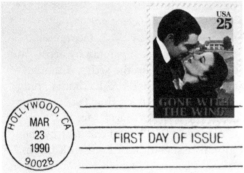

Left. First-day issue *GWTW* stamp. *Above.* Mammy, Scarlett, and Rhett fans. *(The Turner Store)*

Delivery: UPS, USPS
Returns: Items in salable condition may be returned within fourteen days of receipt for refund, less the cost of shipping and handling.

The Turner Store
One CNN Center
Box 105366
Atlanta, GA 30348-5366
Phone: 404-827-4406
FAX: 404-827-3696
Specialties: Gone With the Wind paper dolls, replica of the original 1940 18-doll edition; #GW 57.

Catalog: Free (call 404-827-2500 to order). Stock is subject to change. Collectors should contact The Turner Store to check the current availability of *GWTW*–related items.
Payment: C, MO, V, MC
Delivery: UPS, USPS, Federal Express
Returns: Return item within thirty days in original packaging with sales receipt.

Plates

IN 1978 the Edwin M. Knowles China Company, under the aegis of Metro–Goldwyn–Mayer, introduced the official *Gone With the Wind* commemorative plate collection. The beautiful *Gone With the Wind* series was painted by artist Raymond Kursár.

"Scarlett," the first issue in the series, originally sold for $21.50. But the limited-edition, hand-numbered plate proved so

"Fiery Embrace" collector's plate. *(The Bradford Exchange)*

popular that its value has skyrocketed to nearly $300. The plate depicted Scarlett, with billowing organdy skirts in hand, dashing through azaleas and dogwood, with Tara in the background.

The second plate in the series was "Ashley." The artist portrayed a uniformed Ashley descending the Twelve Oaks staircase as he is about to ride away to war. However, the reserved, aristocratic Mr. Wilkes wasn't a hit with collectors, who bypassed this quintessential Southern gentleman in favor of the third plate, "Melanie," and the fourth plate, "Rhett." "Melanie" showed the gentle Mrs. Wilkes waiting outside Aunt Pittypat's house for Ashley's return. "Rhett" pictured Mr. Butler, outspoken and independent, against the extravagantly decorated library in Scarlett's Atlanta house.

Suddenly collectors decided "Ashley" was the one for them after all. Collectors scrambled to complete their series but found that the price for "Ashley" in the secondary markets soared as high as $225. The remaining issues in the nine-plate series were: "Mammy Lacing Scarlett," "Melanie Gives Birth," "Scarlett's Green Dress," "Rhett and

Bonnie," "Scarlett and Rhett: The Finale."

In 1988, as a follow-up to the first series, MGM and Turner Entertainment Company authorized the "*Gone With the Wind* Golden Anniversary" series. Painted by artist Howard Rogers, this limited-edition, hand-numbered, twelve-plate series carried the hallmark of W. S. George Fine China. The first plate in the series had an issue price of $24.50 but has since appreciated in value to $85. The series included

1. "Scarlett and Her Suitors"
2. "The Burning of Atlanta"
3. "Scarlett and Ashley after the War"
4. "The Proposal"
5. "Home to Tara"
6. "Strolling in Atlanta"
7. "A Question of Honor"
8. "Scarlett's Resolve"
9. "Frankly, My Dear"
10. "Melanie and Ashley"
11. "A Toast to Bonnie Blue"
12. "The Honeymoon"

In 1991 a third series of collector plates, called "Critic's Choice: *Gone With the Wind*," was issued by W. S. George Fine China. Twelve plates, painted by artist Paul Jennis, will make up the series, although according to the Bradford Exchange, only nine have been planned thus far. The first plate in the series, "Marry Me, Scarlett," was named 1992 Plate of the Year by the National Association of Limited Edition Dealers. The series, which will probably conclude in 1993, includes:

1. "Marry Me, Scarlett"
2. "Waiting for Rhett"
3. "A Declaration of Love"
4. "The Paris Hat"
5. "Scarlett Asks a Favor"
6. "Scarlett Gets Her Way"
7. "The Smitten Suitor"
8. "Scarlett's Shopping Spree"
9. "Buggy Ride"

A fourth series of *Gone With the Wind* collector plates is running concurrently with "Critic's Choice." Artist Paul Jennis is also painting this latest series, called "The Passions of Scarlett O'Hara." The series is open-ended, and the first four plates include:

1. "Fiery Embrace"
2. "Pride and Passion"
3. "Dreams of Ashley"
4. "The Fond Farewell"

Collectors wanting to complete their plate series with back issues can take advantage of the Bradford Trading Floor, part of the Bradford Exchange. Bradford brokers can help collectors to buy (and also sell) back issues via the telephone or through the mail. Once the Exchange has confirmed a match, that transaction is guaranteed for both parties. Collectors selling through the Exchange are charged a 30-percent commission while buyers pay a 4-percent commission or $4 if the plate is less than $100. For information, contact the Bradford Trading Floor at 800-323-8078 or if calling in Illinois, at 708-966-1900.

Aunt Edye's Show Plates, Collectibles & Gifts
9832 Albemarle Road
Charlotte, NC 28227
Phone: 704-545-2658
Specialties: Gone With the Wind collector plates.
Catalog: None. Stock is subject to change. A list of items offered by Aunt Edye's is available by sending a request and enclosing a SASE.
Payment: C, V, MC
Delivery: UPS
Returns: If an item should be unsatisfactory, telephone Aunt Edye's to discuss a return or exchange.

Bluff Park Rare Books
2535 East Broadway
Long Beach, CA 90803
Phone: 310-438-9830
Specialties: Gone With the Wind collector plates.
Catalog: None. Stock is subject to change. Collectors should notify Bluff Park Rare Books of particular wants by sending a letter of inquiry with a SASE.
Payment: C

Delivery: UPS, USPS, Federal Express
Returns: Any item may be returned within ten days for refund if not as described.

The Bradford Exchange
9333 North Milwaukee Avenue
Niles, IL 60714
Phone: 708-966-2770 (in Illinois)
800-323-5577
Specialties: Limited-edition *Gone With the Wind* collector plates.
Catalog: Flyers are available on recently issued plates. Catalogs are issued periodically and may or may not contain *Gone With the Wind* plates. Stock is subject to change. Collectors should contact The Bradford Exchange to check the current availability of *GWTW*–related items.
Payment: C, MO, V, MC, D
Delivery: UPS, USPS
Returns: Each new issue purchased from The Bradford Exchange is protected by an unconditional 365-day guarantee. Within one full year after receipt of a plate, it may be returned for any reason if customer is not fully satisfied. The Exchange will issue a refund check (or credit for credit card purchase) for the entire cost of the plate, including postage.

Ceramica Gift Gallery, Inc.
1009 Sixth Avenue
New York, NY 10018
Phone: 212-354-9216
800-666-9956 (orders)
Specialties: Gone With the Wind collector plates.
Catalog: None. Stock is subject to change. Collectors should contact Ceramica Gift Gallery to check the current availability of *GWTW*–related items.
Payment: C, MO, V, MC
Delivery: UPS, USPS
Returns: Any item may be returned with receipt within fourteen days for refund.

Gifts & Accents
9611 Metcalf Avenue
Overland Park, KS 66212

Phone: 913-381-8856
800-822-8856 (orders)
Specialties: Gone With the Wind collector
  plates.
Catalog: None. Stock is subject to change.
  Collectors should contact Gifts &
  Accents to check the current availability
  of *GWTW*–related items.
Payment: C, MO, V, MC, D
Delivery: UPS
Returns: Any item may be returned within
  thirty days for refund.

Hemetro
127 South Main Street
New Hope, PA 18938
Phone: 215-862-5629
800-362-5336 (orders)
Specialties: Gone With the Wind collector
  plates.
Catalog: None. Stock is subject to change.
  Collectors should notify Hemetro of par-
  ticular wants by telephoning or sending a
  letter of inquiry with a SASE.
Payment: C, MO, V, MC, D, AE
Delivery: UPS
Returns: No returns.

Monarch Collectibles
2012 Northwest Military Highway
San Antonio, TX 78213
Phone: 512-341-3655
800-648-3655 (orders)
Specialties: Gone With the Wind collector
  plates.
Catalog: None. Stock is subject to change.
  Collectors should contact Monarch Col-
  lectibles to check the current availability
  of *GWTW*–related items.
Payment: C, V, MC, D, layaways
Delivery: UPS
Returns: Any item may be returned along
  with receipt for exchange or in-store
  credit.

Scarlett's Sales
PO Box 6351
3401 Gentian Boulevard
Columbus, GA 31907
Phone: 706-569-7316

Specialties: Gone With the Wind collector
  plates.
Catalog: $1.00. Cost of catalog may be
  deducted from first order. Stock is subject
  to change. Collectors should contact
  Scarlett's Sales to check the current availability of *GWTW*–related items.
Payment: C, MO, V, MC
Delivery: UPS, USPS
Returns: Items in salable condition may be
  returned within fourteen days of receipt
  for refund, less the cost of shipping and
  handling.

Worldwide Collectibles & Gifts
2 Lakeside Avenue
Berwyn, PA 19312-0158
Phone: 215-644-2442
800-222-1613 (orders)
Specialties: Gone With the Wind collector
  plates.
Catalog: Free. Stock is subject to change.
  Collectors should contact Worldwide
  Collectibles & Gifts to check the current
  availability of *GWTW*–related items.
Payment: C, MO, V, MC, D, AE
Delivery: UPS, USPS
Returns: Any item may be returned within
  thirty days for refund.

Posters, Prints, and Photographs

FIRST release and reissue posters, inserts, lobby cards, and black-and-white
movie stills are appreciated not only for
their beauty but for the nostalgic feelings of
a bygone era which they evoke. Unfortunately, original items command high prices.
Luckily, the average collector can capture
the same wistful feelings at a much more
affordable cost with high-quality reproductions.

Reproduction posters, inserts, and lobby
cards are printed on stock that differs in
texture from the originals. But the materials
often carry the flavor of the item from
which it was reproduced. For example, on
the reproduction poster you may be able to
see evidence of the fold marks of the original.

"Marry Me, Scarlett" collector's plate. *(The Bradford Exchange)*

Scarlett poster. *(O.S.P. Publishing, Inc.)*

Reproduction black-and-white eight-inch by ten-inch stills, known as "dupes," bring different dimensions to a collection, depending upon the category into which the photograph is classified. The categories include:

• **Outtakes.** Publicity photographs were often taken during dress rehearsals or before the director's official take of a scene and then distributed before the movie was completed. Sometimes the scene was later reshot with different costumes or hairstyles, and other times the scene in the still was edited out of the film's final version. For example, publicity stills from *Gone With the Wind*'s opening scene on Tara's porch show Vivien Leigh in the green-sprig barbecue dress. However, the scene was reshot much later with Leigh wearing the white ruffled gown, and this scene was the one used in the final version of the film.

• **Close-ups.** These stills were head shots of an actor or actress in a memorable movie moment.

• **Behind-the-scenes.** These photographs might show the stars relaxing on the set between takes or might show the director, cast, and crew setting up a scene.

• **Portrait stills.** Shot on the set or in a photographer's studio, these publicity stills captured the stars in glamorous poses.

Reproduction posters and black-and-white stills allow collectors to capture the feelings of the originals without incurring the high costs.

Atlanta Historical Society Museum Shop
3101 Andrews Drive, NW
Atlanta, GA 30305
Phone: 404-261-1837
Specialties: Poster of Scarlett and Rhett from the New Orleans honeymoon scene, black-and-white.
  Scarlett's portrait poster, features Scarlett's portrait from Rhett's bedroom, color.
Catalog: None. Stock is subject to change. A list of items offered by the Museum Shop is available by sending a request and enclosing a SASE.
Payment: C, MO, V, MC
Delivery: UPS
Returns: Only items damaged in shipping may be returned.

Aunt Edye's Show Plates, Collectibles & Gifts
9832 Albemarle Road
Charlotte, NC 28227
Phone: 704-545-2658
Specialties: Framed *Gone With the Wind* lithographs.
Catalog: None. Stock is subject to change. A list of items offered by Aunt Edye's is available by sending a request and enclosing a SASE.
Payment: C, V, MC
Delivery: UPS
Returns: If an item should be unsatisfactory, telephone Aunt Edye's to discuss a return or exchange.

Cinema Collectors
1507 Wilcox Avenue
Hollywood, CA 90028
Phone: 213-461-6516
Specialties: Gone With the Wind stills and posters.
Catalog: Free. Stock is subject to change. Catalog contains listings of stills only. Collectors should contact Cinema Collectors to check the current availability of *GWTW* posters.
Payment: C, MO, V, MC, AE
Delivery: UPS, USPS
Returns: Damaged items may be returned for exchange or store credit. No refunds.

Collectors Book Store
1708 North Vine Street
Hollywood, CA 90028
Phone: 213-467-3296
FAX: 213-467-4536
Specialties: 8″ by 10″ black-and-white stills and 35-mm mounted slides from *Gone With the Wind.*
Catalog: None. Stock is subject to change. Collectors should notify Collectors Book Store of particular wants by telephoning or sending a letter of inquiry with a SASE.
Payment: C, MO, V, MC, D, AE
Delivery: UPS, USPS
Returns: Any item may be returned for full refund or credit if returned in good condition within fourteen days.

Proposal-embrace poster. *(O.S.P. Publishing, Inc.)*

Larry Edmunds Bookshop
6644 Hollywood Boulevard
Hollywood, CA 90028
Phone: 213-463-3273
Specialties: 8″ by 10″ black-and-white stills from *Gone With the Wind.*
Catalog: None. Stock is subject to change. Collectors should notify Larry Edmunds Bookshop of particular wants by sending a letter of inquiry with a SASE.
Payment: C, MO, V, MC
Delivery: UPS
Returns: All sales final. No returns, credits or exchanges.

Film Favorites
PO Box 133
Canton, OK 73724
Phone: 405-886-3358
Specialties: Reproduction photographs of *Gone With the Wind*'s stars and supporting cast.
Catalog: None. Collectors should notify Film Favorites of particular wants by sending a letter of inquiry with a SASE. Film Favorites will supply photocopies of photographs at a cost of ten cents each, from which collector can make a selection.
Payment: C, MO

Rhett poster. *(O.S.P. Publishing, Inc.)*

Delivery: UPS, USPS
Returns: Since each order is considered custom made, no returns are permitted.

The Last Moving Picture Company
2044 Euclid Avenue
Cleveland, OH 44115
Phone: 216-781-1821
Specialties: Reproduction *Gone With the Wind* posters, lobby cards, stills.
Catalog: None. Stock is subject to change. Collectors should contact The Last Moving Picture Company to check the current availability of *GWTW*–related items.
Payment: C, MO, V, MC
Delivery: UPS, USPS, Federal Express, Air Express
Returns: Only if item has been incorrectly described.

The Last Moving Picture Company
6307 Hollywood Boulevard
Hollywood, CA 90028
Phone: 213-467-0838

Specialties: Reproduction *Gone With the Wind* posters, lobby cards, stills.
Catalog: None. Stock is subject to change. Collectors should contact The Last Moving Picture Company to check the current availability of *GWTW*–related items.
Payment: C, MO, V, MC
Delivery: UPS, USPS, Federal Express
Returns: Only if item has been incorrectly described.

Legends By Lund
PO Box 34
Olyphant, PA 18447
Phone: 717-383-1282
Specialties: Signed and numbered limited-edition prints of artwork inspired by *Gone With the Wind*. Prints are black-and-white or sepia.
Catalog: Free for a SASE. Stock is subject to change. Collectors should contact Legends by Lund to check the current availability of *GWTW*–related items.
Payment: C, MO
Delivery: USPS
Returns: No returns.

The Marks Collection
1590 North Roberts Road, Suite 308
Kennesaw, GA 30144
Phone: 800-849-3125
Specialties: 32 ″ by 24 ″ limited-edition print, "Tara," showing Scarlett running down the driveway from Tara. Prints are reproduced from an original oil painting by William Maughan. Each edition is signed and numbered by the artist and printed on the very finest heavy-weight art stock. 30 ″ by 23 ″ limited-edition print, "The Confederate Ball," showing Scarlett and Rhett beginning to dance the Virginia Reel at the Atlanta bazaar. Prints are reproduced from an original oil painting by William Maughan. Each edition is signed and numbered by the artist and printed on the very finest heavy-weight art stock.
Catalog: Flyers only. Stock is subject to change. Collectors should contact The Marks Collection to check the current availability of *GWTW*–related items.

Payment: C, MO, V, MC, AE
Delivery: UPS
Returns: Only damaged or defective items
may be returned.

Movie Gallery
2072 Front Street
East Meadow, NY 11554
Phone: 516-794-0294
Specialties: Gone With the Wind fiftieth
anniversary poster, 22″ by 28″.
Catalog: None. Stock is subject to change.
Collectors should contact Movie Gallery
to check the current availability of
GWTW–related items.
Payment: C, MO, V, MC
Delivery: UPS
Returns: Items may be returned for refund
or exchange for any reason.

Movie Poster Gallery
308¹/₂ South State Street #25
PO Box 2745
Ann Arbor, MI 48106
Phone: 313-665-3151 (11 A.M. to 8 P.M.
Eastern Time Monday–Friday)
Specialties: Reproduction *Gone With the
Wind* posters, lobby cards, photographs,
both U.S. and foreign.
Catalog: $3.00. Stock is subject to change.
Collectors should telephone Movie Poster
Gallery to determine current availability
of *GWTW*–related items.
Payment: C, MO, V, MC
Delivery: UPS, USPS
Returns: Exchanges only. No refund or
credit of shipping charges.

Movie Poster Place
PO Box 128
Lansdowne, PA 19050-0128
Phone: 215-622-6062
FAX: 215-622-6062
Specialties: Gone With the Wind Belgian
window card reproductions, 14″ by
22″.
Gone With the Wind poster reproduction,
20″ by 30″.
Gone With the Wind title card reproduc-
tion.
Clark Gable pinup poster, 20″ by 30″.

Star portraits, b&w, 8″ by 10″.
Still photographs, b&w and color, 8″ by
10″.
Catalog: $1.00, which can be deducted
from first order. Stock is subject to
change. Collectors should contact Movie
Poster Place to check the current avail-
ability of *GWTW*–related items.
Payment: C, MO, V, MC
Delivery: UPS, USPS, Federal Express
Returns: Any item may be returned for re-
fund or exchange for any reason.

Movie Star News
134 West 18th Street
New York, NY 10011
Phone: 212-620-8160
FAX: 212-727-0634
Specialties: An extensive collection of movie
photos and posters.
Catalog: Free. Items in catalog represent
only a small percentage of inventory.
Collectors should notify Movie Star
News of particular wants by sending a
letter of inquiry with a SASE.
Payment: C, MO, V, MC, AE. Minimum
order of $10.00 if check or money order
is sent; minimum order of $20.00 for
credit card charge
Delivery: UPS
Returns: Contact Movie Star News for in-
formation on making returns.

Movie World
200 North San Fernando Road
Burbank, CA 91502
Phone: 818-846-0459
Specialties: Reproduction *Gone With the
Wind* posters and black-and-white stills.
Catalog: None. Stock is subject to change.
Collectors should notify Movie World of
particular wants by sending a letter of
inquiry with a SASE.
Payment: C, MO, V, MC, D
Delivery: UPS
Returns: No refunds or credit.

S. and P. Parker's Movie Market
PO Box 1868
Laguna Beach, CA 92652
Phone: 714-376-0326

Specialties: 8″ by 10″ color and black-and-white photos; 16″ by 20″ color and black-and-white photos.

Catalog: Free. The Movie Market produces 2 main catalogs a year plus 6 supplements. Stock is subject to change. Collectors should contact company to check the current availability of *GWTW*–related items.

Payment: C, MO, V, MC

Delivery: USPS

Returns: Any item may be returned within fourteen days for refund or exchange.

R & R Associates
PO Box 65
Monterey Park, CA 91754

Phone: No phone orders.

Specialties: Poster of Rhett Butler leaning against a pillar; #28-586.
Poster of Scarlett, a head shot showing Vivien Leigh; #28-587.
Poster of Scarlett, tinted head shot; #2046.
Poster of Rhett playing cards, tinted; with fiftieth-anniversary logo; #28-619.
Poster of proposal embrace, tinted; with fiftieth-anniversary logo; #28-620.

Catalog: Free. Stock is subject to change. Collectors should contact R & R Associates to check the current availability of *GWTW*–related items.

Payment: C, MO

Delivery: UPS, USPS

Returns: None.

Scarlett's Sales
PO Box 6351
3401 Gentian Boulevard
Columbus, GA 31907

Phone: 706-569-7316

Specialties: 1989 poster for the book, *The Art of GONE WITH THE WIND* with color photo of Scarlett and Rhett.
Turner commemorative poster of the fiftieth anniversary of *Gone With the Wind;* image is the same as on the 1939 original program. Around the border is a listing of events in Atlanta for the week-long celebration.

Scarlett poster. *(O.S.P. Publishing, Inc.)*

Color and black-and-white movie and publicity stills.

Catalog: $1.00. Cost of catalog may be deducted from first order. Stock is subject to change. Collectors should contact Scarlett's Sales to check the current availability of *GWTW*–related items.

Payment: C, MO, V, MC

Delivery: UPS, USPS

Returns: Items in salable condition may be returned within fourteen days of receipt for refund, less the cost of shipping and handling.

The Turner Store
One CNN Center
Box 105366
Atlanta, GA 30348-5366

Phone: 404-827-4406

FAX: 404-827-3696

Specialties: Scarlett's portrait poster, 23³/4″ by 37¹/2″; features Scarlett's portrait from Rhett's bedroom; printed on heavy, high-gloss paper; #GW 85.

Catalog: Free (call 404-827-2500 to order). Stock is subject to change. Collectors should contact The Turner Store to check the current availability of *GWTW*–related items.

GWTW photo stills. (The Turner Store)

Payment: C, MO, V, MC
Delivery: UPS, USPS, Federal Express
Returns: Return item within thirty days in original packaging with sales receipt.

Yesterday
1143 West Addison Street
Chicago, IL 60613
Phone: 213-248-8087
Specialties: Reproduction *Gone With the Wind* posters, lobby cards and stills.
Catalog: None. Stock is subject to change. Collectors should notify Yesterday of particular wants by sending a letter of inquiry with a SASE. Company maintains a "want card" system and will inform collectors of new material which meets collecting interests.
Payment: C, MO
Delivery: USPS
Returns: Any item may be returned for full refund if not satisfied.

Scripts

DAVID O. SELZNICK selected Sidney Howard, a Pulitzer Prize–winning writer and one of America's leading playwrights, to turn Margaret Mitchell's novel into a movie script.

Howard worked on the script in early 1937, using a copy of the novel that contained Selznick's comments jotted in the margins. Writing at a breakneck, sixteen-hour-a-day pace, Howard completed the script—all 400 pages of it—in six weeks. However, the script had a playing time of nearly six hours.

In early 1938 Selznick and Howard hammered out the second, third, and fourth drafts of the script. Selznick, ever the perfectionist, was still not completely satisfied. He put the script on a shelf but browsed through it occasionally during the next few months, making notes on areas for revision.

In October 1938 Selznick tried to coax Howard back for another script revision. Because of prior commitments, Howard refused. Selznick then selected one writer after another to work on the script, but he viewed all the attempts as unsuccessful. Undaunted, Selznick undertook to write the script himself.

By the time Victor Fleming assumed the directorial reins, the script was in serious trouble. Selznick turned to Ben Hecht, a famous script doctor who had a reputation for working miracles. Hecht agreed to base his rewrite not on the existing script, but on Sidney Howard's two-year-old draft, which Hecht called a "superb treatment." In five days of nonstop work, Hecht revised the entire first half of the script.

The grueling pace discouraged Hecht from attempting the second part of the script, and he left. With Hecht gone, Selznick undertook the writing of the second half on his own. By April 1939, he was hopelessly behind in the rewriting, and the filming was floundering. He sent out a desperate SOS to Sidney Howard.

Howard agreed to work on the script for one week. During that time he rewrote several major scenes in the second part, including the final scene in which Rhett leaves Scarlett. Howard was sure that Selznick would rewrite the rewrite, then call him back again to salvage the script. Selznick did attack the script again, but Howard never worked again on it. In August 1939 Howard was killed in an accident on his seven-hundred-acre cattle farm in Tyringham, Massachusetts.

Sidney Howard's work on *Gone With the Wind* was recognized by the Academy of Motion Picture Arts and Sciences. In February 1940, at the twelfth annual awards presentation held in Los Angeles, Howard was awarded the Oscar for Best Screenplay, making him the first posthumous Academy Award winner.

Script City
8033 Sunset Boulevard
Suite 1500
Hollywood, CA 90046
Phone: 213-871-0707
800-676-2522 (orders)
Specialties: Script for *Gone With the Wind.*
Catalog: Free. Stock is subject to change. Collectors should contact Script City to check the current availability of *GWTW*–related items.
Payment: C, CC, V, MC, AE, DC, CB
Delivery: UPS, USPS, offers rush and super-rush delivery
Returns: All sales are final. Contact company immediately for information concerning damaged goods.

The Turner Store
One CNN Center
Box 105366
Atlanta, GA 30348-5366
Phone: 404-827-4406
FAX: 404-827-3696
Specialties: GONE WITH THE WIND: The Screenplay by Sidney Howard. Edited by Herb Bridges and Terryl C. Boodman.
Catalog: Free (call 404-827-2500 to order).

Stock is subject to change. Collectors should contact The Turner Store to check the current availability of *GWTW*–related items.
Payment: C, MO, V, MC
Delivery: UPS, USPS, Federal Express
Returns: Return item within thirty days in original packaging with sales receipt.

Stationery

THE pen, indeed, is mightier than the sword. In *Gone With the Wind,* audiences witness letters that have important repercussions. For instance:

• "Though he was not vouchsafed a hero's death upon the field of glory, he was nonetheless a hero, dying of pneumonia, following an attack of measles."

News from Colonel Wade Hampton of Charles Hamilton's death plunges Scarlett into "mourning." Ellen O'Hara, wishing to comfort her "bereaved" daughter, suggests that Scarlett might enjoy visiting. Savannah sounds dull to the Widow Hamilton but Atlanta, bustling with activity, has a definite appeal. Mrs. O'Hara tells Scarlett to stop her crying and then coaxes a smile. Before she withdraws, Ellen O'Hara states, "I'll go write the necessary letters." Colonel Hampton's letter and Mrs. O'Hara's letters to Melanie and Aunt Pittypat lead Scarlett to a momentous albeit unwelcome reunion with Rhett Butler.

• "When I return from Paris I shall take the liberty of calling in person to express my admiration for the courage and sacrifice of a very great lady."

Rhett's letter to Melanie literally opens the door to his calling upon Melanie and Scarlett. He presents the Paris hat to Scarlett, and the two flirt with one another. But the hint of romance is quickly dashed when Rhett realizes that Scarlett still hasn't gotten "the wooden-headed Mr. Wilkes" out of her mind. The letter results in Rhett and Scarlett being at crossed purposes on a romantic collision course.

• "Three days' Christmas furlough is hereby granted to Maj. Ashley Wilkes of Cobb's Legion in consideration of meritorious service during the Pennsylvania campaign."

The letter granting Ashley's leave brings him back to Atlanta. Ashley, Melanie, Scarlett, and Aunt Pittypat feast on the last chicken in the city and the last of the fine Madeira. At the end of his leave, as Ashley prepares to depart, he asks Scarlett to look after Melanie for him. The letter that held the promise of joy at Ashley's return results in a promise that inextricably binds Scarlett to Melanie.

Letters are important. Whether the ones you write share personal happenings, detail family news, or extend invitations, you can showcase your message by using *Gone With the Wind* stationery. Presentation folders of rich-looking sheets and envelopes are available from these sources.

Hemetro
127 South Main Street
New Hope, PA 18938
Phone: 215-862-5629
800-362-5336 (orders)
Specialties: Gone With the Wind stationery.
Catalog: None. Stock is subject to change. Collectors should notify Hemetro of particular wants by telephoning or sending a letter of inquiry with a SASE.
Payment: C, MO, V, MC, D, AE
Delivery: UPS
Returns: No returns.

Legends by Lund
PO Box 34
Olyphant, PA 18447
Phone: 717-383-1282
Specialties: Single note cards or packets of 10. Notes feature artwork inspired by *Gone With the Wind.*
Catalog: Free for a SASE. Stock is subject to change. Collectors should contact Legends by Lund to check the current availability of *GWTW*–related items.
Payment: C, MO

Delivery: USPS
Returns: No returns.

Scarlett's Sales
PO Box 6351
3401 Gentian Boulevard
Columbus, GA 31907
Phone: 706-569-7316
Specialties: Gone With the Wind stationery.
Catalog: $1.00. Cost of catalog may be deducted from first order. Stock is subject to change. Collectors should contact Scarlett's Sales to check the current availability of *GWTW*–related items.
Payment: C, MO, V, MC
Delivery: UPS, USPS
Returns: Items in salable condition may be returned within fourteen days of receipt for refund, less the cost of shipping and handling.

The Turner Store
One CNN Center
Box 105366
Atlanta, GA 30348-5366
Phone: 404-827-4406
FAX: 404-827-3696
Specialties: "Portrait of Scarlett" stationery, 12 foil-stamped, soft peach sheets and envelopes featuring Scarlett's portrait from Rhett's bedroom; includes 12 second sheets and blue presentation folder with tassel; #GW 88
Notecards, set of ten 4" by 6" cards and envelopes in folder; #GW 90.
Catalog: Free (call 404-827-2500 to order). Stock is subject to change. Collectors should contact The Turner Store to check the current availability of *GWTW*–related items.
Payment: C, MO, V, MC
Delivery: UPS, USPS, Federal Express
Returns: Return item within thirty days in original packaging with sales receipt.

This and That

THE scent of miscellany is in the air! Unusual collectibles abound to tickle your fancy!

For Clark Gable fans, there are key chains and coasters marking his birthplace, Cadiz, Ohio. For *Gone With the Wind* fans in general, there are matchboxes, magnets, pins, commemorative stamps, and souvenir spoons. Details follow.

Clark Gable Foundation
PO Box 65
Cadiz, OH 43907
Phone: 614-942-GWTW
Specialties: Key chain with map of Ohio marking Clark Gable's birthplace.
Round rubber coasters, 3" diameter, available in a variety of colors, with map of Ohio marking Clark Gable's birthplace.
Catalog: None. Stock is subject to change. Collectors should contact the Clark Gable Foundation to check the current availability of items.
Payment: C, MO, V, MC
Delivery: UPS, USPS
Returns: Any item may be returned for refund.

Painting the Town, Inc.
530 Park Avenue, 7G
New York, NY 10021
Phone: 212-888-0281
Specialties: Gone With the Wind reusable plastic matchboxes, 2" by 2".
Catalog: None. Stock is subject to change. A list of items offered by Painting the Town, Inc., is available by sending a request and enclosing a SASE.
Payment: C, MO, COD
Delivery: UPS
Returns: Returns are not accepted unless item is damaged in shipping. Contact Painting the Town before returning damaged item.

Scarlett's Sales
PO Box 6351
3401 Gentian Boulevard
Columbus, GA 31907
Phone: 706-569-7316
Specialties: Gone With the Wind souvenir spoons with oval color portrait on the handle of Scarlett and Rhett in the

GWTW notecards. *(The Turner Store)*

Framed *GWTW* stamp. *(The Turner Store)*

proposal scene, in gold or silver.
Gone With the Wind pins, magnets, and key chains.

Catalog: $1.00. Cost of catalog may be deducted from first order. Stock is subject to change. Collectors should contact Scarlett's Sales to check the current availability of *GWTW*–related items.

Payment: C, MO, V, MC

Delivery: UPS, USPS

Returns: Items in salable condition may be returned within fourteen days of receipt for refund, less the cost of shipping and handling.

The Turner Store
One CNN Center
Box 105366
Atlanta, GA 30348-5366

Phone: 404-827-4406

FAX: 404-827-3696

Specialties: Gone With the Wind stamp, mounted on a foil-embossed matte, sealed by glass in a solid brass, tarnish-proof frame with brass-bow hanger. Comes with acrylic stand in gift box, measures $2^3/8$" by $2^3/4$"; #GW 89.

"Scarlett" coaster set, 6 different images of Scarlett. Acrylic coating on top protects against staining; cork backing prevents slipping; #GW 91.

Scarlett tin, 7" by $5^1/4$" by $2^3/4$"; #GW 16.

Gone With the Wind Address Book. Step-indexed for easy use, with ample space for 476 entries, including birthdays and fax numbers. Contains more than twenty color photos from the film plus

all the famous lines. Hardcover, $8^{1/4}$"
by $6^{1/2}$", 96 pages; #GW 87.

Frosted glasses, 14-ounce with florentine
gold-finish; #GW 25.

Catalog: Free (call 404-827-2500 to order).
Stock is subject to change. Collectors
should contact The Turner Store to check
the current availability of *GWTW*–related
items.

Payment: C, MO, V, MC

Delivery: UPS, USPS, Federal Express

Returns: Return item within thirty days in
original packaging with sales receipt.

Tote Bags

IF you shop 'til you drop, you'll love *Gone
With the Wind* totes. Each roomy bag
depicts a scene from the film on heavy,
glossy paper and comes with a corded handle. Don't be bogged down with bundles.
Choose *Gone With the Wind* totes—for all
your weary loads.

Tara tote bag. *(The Turner Store)*

Scarlett's
247 East Main Street
Ashland, OR 97520
Phone: 503-488-2745
Specialties: Gone With the Wind tote bags,
various sizes.
Catalog: None. Scarlett's has a large inven-
tory of items. Write or telephone with
specific wants for a price quote.
Payment: C, MO, V, MC, D, AE
Delivery: UPS
Returns: Items may be returned for ex-
change or refund within thirty days of
receipt.

Scarlett's Sales
PO Box 6351
3401 Gentian Boulevard
Columbus, GA 31907
Phone: 706-569-7316
Specialties: Gone With the Wind tote bags,
various sizes.
Catalog: $1.00. Cost of catalog may be
deducted from first order. Stock is subject
to change. Collectors should contact

Scarlett's Sales to check the current availability of *GWTW*–related items.
Payment: C, MO, V, MC
Delivery: UPS, USPS
Returns: Items in salable condition may be
returned within fourteen days of receipt
for refund, less the cost of shipping and
handling.

The Turner Store
One CNN Center
Box 105366
Atlanta, GA 30348-5366
Phone: 404-827-4406
FAX: 404-827-3696
Specialties: Gone With the Wind tote bag,
made of heavy, glossy paper with corded
handle, $9^{3/4}$" by 8"; #GW 17.
Catalog: Free (call 404-827-2500 to order).
Stock is subject to change. Collectors
should contact The Turner Store to check
the current availability of *GWTW*–related
items.
Payment: C, MO, V, MC
Delivery: UPS, USPS, Federal Express
Returns: Return item within thirty days in
original packaging with sales receipt.

Scarlett's Chocolates. *(The Turner Store)*

Acquiring Vintage GWTW Collectibles

How to Judge Authenticity

WHILE circulating among the tables at a giant, open-air flea market, I spied a number of makeshift book cases crammed with hardcovers and paperbacks. I scanned the spines for interesting possibilities, and there, wedged between *Jane Eyre* and *A Writer's Guide and Index to English,* I spotted a Confederate-gray cloth binding and the title *Gone with the Wind* in blue-gray lettering.

I gently turned the pages to the one listing the copyright. After the "all rights reserved" paragraph, I noticed the publication history: published in June 1936, reprinted twice in June, three times in July, and six times in August 1936. I decided this would make a good reading copy for my mom, so I took it to the young woman sitting nearby in a lawn chair with a metal cash box in her lap.

"You're getting a good deal," she said as I handed her the book and reached for my wallet. "This is a first edition, but because it doesn't have a dust jacket, I can let you have it for fifty dollars."

That was one bargain I managed to pass up that day. The copy of *Gone with the Wind* I found was not a first edition and certainly not worth the asking price. In the world of collectibles, the principle of *caveat emptor* ("let the buyer beware") is paramount. But how can you judge if a collectible is what the seller claims it to be?

First, establish a solid base of knowledge before you begin buying. Become familiar with original collectibles. Study books of *Gone With the Wind* memorabilia so that you know, for example, what an original first-release one-sheet looks like. Visit exhibits of *Gone With the Wind* collectibles so that you gain a sense of the size, color, texture, quality, and so forth, of various original items. Befriend experienced collectors and gain entrée to their private collections. They may allow you to handle some of the original pieces. Discuss with collec-

---

Highly Desired
Gone With the Wind Collectibles
• an autographed first edition of Margaret Mitchell's novel with dust jacket.
• an original 1939 movie poster.
• Madame Alexander Scarlett O'Hara composition dolls from 1937 to 1943.

Tiny Betty Scarlett doll of 1937. *(Jan Lebow,* The Fashion History of Alexander Scarlett O'Hara Dolls, 1937–1992*)*

tors those special features to look for when considering a collectible purchase.

Second, do business only with reputable dealers. A reputable seller should offer you more than just a verbal promise that an item is original. The dealer should not only authenticate the collectible but guarantee its authenticity in writing. For example, most reputable autograph dealers stand behind every item offered for sale with a lifetime guarantee of authenticity.

Third, know the signs of authenticity for the various vintage items you plan to collect.

First-Edition Copies of GONE WITH THE WIND. In publishing, first edition copies are those produced during the first press run. Characteristics that identify a first edition are known as "points." A true first edition of *Gone with the Wind* has the words "Published May, 1936" on the copyright page with no indication of any other printings. A first-printing dust jacket has the heading "Macmillan Spring Novels" on the back panel with seventeen titles listed.

Gone with the Wind appears second from the top in the right-hand column.

Original First-Release One-Sheets. One-sheets are standard 27-inch by 41-inch theatrical posters. Reproduction posters are sometimes smaller. During *Gone With the Wind*'s first release, the artwork for the posters varied, but below the title the billing on most one-sheets indicated "starring Clark Gable as Rhett Butler" which was followed by the names Leslie Howard and Olivia de Havilland, and ended with "and presenting Vivien Leigh as Scarlett O'Hara." Authentic posters will probably also bear signs of their original folded position.

Original Madame Alexander Scarlett O'Hara Dolls. Authenticity can have a wide scope with Scarlett O'Hara dolls. The doll should have the correct costume, proper undergarments, jewelry, shoes, wrist tag, clothing tags, correct hair style, and so forth. For example, the first Scarlett doll produced by Madame Alexander was the Tiny Betty Scarlett of 1937. This seven-inch, pre-movie, composition Scarlett doll wore a simple yellow organdy dress with a matching ruffled-hem trim and had an attached gauze petticoat. The doll's accessories included cotton pantaloons and a natural straw hat decorated with flowers. Her eyes, shoes, and socks were hand painted. All of these elements should be present for the doll to be considered authentic. The most comprehensive source of information on Madame Alexander Scarlett doll authenticity is *The Fashion History of Alexander Scarlett O'Hara Dolls 1937–1992, Volume 2* by Jan Lebow. (See listing under "Books" or "Dolls.")

Autographs. Authenticity is a major concern for autograph collectors, who have to contend with facsimile signatures, those signed by secretaries and Autopen machines, and signatures that are outright forgeries.

Some celebrities rely on a mechanical device to duplicate a signature. The celebrity signs his or her name, and the Autopen machine reproduces the signature on each letter fed into it. Autopen signatures are difficult to distinguish from an original signature. The best approach is to compare the signature in question with a known Autopen signature. Place the suspected signature over the Autopen signature and move them around while holding them up to a strong light. If you can match sections, it is likely that the suspected signature was done by mechanical reproduction. No person can sign his or her name the same way twice.

Secretarial signatures can be easier to spot since they tend to be dissimilar to the actual signature of the celebrity. Usually secretaries aren't concerned about forging a signature. They simply want to sign the letter in their own handwriting and post it to the mail. Comparison of a suspected secretarial signature with a genuine signature is often enough to differentiate between the two.

However, some secretaries do forge the signatures of their employers. Forgeries produced by secretaries as well as those perpetrated by nefarious characters are much more difficult to detect. A reputable dealer is the best defense against purchasing forged autographs.

The Pen and Quill, the bimonthly journal of the Universal Autograph Collectors Club, keeps members aware of disreputable dealers, forgers, and the use of secretarial and Autopen signatures.

And last, trust your instincts. If you have any doubts about a potential purchase, get more information before investing a large sum of money.

Knowledge is power, and the more knowledge you have the better able you will be to make buying decisions concerning original collectibles.

Assessing the Condition of a Collectible

MOST *Gone With the Wind* collectors would probably give their eye teeth to own a mint first edition of Margaret Mitchell's novel. Along with their upper canines, they also would have to shell out perhaps $10,000 or more.

The condition of a collectible determines its desirability and value. Most collectors strive to obtain items in the best possible condition, and mint is as good as it gets. Since there are few remaining first editions in mint condition, those volumes bring the highest prices.

Collectibles are generally graded from mint (excellent condition with no defects), fine (only a few signs of wear), good (in average condition), fair (noticeable signs of wear), to poor (damaged or incomplete). There may also be grades in between such as near mint, very fine, and very good. All of this can be confusing, especially for the beginning collector.

The best way to overcome the confusion is to become educated. Read price guides and catalogs for descriptions of condition but don't stop there. Look at collectibles. Handle them. Only by physically touching items that are accurately graded will you be able to gain knowledge about condition. When you are knowledgeable, you will be able to spot the defects that affect the value of a collectible.

Paper. Examine paper collectibles in a methodical, inch-by-inch fashion. Rips, folded corners, creases, soiling, pen or pencil marks all downgrade the condition of a paper collectible. For a first edition book, is it without its dust jacket? Is the binding loose? Are pages missing? Is there a bookplate from a previous owner?

Is foxing (yellowish-brown spots or stains) present? Any evidence of mold? Is the paper browned and brittle? Are there pin holes or evidence of a collectible having been taped to a surface? Does the item have stains? Has the item been trimmed? Are any pieces missing? Can you detect any repairs to the paper?

Ceramics. Hold the collectible in a well-lit area and rotate the item slowly, observing carefully from top to bottom. Are there hairline cracks? Are any pieces missing? Is the collectible chipped? Can you see any areas that have been repaired? Pay particular attention to elaborately decorated objects, which can easily hide signs of repair. Concerning music boxes, is the wind-up mechanism functional? Are any fittings such as hinges operational?

Glass. As with ceramics, hold the glass collectible in a well-lit area and rotate the object slowly. Can you see any cracks or glued portions? Do any of the sections seem to have been ground down? Run your fingers slowly over the entire piece. Can you feel any slight indentations that would indicate chips?

Cloth. Garments or other cloth collectibles require inch-by-inch examination under good light. In a wool garment, are there moth holes? Does the collectible have spots or stains? Are there signs of mending? Are there threadbare or frayed areas?

Dolls. In good light, place your hand under the doll's dress and grasp her around the waist. Examine the doll first from head to toe, her costume next and then her box, if present. In general, you can count on the presence of a box with dolls created from 1965 to the present time.

Has the hair been combed, or is the wig hair sparse in places? Are the eyes cracked or crazed? Are there visible cracks around the eyes? Is any part of the complexion altered? Have painted-on cosmetic features worn off? Is there color missing? Are there stains, scratches, or breaks on the body? Is there excessive, irreparable joint wear? (Irreparable joint wear exists if the doll cannot be restrung.) If composition, is there extensive crazing or flaking on the body? Are fingers missing or replaced?

Is the doll costumed correctly? Are garments or accessories missing? Has the clothing been washed or replaced? Is the costume weathered? Are there stains on the clothing? Is the clothing soiled or torn?

Is the box the correct one? Has the label on the box been changed? Has the name or number on the box been altered? Is the doll without her box?

Records. In a well-lit area, hold the record by the edges and examine it at different angles so you can view all surfaces. Is the record warped? Has the disk lost its original sheen? Is the record scuffed or visibly worn from overplay? Are there cracks, chips, or gouges? Are there scratches? Run your index finger over the scratch as a test. You will be able to feel a deep scratch, and it will affect the play of the record.

For albums, examine the cover or slip jacket. Is it badly worn or stained? Are there rips or tears? Has the cover been repaired with tape? Has the cover been defaced with pen or pencil? Does it bear the name of the previous owner?

Wood. Hold the music box or figurine in good light and rotate the item slowly. Has the piece been refinished? Are there scratches, chips, or stains? Is the item warped? Regarding music boxes, is the wind-up mechanism functional? Are any fittings such as hinges operational?

Metals. Hold the metal collectible in good light and rotate the item slowly. Can you see any deep scratches or dents? Do engraved sections show signs of wear? Are there any raised portions that are chipped or worn down?

GWTW EP and LP record albums. *(The collection of John Wiley Jr.)*

Defects affect the value of a collectible. Use information about condition to ensure that the items you add to your collection are in the best state of preservation.

Finding and Buying Collectibles

COLLECTIBLES of all kinds can be found at flea markets, garage and estate sales, auctions, collectible shops and shows, thrift and antique shops. Baseball cards, mechanical banks, comic books, radio premiums, and other kinds of memorabilia abound, but what are your chances of finding *Gone With the Wind* collectibles? Here's what you need to know.

Flea Markets. The flea market of today is a direct descendant of the *Marché aux Puces,* a giant gathering of vendors that began in Paris in the 1860s. American flea markets range in size from small—only a handful of dealers—to large—several hundred vendors. Whether outdoor or indoor, flea markets promise the collector an interesting contrast of wares from trash to treasure.

For the experienced collector, flea markets sometimes offer that diamond in the rough often called a "score." A "score" is a piece of memorabilia offered by a dealer who doesn't realize the item's worth to the collector. Although scores tend to be few and far between, experienced collectors are prepared to scoop them up because they know what they are buying. Experienced collectors also know that any diamonds in the rough have to be uncovered early. Those collectors arrive at the flea market site while the dealers are setting up—as early at 8:00 A.M.—to find jewels rather than junk.

Flea markets are definitely not the place for a beginning collector to wander up and down the aisles seeking scores. Flea market dealers have well-earned reputations as salespeople, and they often convince neophyte collectors that an item is worth more than the selling price. Beware and buy only what you know. When in doubt, walk away.

Garage Sales. Rarely do garage sales and their kissing cousins—house, rummage, and white-elephant sales—offer the collector any noteworthy memorabilia items. At best you'll probably only be able to find collectibles such as reproduction posters or *Gone with the Wind* paperbacks.

If scouring garage sales is a particular

passion for you, indulge. Keep your eyes open for collectibles, but don't be surprised if the only bargains you find are in the area of kitchen gadgets, men's neckties, and children's games with some of the pieces missing.

Estate Sales. Since estate sales involve the selling of an individual's or family's possessions, you never know what you'll find. Often estate sales are excellent opportunities for the collector.

Estate sales are usually run by a firm specializing in estate liquidation. For a commission, the company appraises the estate's contents, advertises the sale in the newspaper and handles the actual selling.

The newspaper advertisement usually provides a list of items that will be offered, the date and time of the sale, as well as the firm's name and telephone number. If the ad mentions "movie memorabilia," "collectibles," "rare books," "ephemera," or other similar key words, telephone the firm to determine if any *Gone With the Wind* items will be included. Keep in mind that many of these companies are used to dealing more with furniture and furnishings, so you may have to be specific about the items for which you are looking. Frequently, the firm will also be able to tell you how much the collectibles will cost. Calling in advance and checking the inventory will prevent you from wasting time and gas driving to a sale that holds nothing of interest for you.

If a sale sounds promising, plan to arrive about two hours before the sale begins. Many estate liquidation companies distribute admission numbers about an hour before the doors open. The numbers allow the firm to regulate the flow of potential buyers who enter the premises at a given time. If you're not there early enough to be one of the first groups through the doors, you risk losing out on the best buys. Best buys are usually snapped up in the first two hours of a sale.

Estate sales operate briskly, and you the buyer must move fast as well. As you stride through the sale area and see an item of interest, grab it immediately. Staking your

claim in this way prevents another buyer from purchasing the item while you're making up your mind and also gives you a chance to examine the collectible more closely. Since you are not obligated to buy the items you pick up, feel free to put back the ones you have decided against.

In estate-sale buying, the experienced as well as the beginning collector must move quickly and decisively around the buying floor. Clearly, the collector who hesitates risks losing the opportunity to acquire fine collectibles.

Auctions. Auctions can be where the action is, for collectors. Large, prestigious auction houses routinely offer movie memorabilia, including vintage *Gone With the Wind* collectibles. Specialized auction houses offer *Gone With the Wind* dolls.

Auction houses produce catalogs which list the items to be offered in upcoming sales. Perusing the catalog allows a collector an opportunity to consider the offerings, research prices paid in the past, and decide upon a bidding maximum. Most auction houses accept absentee bids, either by telephone, FAX or mail, so that collectors don't have to be in attendance to bid on an item.

But part of the fun of buying at auction is attending. You may not be able to get to Christie's in New York City for their auctions, but there are probably small and medium-sized houses in your area, holding auctions that you may be able to attend.

Instead of producing slick, glossy preview catalogs, these smaller auction houses distribute modest brochures or flyers, or advertise in the newspaper. Often, these houses liquidate estates, private collections, and the property of bankrupts. Experienced collectors can find wonderful buys at what are generally wholesale prices. For the beginning collector, however, buying at auction can be fraught with peril. But that doesn't mean that the beginner can't become educated about the ins and outs of auction action. (See the section "The Action at Auctions.")

Collectible Shops. Collectible shops are

Melanie collector's plate.

"Tara . . . Scarlett's Pride" miniature set. *(Hawthorne Architectural Register)*

found in and around major American cities and allow the collector to walk through the door on a regular basis and find posters, tote bags, books, and other items related to the collecting specialty. Collectible shops either include some *Gone With the Wind* items in their inventory or handle *Gone With the Wind* memorabilia exclusively.

For the collector at a distance, many collectible shops also offer mail-order sales. The shops publish catalogs, brochures, information sheets or flyers, indicating the available new and/or vintage items. These printed materials are useful to save not only for future ordering but also as references to collectible market values.

With vintage *Gone With the Wind* collectibles, keep in mind that because the items are usually one of a kind, they are subject to prior sale. If in a catalog you see a desired, vintage collectible, telephone the shop to find out if the item is still available.

Since you are buying through the mail, you need to rely on the dealer's grading standards. Test the accuracy by placing a few trial orders of inexpensive items. You will then be able to tell if the dealer's grading standards are accurate.

The listings in this book will lead collectors to mail-order sources of *Gone With the Wind* memorabilia from the past as well as the present. Each listing provides information about the specialties of each dealer, whether a catalog is available, the methods of payment and delivery, and the return policy. Keep in mind that most dealers want to please their customers and will permit returns for merchandise that proves to be unsatisfactory.

If you can't drop into a collectible shop, buying by mail is the next best thing.

Collectible Shows. Imagine an indoor arena filled to overflowing with dealers from all over the country. Think of hundreds or thousands of collectors circulating among the various tables, looking over and making deals on Madame Alexander Scarlett dolls, *Gone With the Wind* postcards or collector plates. The collectible show is a dream come true for the experienced as well as the beginning *Gone With the Wind* collector.

There are collectible shows of all sizes that feature collectibles in particular categories such as dolls, ephemera, movie memorabilia, and so forth. The shows draw collectors from coast to coast by offering two to four days of buying, selling, guest speakers, exhibits, auctions, raffles, and seminars.

Small, one-day shows are strictly for buying and selling, but they still allow the collector the chance to examine original items and compare them to reproductions, purchase sought-after collectibles, learn about pricing and grading, talk with dealers and other collectors, and gather information about the specialized area of collecting.

Because they provide the opportunity to buy just about any item of memorabilia you want, collectible shows will be the highlight of the year for you. You'll have to pinch yourself to make sure you're not dreaming, and you'll be more than delighted to find out that you're not.

Thrift Shops. Charitable organizations run thrift shops which almost always feature clothing donated by members of the community. Any collectibles that may arrive on the doorstep of the thrift shop—paperback books, for instance—probably have little value.

Antique Shops. Antique shops are known to specialize in furniture, artwork, china, crystal, jewelry and other fine-quality items. Today many antique shops are incorporating collectibles into their inventories as well.

Take a handful of your collecting business cards and visit the antique-shop owners in your local area. Introduce yourself, explain your area of collecting interest, and ask the proprietor about the likelihood of his or her having *Gone With the Wind* items for sale. You will probably find antique shops that handle absolutely no *Gone With the Wind* collectibles, a few that offer items from time to time, and others that regularly sell the collectibles in which you are interested.

Leave your cards with the proprietors

who seem the most promising as sources for collectibles. The owner will add your card to a file of prospective buyers and will call you when an item of interest is available.

Visit the shops every few months to remind the proprietor that you are still interested in buying. Once you have gotten to know and trust a proprietor's judgment, you might also ask if he or she would be willing to scout for *Gone With the Wind* collectibles for you. Since antique-shop owners often go on buying excursions, they can keep their eyes peeled for your special requests.

Cultivating a good working relationship with antique-shop owners in your area can result in your adding fine *Gone With the Wind* items to your collection at reasonable prices.

The Action at Auctions

BIDS reverberate through the auction hall like ricocheting bullets. Then the gavel falls, the auctioneer yells "Sold!" and an-

other successful bidder claims a valuable lot of *Gone With the Wind* memorabilia. Maybe.

If you are an inexperienced auction goer, buying at auction can be like walking through a mine field. Initially, you might think you've captured a rare bit of *Gone With the Wind* memorabilia. Only later do you realize you've paid too much for something not the least bit extraordinary or valuable. Knowing the twists and turns in auction action will help you steer clear of the usual pitfalls and allow you to have a positive auction experience.

When you learn about an upcoming auction, obtain a copy of the auction catalog. The catalog lists or describes the items to be offered and often includes photographs of the collectibles. Items are offered in lots which can include one or several collectibles. Sometimes lots are offered subject to a reserve, and this is frequently noted in the catalog.

A reserve is the confidential minimum price established by the auctioneer and the seller below which the lot will not be sold.

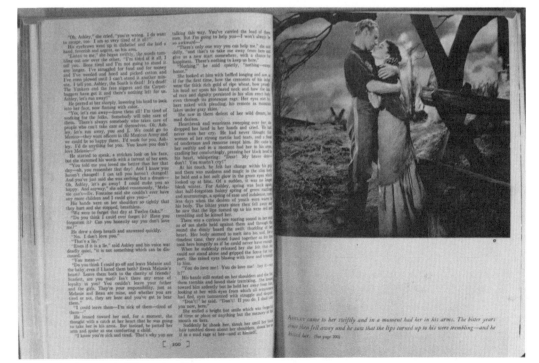

Original hardcover *GWTW* movie edition.

The reserve benefits the seller in case the auction is poorly attended. If the bidding does not reach the lot's reserve, the auctioneer can declare the lot "passed," "withdrawn," "returned to owner," or "bought-in." "Bought-in" means the auction house has purchased the lot.

By perusing the catalog, you can consider the offerings and research the prices paid in the past. Large auction houses generally produce slick, glossy preview catalogs; smaller auction houses distribute modest brochures or flyers. Some small houses simply place an advertisement in the newspaper.

The catalog, brochure, or advertisement will indicate a date and time for the auction preview. Plan to attend the preview so that you can inspect the collectibles. Bring to the preview the catalog, a notebook and pen, a small flashlight, and a magnifying glass.

Armed with these accouterments, you are ready to walk around the auction hall to see where items are located. Zero in on those items of interest and examine them in detail, using the flashlight to provide better light and the magnifying glass to focus on the minute details of a piece. In the notebook, indicate the good and bad points of each collectible's condition. If you have any questions about the items, ask the auction house staff for clarification. Then determine the maximum you will bid for each piece.

Some catalogs provide a presale estimate or range of value for each lot. For example, the value of a Scarlett O'Hara doll may be estimated at between $500 and $800. Use this range only as a guideline. Rely on the pricing knowledge you have gained by visiting shows and collectible shops and by reading publications in the field. When you decide on the maximum bids, jot the figures in the catalog next to each lot number.

Decide on a bidding limit with a cool, reasoned head and do it before you enter the heat of auction battle. Auction fever is a genuine affliction. Caught up in the excitement, many inexperienced auction goers find themselves out of control, bidding

more than they know the lot is worth.

The bidding process can vary from house to house. At some houses, a potential bidder is given a cardboard paddle with a bidding number. If you wish to bid, you simply raise the paddle. At other houses, oral bidding is permitted. You say "bid," "here," or state the next increment in the bidding such as "fifty dollars." Auction houses also permit silent bidding.

Silent bidding occurs when an auction attendee does not wish to call attention to the fact that he or she is bidding. The individual will prearrange with the auctioneer a special signal. The signal could be a hand gesture, a facial expression or some movement that will indicate the desire to bid. Since these signals are established in advance, you don't have to fear that, for example, your waving at a friend across the room will be misinterpreted as a bid.

The auctioneer starts the auction by introducing the collectible to be sold and then either setting an opening bid—"Let's have five dollars for this set of lobby cards"—or asking for an opening bid—"What am I bid for this poster?" The auctioneer has the right to refuse your bid if it is judged to be unreasonable, and can withdraw a lot if it doesn't attract at least two or sometimes three bids, or the reserve.

Once the opening bid has been accepted, the auction continues with the auctioneer accepting bidding increments. Watch and listen to the auctioneer to determine what are acceptable increments. As a rule of thumb, you can bid one or two dollars at a time for lots worth up to $20, five or ten dollars at a time for lots worth up to $100, and twenty to fifty dollars at a time for lots worth up to $1,000. Some prestigious auction houses list acceptable bidding increments in their catalogs.

Participating in auctions is an education in psychology. You have to decide whether to bid early or bid late. You must try to win your desired lots without arousing the suspicion of other bidders around you. If they sniff out your interest, they may begin a bidding war to discourage you, and that will raise the final price. The competition includes individuals in the audience who bid with the expressed purpose of escalating the price, and "rings." A "ring" consists of a group of bidders who agree among themselves not to compete for the same lot in an attempt to hold down prices. To avoid auction hassle, experts recommend keeping track of your competitors, making sure the auctioneer knows you are a bidder, and sticking to the maximum bids previously determined.

When you are the high bidder for a lot, you will next have to concern yourself with paying for and receiving the merchandise. Beware the buyer's premium. Some auction houses charge the buyer ten percent or more of the total price for which the lot is sold, known as the hammer price. The notice of a buyer's premium appears in the catalog, brochure, or newspaper advertisement.

Payment procedures vary, depending upon the auction house. This information is listed in the auction catalog, so it's advisable to read this information before you attend the auction. Some houses require prospective bidders to register at the beginning of the auction then pay for and receive their collectibles at the end of the day. Other houses ask for a cash deposit at the beginning of the auction or as lots are sold. Auction houses accept cash, certified checks, traveler's checks, and some accept credit cards. Many are opposed to accepting personal checks, which frequently turn out to be of the rubber variety.

Once you have paid for your collectibles, obtain a detailed receipt for each item and then pack them for the trip home. Most collectibles can easily fit into cardboard boxes, so bring a few with you to cart to your car.

Remember that auction merchandise is sold "as is," and that the rule of *caveat emptor* prevails. However, if you discover that the condition of the collectible differs greatly from the description in the catalog or from what you recall from the preview, bring your concerns to the auction staff. In certain cases, returns can be accommodated.

Locating Opportunities to Buy

YOU can locate opportunities to buy *Gone With the Wind* collectibles through:

Newspaper Advertisements. Estate sales and local auctions usually run advertisements in the classified section of area newspapers. A typical ad lists the date and time of the sale, the time of the auction preview, the sale location, name and telephone number of the dealer, a sampling of the available items, the terms of the sale (cash, good check, traveler's check, credit card), and the percentage of the auction buyer's premium, if any. Be sure to telephone the dealer in advance of the sale or auction to determine the kind of *Gone With the Wind* items that will be offered.

Auction Information. Most auction houses provide printed materials—catalogs, brochures, information sheets, flyers—that announce forthcoming auctions and the kinds of collectibles that will be offered. The addresses and telephone numbers of auction houses that handle *Gone With the Wind* collectibles are included in this book so that you can order their printed materials, usually for a fee. Many houses offer their auction information on a yearly subscription basis.

Collecting Periodicals. Almost every area of collecting has some periodical— magazine, tabloid, or newsletter—that provides specialized information to collectors. These periodicals are excellent sources for the collector looking to buy.

The periodicals not only include advertisements for auctions and collector shows but feature ads from readers with collectibles for sale. For example, *The GONE WITH THE WIND Collector's Newsletter*— the only publication devoted exclusively to the area of *Gone With the Wind* collectibles— has at least a full page of ads in every eight-page issue. Typical items listed for sale include sepia still reproduc-

Two-volume edition of *GWTW* published to commemorate the film's 1939 premiere. *(The collection of John Wiley Jr.)*

tions; foreign, movie, and first editions of *Gone with the Wind;* premiere movie programs; collector plates; Scarlett dolls and doll clothing; sheet music; and autographed items.

Addresses for *The GONE WITH THE WIND Collector's Newsletter* and other publications that are sources for *Gone With the Wind* collectibles are listed in this book under "Periodicals." For a modest price, single-issue copies are often available as samples so you can decide before you subscribe if the publication will meet your collecting needs.

Placing Your Own Ad. In addition to carrying ads to sell, collector publications also run ads from subscribers who want to buy collectibles. Generally, advertisement rates are low, and discounts are often given if you run the ad in more than one issue.

Check the periodical for its section on classified advertising information. This section will tell you the ad rates, applicable discounts, deadline for receipt of ad copy, and how to prepare your advertisement.

Scanning the periodical's want-ad section will give you an idea of the style your ad should take. Write your ad carefully and clearly in as few words as possible. Indicate exactly what collectibles you are interested in obtaining. Here are some examples of want-to-buy ads:

WANTED: *Gone With the Wind* standees from all theatrical and video releases, 1939 to present; interested in all sizes (countertop to giant-size lobby displays) and will accept in very good to mint condition.

WANTED: Mass market paperbacks of *Gone with the Wind* from 1954, 1958, and 1971, and trade paperbacks from 1961, 1972, and 1976.

WANTED: Plates from original Edwin M. Knowles *Gone With the Wind* series. Will pay top dollar.

Search Services. Have you had difficulty locating a particular *Gone With the Wind* collectible? Turn the problem over to a collectible search service, and that item may be in your collection before you know it.

Some services confine their searches to

books, but others will try to locate just about any type of collectible. Many services are free—although you will, of course, have to pay for the found collectible. Other services charge a search fee.

Generally, you contact the search service with a complete description of the wanted collectible and provide your name, address, and telephone number. The service will notify you when the collectible is located, will report on the item's condition, and provide a price quote. There is usually no obligation to buy. If you do decide to buy, the service will arrange to purchase the collectible and ship it to you. A list of services that will search for *Gone With the Wind* collectibles is included in this book under "What a Search Service Can Offer to a Collector."

Networking. Wherever *Gone With the Wind* collectors gather, you should be there, too. Attend collectible shows where you can talk to dealers and other collectors and pass around your collector's business card. Write on the back of the card the specific items you are hoping to add to your collection. If the dealer or collector comes across your wanted collectible in the months after the show, he or she will most likely contact you. *Gone With the Wind* collectors are generous individuals and are always happy to share expertise or leads to collectibles.

Join a national *Gone With the Wind* organization or begin a local *Gone With the Wind* club. (See the section of this book entitled "How to Get Connected to a Collector's Network.") Networking nationally and locally can create all kinds of opportunities to buy collectibles, and it's terrific fun in the process.

How to Get Connected to a Collector's Network

COLLECTING can be a lonely pursuit. Who will share your excitement when you acquire your latest *Gone With the Wind* collectible? Friends usually act bored. Significant others only feign interest. Family members may secretly roll their eyes. Noth-

ing can dampen the ardor of collecting more than sharing your joy with those who cannot match your own enthusiasm. That's why collector's networks are invaluable.

Why Get Connected? A collector's network brings together those with similar interests wishing to share information. Many organizations publish a newsletter which usually contains news and features about the collectible area, buy-and-sell ads for items, and information about collector get-togethers.

Some organizations even sponsor conventions and symposia, which provide opportunities to meet other collectors; mingle with important representatives of the collecting area; hear renown guest speakers; attend special events; and buy, sell, and trade collectibles.

Not only can you locate that unusual item for which you've been searching, you can also find something more valuable: the friendship and camaraderie of people who share your passion. Meeting those who are as excited as you are about *Gone With the Wind* dolls, posters, autographs, plates, or first editions of Mitchell's novel is an intoxicating experience, and many of the relationships established through a collector's network last a lifetime.

Networks of Note. Get connected with *Gone With the Wind* aficionados who have across-the-board interests, those just wild about Gable, lovers of autographs, or Madame Alexander Scarlett dolls. Here are the details:

The GONE WITH THE WIND Collector's Newsletter
PO Box 2072
Dublin, GA 31040-2072

This network unites *Gone With the Wind* fans through a quarterly 8-page newsletter which contains news and features about *Gone With the Wind* plus buy-and-sell ads. The newsletter also sponsors collector forums.

Clark Gable Foundation
PO Box 65
Cadiz, OH 43907

Gone With the Wind
Forum-1991 gifts.

Telephone: 614-942-GWTW

This organization, dedicated to keeping Clark Gable's spirit alive throughout the United States, publishes a quarterly newsletter and sponsors get-togethers during the year in Clark Gable's hometown of Cadiz, Ohio.

The Madame Alexander Doll Club
PO Box 330
Mundelein, IL 60060-0330

The Club encourages research and preservation of Madame Alexander dolls, sponsors symposia and an annual convention, publishes a quarterly newsletter and 6 shoppers (listing dolls wanted and for sale by members).

Universal Autograph Collectors Club
PO Box 6181
Washington, DC 20044-6181

UACC is the largest organization in the world for autograph collectors. Members receive a 48-page bimonthly journal, *The Pen and Quill,* containing articles about autograph collecting and free buy-sell-or-trade ads for members. The club sponsors a yearly autograph auction and frequent autograph shows.

Typical Events. In November 1991, *The GONE WITH THE WIND Collector's Newsletter* sponsored a weekend *Gone With the Wind* forum at The Jefferson Hotel in Richmond, Virginia.

A kickoff reception was held Friday evening, November 8 (Margaret Mitchell's birthday) to welcome participants and to open a special forum exhibit, *"Gone With the Wind . . . In the Beginning."* The exhibit, from the collection of newsletter editor John Wiley, Jr., included first editions of *Gone with the Wind;* Macmillan Publishing

Company's Spring 1936 catalog in which *GWTW* was featured; magazine ads for the novel; several items autographed by Margaret Mitchell; original Atlanta newspapers from August 1949 covering Mitchell's accident, death, and funeral; foreign editions of *Scarlett: The Sequel to Margaret Mitchell's GONE WITH THE WIND* by Alexandra Ripley.

Registration for the forum began Saturday morning at 9:00 A.M., and after opening remarks, the first speaker of the day was introduced. Herb Bridges, well-known author and owner of the world's largest collection of *Gone With the Wind* memorabilia, spoke to the attendees on "Collecting *Gone With the Wind* Memorabilia." The next speaker was yours truly—Pauline Bartel—author of *The Complete GONE WITH THE WIND Trivia Book,* and my topic was "The First Sequel to *Gone with the Wind.*"

Following lunch, Elizabeth Hanson, an assistant professor of English at Temple University in Philadelphia and author of *Margaret Mitchell,* addressed the audience regarding "Margaret Mitchell: A Storyteller's Stories."

Autograph sessions dotted the day, and in the late afternoon a sales room offered two hours of nonstop buying, selling, and trading of *Gone With the Wind* collectibles. The day was capped off with a dinner cruise aboard the 108-foot paddle wheel riverboat *Annabel Lee.* The moonlight cruise on the James River featured a tempting buffet dinner and a fabulous riverboat review which mixed song, dance, history, and humor. Newsletter publisher Kenneth Nix presented each forum attendee with a grab bag of *Gone With the Wind* goodies, including a specially designed forum 1991 tote bag, collector's mug, souvenir paper dolls, note cards, and commemorative booklets and brochures.

The schedule for Sunday featured three speakers: Jan Lebow, authority on Madame Alexander Scarlett O'Hara dolls, spoke on the topic, "Scarlett O'Hara Dolls: Alexander and Beyond." Marcella Rabwin, former

Will these *GWTW* collectibles—Scarlett tin, tote bag, mug, and music box—be considered vintage items in the future? *(The Turner Store)*

executive assistant to David O. Selznick during the making of *Gone With the Wind,* talked about *"Gone With the Wind* Today." Darden Asbury Pyron, a professor of history at Florida International University in Miami and author of *Southern Daughter: The Life of Margaret Mitchell,* addressed the attendees on "Pansy, Prissy, Peggy: The Bad Girls of *Gone with the Wind."*

The weekend reached its close Sunday afternoon with additional autograph sessions, special gifts of thanks to the speakers, and raffle prize drawings. Everyone left The Jefferson Hotel exhausted, exhilarated and eager for the next *Gone With the Wind* Forum.

Start Your Own Network. National networks are terrific but don't overlook the potential of connecting with *Gone With the Wind* collectors right in your own backyard. Post flyers announcing the formation of a local club along with your name and phone number on supermarket or community center bulletin boards. Place small ads in community newspapers or in collector periodicals. Here's an example:

Great balls of fire! A *Gone With the Wind* club is forming. Send an SASE for information to (your name and address).

To all those who respond, send a photocopied sheet providing information about yourself, the name of the club and how you hope to structure the organization. Keep the list of names and addresses, and when you have six or more potential members, arrange a membership meeting at the local library or community room.

Participation from even a small group of *Gone With the Wind* collectors is often all you need to get a club off and running. You can eventually elect officers, decide to publish a newsletter, sponsor local events, and expand your outreach to other areas of your state. You might even consider having your organization listed in subsequent editions of this book in order to attract more members. (See the back of this book for a questionnaire.)

Local and national networks offer unlimited opportunities for you, including sharing *Gone With the Wind* information; buying, selling, and trading collectibles, and having other people with whom to share the excitement and the fun of collecting *Gone With the Wind* memorabilia.

Bargaining at Collectible Shows

"CAN you do any better on this price?" is usually the first salvo heard in the battle of bargaining that takes place at collectible shows. Many collectors are embarrassed to bargain while others dicker at the drop of a hat.

The good news is that collectible dealers who appear at shows generally expect to bargain with buyers. Coming down in price allows dealers to be generous and win new customers.

Assume that you can get at least ten percent off the marked price of a collectible. For example, if a *Gone With the Wind* poster is priced at $22, you might offer the dealer $20.

There are no hard and fast rules when it comes to bargaining at collectible shows except one: it doesn't hurt to ask. But use your judgment.

If you know that the poster is underpriced at $22 pay the marked amount and be happy with the bargain. This is especially true if there are other potential buyers eyeing the poster. Attempting to dicker under these circumstances could result in one of those other collectors snapping up the poster at the rock-bottom price.

The battle of bargaining at collectible shows turns out to be not a struggle after all. Dealers expect it; customers do it; and in the end, everybody wins.

Trading

The last day of the 1991 *Gone With the Wind* Collectors Forum held at The Jefferson Hotel in Richmond, Virginia, was winding down. Capping off the weekend was a series of raffles of *Gone With the*

Vintage magazines featuring *GWTW*. *(The collection of John Wiley Jr.)*

Wind collectibles, and tickets were selling faster than hot buttermilk biscuits.

Each attendee scrambled to put tickets into the boxes representing the various groups of prizes that he or she hoped to acquire. Determined to win the set of *Gone with the Wind* British editions, a collector from North Carolina shot her wad. She tucked $20 worth of tickets into the box for that prize.

When the winner of that prize was finally announced, it wasn't the woman who had had twenty chances; it was someone who had wagered one lone ticket—yours truly. As I contemplated how I would get the two hefty volumes into my already overloaded suitcases for my trip home, the North Carolina collector came over to congratulate me.

"That's a wonderful prize," she said.

"Yes, it is," I replied. "Unfortunately, I'm not a big fan of foreign editions."

"You're not? Well, would you be willing to trade?"

"Sure. What do you have to offer?"

"Would you accept a signed first edition of *Scarlett*?"

Now that was something I would make some room for in my suitcase. We agreed on the trade, and later, the North Carolina collector very kindly sent me photographs of author Alexandra Ripley signing the very volume which I had added to my collection.

Trading is a cost-effective way of a obtaining items for your collection. Many times you can acquire highly desirable collectibles for much less than if you had purchased them.

As illustrated in the above example, the guiding principle behind trading is to connect with someone who has a collectible you want but who attaches little value to the item. If you have something that a collector wants with which you would be willing to part, you have the right ingredients for a trade.

You can create trading opportunities. Attend local and national collectible shows where you can meet and talk to other collectors to get a sense of the items they have and the ones they want. Let collectors know you are open to trading, mention the items you desire and the ones you would be willing to trade. Items you would be willing to trade can include duplicate items in your collection. In fact, some collectors deliberately buy duplicate items as inventory that they can use in future trades.

If it appears that you and a particular collector are not able to arrange a trade, give the collector one of your business cards and ask the person to spread the word. The collecting grapevine will take over from there and bring potential traders directly to you.

Since many trading situations occur serendipitously, keep in mind that the items involved will probably be many miles away in the collections of the respective owners. Only a collector seriously bent on making a deal will bring with him or her the collectibles to trade.

Make sure you have full information about the condition of the collectible you will be acquiring. Accurately describe to the other collector the condition of the collectible you will be trading. Exchange names, addresses, and telephone numbers, and make arrangements for the actual trade. If

the other collector lives locally, a subsequent meeting at a mutually agreeable time and place will give each of you the chance to examine the trading items. If a face-to-face trade is not possible, consider making the exchange by mail.

Another way to initiate a trade is to place trading ads in collectible periodicals. State up-front the collectible you are looking for and the preferred condition, then mention what you will offer in trade. Be specific about the condition of the item for trade. You might request that interested traders send a letter describing the collectible or a photograph. You will want to have—and provide—as much information as possible so that the trade is concluded successfully and happily for both parties.

Trading opportunities can also occur when you scout the shops of general antique dealers. Someone who is not a specialist in *Gone With the Wind* collectibles may be willing to trade desirable items for ones that hold more familiarity, such as crystal goblets or silver candlesticks.

Become familiar with the various ways of trading. Making a connection with someone for mutual collecting benefit can often yield the collectibles you have always wanted.

GWTW Collectibles from Yesterday

Auctions

AT a Pennsylvania auction house, you are declared the high bidder for a pair of ceramic "Scarlett and Rhett" bookends. That's wonderful news! And you learn about your success while you are at home—two thousand miles away in California.

Auction houses cater to collectors who are unable to be present physically for auctions. Collectors participate as absentee bidders through the mail, via FAX, by telephone, or in combination.

Of course, absentee bidders are usually unable to attend the auction preview. Instead, they must rely on the illustrations and descriptions of items in the catalog plus whatever information they can gather from phone calls to the auction house staff.

The catalog provides a mail-bid sheet, which the house requires that the absentee bidder complete and send or FAX in. The sheet usually asks for the following information:

• name, address, and telephone number
• method of payment
• bank reference
• signature
• desired lot numbers, descriptions, top bidding limits

The top bidding limits stated in the mail bid are treated as such. In fact, most houses state this policy in their catalogs. For example, Christie's East indicates that absentee bids "will be executed at the lowest possible price taking into account the reserve price and other bids."

Auction houses usually require that the mail bids be received by a certain deadline. With many houses, the deadline is three days before the auction. Some auction houses require an accompanying deposit representing a percentage of the total bids submitted. These and other specific policies of each auction house are outlined in the catalog, usually under a section entitled "Information for Prospective Bidders."

The execution of absentee bids by the auctioneer or house staff is a free service offered as a courtesy. Catalogs are quick to point out that the auction house assumes no responsibility for failing to enter bids or for making errors in executing them. If matching bids are entered by two or more bidders, the house gives precedence to the one that arrived first.

In auctions that offer telephone bidding, representatives of the auction house act as agents for one or more absentee bidders. The agents staff a bank of open telephone lines during the auction, advising clients about the state of the bidding and executing their bids.

The Scarlett O'Hara game, Bet Chu Can't. *(The collection of John Wiley Jr.)*

Some auction houses offer a combination of mail and telephone bidding. Absentee bidders submit mail bids prior to the sale but are able to increase their bids by telephone during the auction.

When the bidder calls, a staff member indicates if the individual is the current high bidder or states the minimum amount he or she must bid in order to become the current high bidder for an item. Calls come into the house's multiple phone lines fast and furiously, and absentee bidders frequently encounter busy signals, but this all adds to the excitement of the auction.

The houses that use this type of combination bidding do insure that all bidders get through. At Hake's Americana & Collectibles, for example, phone bidding begins at 10 A.M. and continues past midnight. As long as the line is busy, staff members still accept calls. When ten minutes pass without a call, the bidding officially ends.

Following the auction, successful absentee bidders are notified. The house mails an invoice indicating the lot purchased, total cost, any applicable buyer's premium, and shipping information. Unsuccessful absentee bidders are not notified, but they can telephone to find out the results of the sale. If unsuccessful bidders have made deposits, those are refunded after the auction.

Auction houses that offer mail, telephone or combination bidding provide a convenience for collectors who might otherwise not be able to participate. Whether you're looking for bookends, dolls, or premium brooches, absentee bidding for *Gone With the Wind* collectibles brings the auction action right to you no matter where you live.

Camden House Auctioneers, Inc.
427 North Canon Drive
Beverly Hills, CA 90210
Phone: 310-246-1212
FAX: 310-246-0416
Specialties: Catalogued auctions of original film posters and entertainment memora-

bilia, autographed photographs, letters, manuscripts. Absentee and telephone bidding.
Catalog: $20.00 per issue.

Christie's East
219 East 67th Street
New York, NY 10021
Phone: 212-606-0400
FAX: 212-737-6076
Auction Results: 212-546-1199
Specialties: Catalogued auctions of entertainment memorabilia and collectibles. Absentee and telephone bidding.
Catalog: Available on an annual subscription basis. For subscription information, contact Christie's at 718-784-1480 or write to Christie's Publications, 21-24 44th Avenue, Long Island City, NY 11101.

Cohasco, Inc.
Postal 821
Yonkers, NY 10702
Phone: 914-476-8500
Specialties: Catalogued auctions of autographed material, books, sheet music, movie and entertainment memorabilia. Absentee bidding.
Catalog: $5.00 per issue.

Frasher's
Route 1, Box 142
Oak Grove, MO 64075
Phone: 816-625-3786
FAX: 816-625-6079
Specialties: Catalogued auctions of antique and collectible dolls, including *Gone With the Wind* dolls. Absentee and telephone bidding.
Catalog: $25.00 per issue.

C. E. Guarino
PO Box 49, Berry Road
Denmark, ME 04022
Phone: 207-452-2123
Specialties: Catalogued auctions of antiques and collectibles, including *Gone With the Wind* memorabilia. Absentee and telephone bidding.
Catalog: Free brochures announcing upcoming sales are available by letting C. E. Guarino know of particular interests in a letter including name and mailing address.
  Offers a mail- and phone-bid auction catalog: $7.00 per copy; $20.00 for 3 catalogs sent regular bulk mail; $25.00 for 3 catalogs sent first class mail; $30.00 for 3 catalogs sent to Canada or South America; $35.00 for foreign subscriptions by air post.

Hake's Americana & Collectibles
PO Box 1444
York, PA 17405
Phone: 717-848-1333
FAX: 717-852-0344
Specialties: Catalogued auctions of antiques and collectibles. Absentee and telephone bidding.
Catalog: $25.00 for 5 catalogs mailed to customers in the U.S. and Canada, $35.00 mailed to customers in foreign countries. Longer term rates are available.

McMasters Productions, Inc.
PO Box 1755
Cambridge, OH 43725
Phone: 614-432-4320
800-842-3526
FAX: 614-432-3191
Specialties: Antique and collectible dolls, including *GWTW*–related dolls. McMasters holds auctions in various locations throughout the United States and has 3 types of doll auctions: Catalogued, Mini-Catalogued Specialty Auctions, and Uncatalogued "Treasure Hunts."
Catalog: Catalogued Doll Auctions ($22.00): These auctions are held several times a year. Antique and collectible dolls and related items are featured. All items are photographed and described in detail in a 96-page catalog. Dolls of exceptional quality are featured in color. Absentee and telephone bids are accepted.
  Specialty Doll Auctions ($10.00): These auctions are held several times a year. Dolls sold are of one specific type (Barbie, Madame Alexander, Shirley

Temple, etc.) and are presented in a "mini catalog." Select dolls are featured in black-and-white photos. Absentee bids are accepted.

Uncatalogued "Treasure Hunt" Doll Auctions ($10.00—minimum of 6 lists): These auctions are held during the months in which no Catalogued or Specialty auctions are held. These auctions include dolls of all types, clothing, and accessories. You need to be present to bid.

Phillips West Two
10 Salem Road
Bayswater
London W2 4DL
Phone: 071-229-9090
FAX: 071-792-9201
Specialties: Catalogued auctions of entertainment memorabilia and collectibles. Absentee bidding.
Catalog: 5 pounds sterling per issue. Twelve-month catalog subscriptions are also available.

Sotheby's
1334 York Avenue
New York, NY 10021
Phone: 212-606-7000
FAX: 212-606-7249
Specialties: Catalogued auctions of Hollywood memorabilia, including original posters, scripts, autographed material, costumes, and props.
Catalog: $30.00 per issue.

Swann Galleries, Inc.
104 East 25th Street
New York, NY 10010
Phone: 212-254-4710
FAX: 212-979-1017
Specialties: Catalogued auctions of rare books (including *Gone with the Wind* first editions), autographs, and manuscripts. Absentee and telephone bidding.
Catalog: Available individually (prices vary), by subject subscription (prices vary), or by full annual subscription—$250 U.S., Canada, Mexico; $300 Overseas, Foreign.

Autographs

OBTAINING autographs either through the mail or in person from members of the *Gone With the Wind* family is an exciting way to begin a collection. Unfortunately, there are limitations to such collecting on your own. Certain celebrities refuse to sign, and the stars who now shine brightly in other worlds are unable to. But the skills of a reputable autograph dealer can help to expand your collecting possibilities.

Most dealers are knowledgeable, ethical individuals with a sincere interest in helping clients acquire a fine collection of genuine autographs. These dealers not only research the material they offer but guarantee the authenticity. Should an autograph ever prove to be fraudulent, the dealer will refund your money.

Unfortunately, there are some dealers who do not hold themselves to these high standards. They offer suspect autographs and do not fully guarantee the materials. Avoid doing business with any dealer who is reluctant to stand behind his or her merchandise with a written guarantee of authenticity.

Dealers rely on catalogs to describe the autographs they offer, but catalogs will vary among dealers. Some catalogs may be simple, photocopied lists while others may be elaborate, glossy presentation packets. Don't be put off by either type, as both can contain wonderful, affordable buys.

In their catalogs, dealers describe their offerings by using standard abbreviations. They include:

ADS – autograph document signed (a document such as a check written and signed by the same person)

ALS – autograph letter signed (a letter written and signed by the sender)

ANS – autograph note signed (a note of two or three lines written and signed by the sender)

APcS – autograph postcard signed (a postcard written and signed by the sender)

C – card (a visiting card signed by the visitor)

DS – document signed (a document typed or written by one person and signed by another)

LS – letter signed (a letter handwritten by one person but signed by another)

TLS – typed letter signed (a typewritten letter signed by the sender)

The autograph letter signed (ALS), because it is both written and signed in the hand of the sender, will probably carry the highest price tag.

Acquire as many catalogs as you can so you have information on prices as well as the various kinds of autographed items available. You can start by contacting the autograph dealers listed in the following section because they all handle *Gone With the Wind* autographs. Consider joining the Universal Autograph Collectors Club. As a member, you'll receive autograph catalogs from dealer-members. The UACC's journal, *The Pen and Quill,* carries free ads for members so you can advertise your wants.

And what kind of *Gone With the Wind* autographed items can you expect to acquire? You can collect letters, envelopes, documents, manuscripts, checks, notes, photographs, visiting cards, scripts, programs, and books, just about anything that anyone connected to *Gone With the Wind* handled by putting pen or pencil to paper.

With the wide range of autographed items available, you may be tempted to collect everything all at once. But allow your collection to grow slowly. Add quality items as they present themselves and as your budget permits. Protect and preserve the autographs you acquire.

Last, be sure of the integrity of your dealer. Experts agree that the most expensive autograph you'll ever buy is the one that is fraudulent.

Happy autograph hunting!

Camden House Auctioneers, Inc.
427 North Canon Drive
Beverly Hills, CA 90210

Specialties: Autographed material.
(See listing under AUCTIONS)

Cohasco, Inc.
Postal 821
Yonkers, NY 10702
Specialties: Autographed material
(See listing under AUCTIONS)

C. Dickens Fine, Rare, & Collectible Books
Lenox Square
3393 Peachtree Road NE
Atlanta, GA 30326
Phone: 404-231-3825
800-548-0376 (orders)
Specialties: Signed photograph of Margaret Mitchell; $3750. #AD7931.
Catalog: None. Stock is subject to prior sale. A list of items offered by C. Dickens is available by sending a request and enclosing a SASE. Collectors can request a search for non-inventory items.
Payment: C, MO, V, MC, AE
Delivery: UPS, USPS
Returns: If item ordered is not as described, it may be returned for a refund within five days of receipt.

Jim Hayes, Antiquarian
Drawer 12560
James Island, SC 29422
Phone: 803-795-0732
Specialties: Autographed letters, notes, documents, magazine and newspaper photographs, and more.
Catalog: Free. Items in catalog represent only a small percentage of inventory, and stock is subject to change. Collectors should contact Jim Hayes to check the current availability of *GWTW*–related items.
Payment: C, MO
Delivery: Arranged when order is placed
Returns: Any item may be returned within five days for refund or exchange.

Houle Rare Books & Autographs
7260 Beverly Boulevard
Los Angeles, CA 90036
Phone: 213-937-5858
FAX: 213-937-0091

Specialties: Autographs from the collection of George Cukor.

Other *GWTW*–related autographs, including:

Vivien Leigh, bold signature on halftone of an early portrait with her mother, 17″ by 14″. Framed. $750.

Vivien Leigh, typed letter, signed "Vivien" on letterhead, New York, September 1, 1963; with a still from *Gone With the Wind*, 25″ by 15″. Framed. $895.

Margaret Mitchell, autograph sentiment: "Presented to Mrs. Frank Boland–Oct–1938, by Margaret Mitchell (Mrs. John Marsh)"; with photograph, 11″ by 16″. Framed. $1500.

Catalog: Houle Rare Books & Autographs offers a number of catalogs in various categories, ranging in price from $3.00 to $10.00. George Cukor Collection catalog is $85.00 (hardcover), $20.00 (softcover). Stock is subject to prior sale.

Payment: C, MO, V, MC, AE
Delivery: UPS
Returns: Any item may be returned within ten days for refund or exchange. All autographs are guaranteed without time limit.

Linda's Autographs

PO Box 1
Umpqua, OR 97486
Phone: 503-459-4730
Specialties: Photographs, letters, and other items signed by *Gone With the Wind's* stars and supporting cast.
Catalog: $2.00 for a single copy/$20.00 for a 12-month subscription. Items in catalog represent only a small percentage of inventory, and stock is subject to change. Collectors should notify Linda's Autographs of particular wants by telephoning or sending a letter of inquiry with a SASE.
Payment: C, MO, V, MC
Delivery: Arranged when order is placed
Returns: Any item not satisfactory may be returned within five days after receipt.

William Linehan Autographs

Box 1203
Concord, NH 03301
Phone: 603-224-7226
Specialties: Autographs of *Gone With the Wind's* stars and supporting cast.
Catalog: $2.00
Payment: C
Delivery: USPS
Returns: Items may be returned up to ten days after receipt.

Lone Star Autographs

PO Drawer 500
Kaufman, TX 75142
Phone: 214-563-2115 during business hours
214-932-6050 evenings and weekends
Specialties: Photographs, lobby cards, letters and other items autographed by *GWTW* stars and supporting cast. Prices for items range from $25 to $5000.

One spectacular offering is a 24″ by 36″ framed collection of items: a reproduction lobby card signed by six cast members, a letter signed by Vivien Leigh, a bank check signed by Clark Gable, and a signature of Leslie Howard. $3995.

Catalog: None. Stock is subject to prior sale. Collectors should write or telephone for information on current inventory of *GWTW*–related items.
Payment: C, MO, V, MC, AE
Delivery: USPS
Returns: Unsatisfactory items may be returned within three days of receipt.

Monetary Ltd. of Dallas

8333 Douglas Avenue
Suite 1570
PO Box 12584
Dallas, TX 75225-0584
Phone: 214-691-7005
Specialties: Autographed photos, letters, notes, documents, and more.
Catalog: $25.00 for a one-year subscription. Stock is subject to change. Collectors should contact Monetary Ltd. to check the current availability of *GWTW*–related items. The company maintains a

"want card" system and will inform collectors of new material which meets collecting interests.

Payment: C, MO

Delivery: Arranged when order is placed

Returns: Any item may be returned within five days for refund or exchange.

Phillips West Two
10 Salem Road
Bayswater
London W2 4DL
Specialties: Autographed material.
   (See listing under AUCTIONS)

Profiles in History
Joseph M. Maddalena
9440 Santa Monica Boulevard
Suite 704
Beverly Hills, CA 90210
Phone: 310-859-7701
800-942-8856 (orders outside of California)
800-942-8855 (orders in California)
FAX: 213-859-7329
Specialties: Photographs, letters, and other items signed by those associated with *GWTW,* including:

Vivien Leigh as Scarlett O'Hara in barbecue costume, signed 11 " by 14 " photograph with inscription "for the Members of the Ladies Auxiliaries with best wishes Vivien Leigh". Some surface wrinkling and emulsion cracks; otherwise, in fine condition. Framed. $6500. #15568.

Hattie McDaniel; a candid full-length portrait of McDaniel, dressed in formal wear, standing in front of floor-to-ceiling curtains; signed 8 " by 10 " photograph with inscription "Best Wishes To James R. McCray. From Hattie McDaniel. '45." In fine condition. $1000. #15479.

Margaret Mitchell; engraved calling card, approximately 3 " by 2 "; Mitchell crossed out "Mrs. John Robert Marsh" and wrote in pencil: "If you have a minute—Please! If not, I'll understand. Margaret Mitchell." In fine condition. Call for current price. #14254.

Margaret Mitchell; typed letter signed "Margaret Mitchell" on her personal letterhead. One 8 " by 10 " page, Atlanta, Georgia, February 8, 1937. Written to Mrs. Huston, discussing the suitability of *GWTW* for her fifteen-year-old daughter. In fine condition. $3500. #13956.

Margaret Mitchell; typed letter signed "Margaret Mitchell" on her personal letterhead. One 8 " by 10 " page, Atlanta, Georgia, April 2, 1937. Written to Miss Strong, thanking her for writing. In fine condition. Call for current price. #15792.

Margaret Mitchell; typed letter signed "Margaret Mitchell Marsh" on her personal letterhead. One 8 " by 10 " page, Atlanta, Georgia, April 29, 1942. Written to Mr. Hawkins explaining why she cannot write something for the Navy Relief Society. In fine condition. $3500. #16001.

Margaret Mitchell; typed letter signed "Margaret Mitchell Marsh" on her personal letterhead. Two 8 " by 10 " pages, Atlanta, Georgia, July 23, 1947. Written to Mrs. Johnson, detailing how film rights to *GWTW* were sold. In fine condition. Call for current price. #15764.

Catalog: $20.00. Items in catalog represent only a small percentage of inventory, and stock is subject to prior sale. Collectors should notify Profiles of particular wants. Company maintains a "want card" system and will inform collectors of new material which meets collecting interests.

Payment: C, V, MC, AE, also offers a no-interest layaway plan.

Delivery: Arranged when the order is placed

Returns: Any item may be returned within one day after receipt. Exceptions must be arranged when the order is placed.

The Kenneth W. Rendell Gallery, Inc.
Place Des Antiquaires
125 East 57th Street
New York, NY 10022
Phone: 212-935-6767

FAX: 212-935-6927

Specialties: Photographs, letters, and other items signed by those associated with *GWTW,* including:

Margaret Mitchell; typewritten letter signed, "Margaret Mitchell Marsh," one page, 8″ by 10″, July 7, 1938. To Dr. Mayos. "I read with a sense of almost personal shock the news of the death of your friend Doctor Zeller. He had been so kind to me about the Rock Island Arsenal historical items and I had appreciated his interest so very much. To you, an old friend and a fellow doctor, his passing must have been indeed saddening." Fine condition. Framed with a portrait. $3750.

Vivien Leigh and Clark Gable; signatures of each star framed as an ensemble; his, appearing on a check dated February 14, 1950, and hers on a 2¹/₂″ by 3¹/₂″ sheet. Two fine examples, framed with an original *Gone With the Wind* movie program cover. Framed in peach, terra cotta, and antique beaded gilt, 13″ by 17″. $3500.

Vivien Leigh; autograph letter signed, one full page, approximately 5″ by 7″, circa May 1951. "To dear Lukie" [Ethel Lucas, wardrobe mistress at the St. James's Theatre, London]. "To thank you for dressing me so beautifully and to wish you a really happy holiday." Leigh was at this time playing opposite her husband, Laurence Olivier, in a double bill featuring Shakespeare's *Antony and Cleopatra* and Shaw's *Caesar and Cleopatra*. Fine condition. Framed in buff, mocha, and copper gilt, with a color portrait of Vivien Leigh as Scarlett O'Hara, 14″ by 18″. $1850.

Clark Gable; document signed, one page, oblong 7″ by 5″. November 4, 1942. Second Lieutenant Gable certifies that he has received his "Mask, gas [and] service" and that "the articles listed . . . have not been previously issued to me." A fine example from Gable's military service during World War II. Framed with photograph. $1500.

Butterfly McQueen; signed photograph from *Gone With the Wind,* showing McQueen as Prissy talking with Scarlett O'Hara. The photograph measures 8″ by 10″ and is in fine condition. Framed in gilt. $975.

Olivia de Havilland; half-length portrait photograph of the actress in costume as Melanie, signed "Very best wishes, Olivia de Havilland and Melanie," in the upper left portion. Fine condition. Framed in gilt. $657.

Catalog: $5.00 for a single issue or $30.00 for a year's subscription, which includes 10 issues.

Payment: C, V, MC, AE

Delivery: UPS, USPS

Returns: Items may be returned within three days of receipt. Notify company before making return.

Sotheby's
1334 York Avenue
New York, NY 10021
Phone: 212-606-7000
FAX: 212-606-7249
Specialties: Autographed material.
      (See listing under AUCTIONS)

Swann Galleries, Inc.
104 East 25th Street
New York, NY 10010
Specialties: Autographed material.
      (See listing under AUCTIONS)

Yesteryear Book Shop Inc.
3201 Maple Drive NE
Atlanta, GA 30305
Phone: 404-237-0163
Specialties: A variety of autographed *GWTW*–related items.

Catalog: None. Stock is subject to change. Collectors should notify Yesteryear Book Shop of particular wants by telephoning or sending a letter of inquiry with an SASE. Company will inform collectors of new material which meets collecting interests.

Books about Margaret Mitchell.

Payment: C, MO
Delivery: UPS
Returns: Any item may be returned within five days as long as the merchandise is in the same condition as it was sent to the customer.

Books

MANY collectors know that Margaret Mitchell's novel was released on June 30, 1936. Although that date was the formal debut of the novel, copies published in June 1936 are not considered first editions. Why?

Macmillan originally planned to release *Gone with the Wind* formally on May 5, 1936, and initially placed a print order for 10,000 copies of the novel. (In publishing, first edition copies are those produced during the first press run.) In the meantime, the Book-of-the-Month Club named Mitchell's novel its feature selection for July 1936. Because of the book-club sale, Macmillan delayed the formal release date of the novel

to June 30. However, the publisher still shipped copies of the book to stores in May. Word-of-mouth news about *Gone with the Wind* accelerated the public's demand for the new book, and Macmillan ordered three subsequent printings during the month of June.

That caused confusion among first-edition book collectors. Copies of *Gone with the Wind* purchased at publication bore "Published in June" on the copyright page, yet earlier copies carried "Published in May." Collectors flooded Macmillan with requests for clarification. As a result, Macmillan was compelled to send out form letters explaining that copies of the novel with the May publication date were the real first editions.

Today the value of a *Gone with the Wind* first edition depends upon the book's overall condition, the presence or absence of a dust jacket, and whether or not the book is autographed.

Book dealers use the following general terms to describe a book's condition:

Mint—a perfect copy, bright and fresh as the day it was published

Fine—nearly perfect, showing slight signs of wear but no defects

Very Good—rather worn, but no defects

Good—shows normal wear and aging; textually complete, but below grade

Fair—worn, probably with cover tears and other defects

Poor—very worn, with major defects; the worst possible condition

Since there are few remaining first edition copies of *Gone with the Wind* in mint condition, those volumes bring the highest prices. The value of the book is increased if there is an intact dust jacket.

A dust jacket or dustwrapper is the printed or pictorial cover used to protect a book's binding. Because it is a thick book, *Gone with the Wind* takes longer to read than a thinner volume, and its dust jacket wears much faster because of the increased handling the volume must endure. Therefore, *Gone with the Wind* dust jackets in fine condition are scarce.

The value of a first-edition copy of *Gone with the Wind* with a fine dust jacket usually will be twice that of the same copy without the jacket. The value for a first-edition copy with a tattered dust jacket will probably fall somewhere between those two prices, depending upon the amount of wrapper wear.

The presence or absence of Margaret Mitchell's autograph will also affect a first edition's value. An autographed first edition usually will have twice the value of an unsigned copy.

Mitchell hated to give autographs to people other than family and friends. She wrote to her editor, Lois Cole, that "when a stranger asks me for an autograph I feel just as if he (or she) had asked me for a pair of my step-ins and it makes me just as sore." Mitchell was so overwhelmed with requests for autographs that after December 1936 she refused to sign any copies of *Gone with the Wind* for anyone, including family and friends. She wrote to Kenneth Roberts, author of *Northwest Passage*, that "unfortu-nately, when I came to this decision I had not even inscribed the copies belonging to my brother and other relatives. I have never autographed these copies, for I discovered that I could not pick and choose without offending many people." Because of Mitchell's no-autograph policy, copies of *Gone with the Wind* that do bear her signature have increased value.

There were copies of her novel that Mitchell signed with just her name and others that she inscribed with a sentiment for the recipient. If a signed-inscription copy was for a famous person or someone important in Mitchell's life or work, the volume—known as an association copy—has much more value than the normal autographed first edition.

Bluff Park Rare Books
2535 East Broadway
Long Beach, CA 90803
Phone: 310-438-9830
Specialties: Gone with the Wind first editions, special editions and *GWTW*–related books.
Catalog: None. Stock is subject to change. Collectors should notify Bluff Park Rare Books of particular wants by sending a letter of inquiry with a SASE.
Payment: C
Delivery: UPS, USPS, Federal Express
Returns: Any book may be returned within ten days for refund if not as described.

The Bookstack
112 West Lexington Avenue
Elkhart, IN 46516
Phone: 219-293-3815
Specialties: Gone With the Wind–related books.
Catalog: None. Stock is subject to change. Collectors should notify The Bookstack of particular wants by telephoning or sending a letter of inquiry with a SASE.
Payment: C, MO
Delivery: USPS
Returns: Any book may be returned within ten days as long as The Bookstack has been notified in advance.

GWTW-related books.

Caravan Book Store
550 South Grand Avenue
Los Angeles, CA 90071
Phone: 213-626-9944
Specialties: Gone With the Wind–related
books.
Catalog: None. Collectors should notify
Caravan Book Store of particular wants
by sending a letter of inquiry with a
SASE.
Payment: C, MO
Delivery: UPS, USPS
Returns: Any book may be returned for
exchange credit only.

Cinemage Books
105 West 27th Street
New York, NY 10001
Phone: 212-243-4919
Specialties: Gone With the Wind–related
books.
Catalog: $1.00 in cash (no checks or
stamps). Stock is subject to change. Collectors should notify Cinemage Books of
particular wants by sending a letter of
inquiry with a SASE.
Payment: C, MO

Delivery: USPS
Returns: Any book may be returned for
refund or exchange within seven days if
packaged and insured as received.

Cobweb Collectibles
9 Walnut Avenue
Cranford, NJ 07016
Phone: 908-272-5777 (11 A.M. to 5 P.M.
Eastern Time, Monday through Saturday)
Specialties: Gone with the Wind first edi-
tions and related books.
Catalog: None. Collectors should notify
Cobweb Collectibles of particular wants
by sending a 3″ by 5″ postcard. Com-
pany maintains a "want card" system and
will inform collectors of new material
which meets collecting needs.
Payment: C, MO, V, MC, D
Delivery: UPS, USPS
Returns: All sales are final. No returns or
exchanges.

Cohasco, Inc.
Postal 821
Yonkers, NY 10702

Specialties: Books.
(See listing under AUCTIONS)

Collectors Book Store
1708 North Vine Street
Hollywood, CA 90028
Phone: 213-467-3296
FAX: 213-467-4536
Specialties: Gone With the Wind–related books.
Catalog: None. Stock is subject to change. Collectors should notify Collectors Book Store of particular wants by telephoning or sending a letter of inquiry with a SASE.
Payment: C, MO, V, MC, D, AE
Delivery: UPS, USPS
Returns: Any item may be returned for full refund or credit if returned in good condition within fourteen days.

C. Dickens Fine, Rare, & Collectible Books
Lenox Square
3393 Peachtree Road NE
Atlanta, GA 30326
Phone: 404-231-3825
800-548-0376 (orders)
Specialties: GONE WITH THE WIND Paint Book, first edition, partially colored in. $700. AB8283.
Gone with the Wind, 1939 motion picture edition. $325. AB1473.
Gone with the Wind, 1938, inscribed "To Rose my neighbor and my friend. Love Margaret" $3500. AC3385.
Gone with the Wind, first edition, advance copy in glassine with review slip laid in; unread and hence unreviewed copy. $25,000. AD6468.
Gone with the Wind, first edition. $1200. AA7934.
Million Dollar Legends: Margaret Mitchell by Norman Shavin, first edition, 1974. $75. AC0349.
Catalog: None. Stock is subject to prior sale. A list of items offered by C. Dickens is available by sending a request and enclosing a SASE. Collectors can request a search for non-inventory items.
Payment: C, MO, V, MC, AE

Delivery: UPS, USPS
Returns: If book ordered is not as described, it may be returned for a refund within five days of receipt.

Eugenia's Place
1574 Cave Road NW
Atlanta, GA 30327
Phone: 404-261-0394 (weekdays)
404-458-0682 (weekends)
Specialties: Gone with the Wind special editions and *GWTW*–related books.
Catalog: None. Stock is subject to change. Collectors should notify Eugenia's Place of particular wants by sending a letter of inquiry with a SASE.
Payment: C, MO, V, MC
Delivery: UPS, USPS
Returns: Any book may be returned for store credit only.

Gryphon Bookshops
2246 Broadway
New York, NY 10024
Phone: 212-362-0706
Specialties: Gone with the Wind first and special editions and *GWTW*–related books.
Catalog: None. Gryphon Bookshops has a large inventory of items. Write or telephone with specific wants for a price quote. Company maintains want lists and will inform collectors of new material which meets collecting interests.
Payment: C, MO, V, MC
Delivery: UPS
Returns: Any book may be returned within ten days for refund or exchange.

Hemetro
127 South Main Street
New Hope, PA 18938
Phone: 215-862-5629
800-362-5336 (orders)
Specialties: Gone with the Wind first and special editions and *GWTW*–related books.
Catalog: None. Stock is subject to change. Collectors should notify Hemetro of particular wants by telephoning or sending a letter of inquiry with a SASE.

Payment: C, MO, V, MC, D, AE
Delivery: UPS
Returns: No returns.

Houle Rare Books & Autographs
7260 Beverly Boulevard
Los Angeles, CA 90036
Phone: 213-937-5858
FAX: 213-937-0091
Specialties: Books from the collection of
George Cukor and other *GWTW*–related
books.
Catalog: Houle Rare Books & Autographs
offers a number of catalogs in various
categories, ranging in price from $3.00 to
$10.00. George Cukor Collection catalog
is $85.00 (hardcover), $20.00 (softcover).
Stock is subject to change.
Payment: C, MO, V, MC, AE
Delivery: UPS
Returns: Any book may be returned within
ten days for refund or exchange.

McGowan Book Co.
PO Box 222
Chapel Hill, NC 27514
Phone: 919-968-1121
Specialties: *Gone With the Wind*–related
books.
Catalog: $3.00 for three issues. Stock is
subject to prior sale. Collectors should
contact McGowan Book Co. to check the
current availability of *GWTW*–related
items.
Payment: C, MO
Delivery: UPS, USPS
Returns: Any book may be returned within
fifteen days for refund or exchange.

Matinee Idol
8650 Melrose Avenue
Los Angeles, CA 90069
Phone: 310-659-5569
Specialties: *Gone With the Wind*–related
books.
Catalog: None. A list of items offered by
Matinee Idol is available by sending a
request and enclosing a SASE.
Payment: C, MO, V, MC
Delivery: USPS
Returns: None.

Movie Poster Place
PO Box 128
Lansdowne, PA 19050-0128
Phone: 215-622-6062
FAX: 215-622-6062
Specialties: *Gone with the Wind*, 1939 mo-
tion picture edition, paperback.
Catalog: $1.00, which can be deducted
from first order. Stock is subject to
change. Collectors should contact Movie
Poster Place to check the current avail-
ability of *GWTW*–related items.
Payment: C, MO, V, MC
Delivery: UPS, USPS, Federal Express
Returns: Any book may be returned for
refund or exchange for any reason.

Profiles in History
Joseph M. Maddalena
9440 Santa Monica Boulevard
Suite 704
Beverly Hills, CA 90210
Phone: 310-859-7701
800-942-8856 (orders outside of California)
800-942-8855 (orders in California)
FAX: 213-859-7329
Specialties: *Gone with the Wind*, first edition, first printing (May 1936); boldly
signed "Margaret Mitchell" on the first
blank inside leaf; mint dust jacket, un-
foxed, pages snow white, binding tight,
in a custom leather slipcase. $9500.
#13777.
Catalog: $20.00. Items in catalog represent
only a small percentage of inventory, and
stock is subject to change. Collectors
should notify Profiles of particular wants.
Company maintains a "want card" system
and will inform collectors of new material which meets collecting interests.
Payment: C, V, MC, AE, also offers a no-
interest layaway plan.
Delivery: Arranged when the order is placed
Returns: Any item may be returned within
one day after receipt. Exceptions must be
arranged when the order is placed.

Reading Room Books
264 South Wabash Street
Wabash, IN 46992

Phone: 219-563-6421
FAX: 219-563-4558
Specialties: Gone with the Wind first editions and special editions and *GWTW*–related books.
Catalog: None. Stock is subject to change. Reading Room Books will provide a list of current stock for a SASE. Company maintains a want list system and will inform collectors of new material which meets collecting interests.
Payment: C, MO, V, MC, D
Delivery: UPS, USPS
Returns: Any book may be returned within ten days for a refund. Items damaged or defaced by customer will not be accepted for return.

The Kenneth W. Rendell Gallery Inc.
Place Des Antiquaires
125 East 57th Street
New York, NY 10022
Phone: 212-935-6767
FAX: 212-935-6927
Specialties: Gone with the Wind, signed, inscribed "For Edwin O Grover, with many thanks for a fine visit" and dated "July 1936" on the front free endpaper. Original dust jacket. In normal, well-read condition. Attractively presented in a tan and brown fall-back box. $3750.
Catalog: $5.00 for a single issue or $30.00 for a year's subscription, which includes ten issues.
Payment: C, V, MC, AE
Delivery: UPS, USPS
Returns: Items may be returned within three days of receipt. Notify company before making return.

Ellen Roth Books
47 Truman Drive
Marlboro, NJ 07746
Phone: 908-536-0850
Specialties: Gone With the Wind–related books.
Catalog: None. Stock is subject to prior sale. Collectors should contact Ellen Roth Books by telephoning or sending a letter of inquiry with a SASE. Company maintains a want list and will inform

collectors of new material which meets collecting interests.
Payment: C, MO
Delivery: UPS, USPS
Returns: Items may be returned if they are not as described.

Swann Galleries, Inc.
104 East 25th Street
New York, NY 10010
Specialties: Books.
　　(See listing under AUCTIONS)

Tattered Cover Book Shop
2023 Boston Pike
Richmond, IN 47374
Phone: 317-935-6293
Specialties: Gone with the Wind first and special editions and *GWTW*–related books.
Catalog: None. Stock is subject to change. Collectors should notify Tattered Cover Book Shop of particular wants by sending a letter of inquiry with a SASE. Company maintains an ongoing list of wants and will inform collectors of new material which meets collecting interests.
Payment: C
Delivery: UPS, USPS
Returns: Any book may be returned within fourteen days for refund.

Yesteryear Book Shop Inc.
3201 Maple Drive NE
Atlanta, GA 30305
Phone: 404-237-0163
Specialties: Gone with the Wind first editions, foreign editions, special editions and *GWTW*–related books.
Catalog: None. Stock is subject to change. Collectors should notify Yesteryear Book Shop of particular wants by telephoning or sending a letter of inquiry with a SASE. Company will inform collectors of new material which meets collecting interests.
Payment: C, MO
Delivery: UPS
Returns: Any item may be returned within five days as long as the merchandise is in the same condition as it was sent to the customer.

Ceramics

AMONG the hard-to-find *Gone With the Wind* collectibles is the Scarlett O'Hara "Yesteryear" perfume vial, produced by Babs Creations during the 1940s.

The 4-inch-tall, clear-glass vial image of Scarlett was accented by a small ribbon-and-felt flower corsage at her hands. The vial rested on a circular brass base which was 3¹/₂ inches in diameter. On the front edge of the base was a foil sticker bearing the name "Yesteryear." A clear-glass, vertical dome covered the vial, and with the dome in place the collectible reached 5¹/₂ inches in height.

A Scarlett O'Hara "Yesteryear" perfume vial complete with dome and perhaps some remaining fragrance is a rare and "scent-sational" find.

Bluff Park Rare Books
2535 East Broadway
Long Beach, CA 90803
Phone: 310-438-9830
Specialties: Original *Gone With the Wind* figurines.
Catalog: None. Stock is subject to prior sale. Collectors should notify Bluff Park Rare Books of particular wants by sending a letter of inquiry with a SASE.
Payment: C
Delivery: UPS, USPS, Federal Express
Returns: Any item may be returned within ten days for refund if not as described.

C. Dickens Fine, Rare, & Collectible Books
Lenox Square
3393 Peachtree Road NE
Atlanta, GA 30326
Phone: 404-231-3825
800-548-0376
Specialties: Original *Gone With the Wind* perfume bottles.
Catalog: None. Stock is subject to prior sale. A list of items offered by C. Dickens is available by sending a request and enclosing a SASE. Collectors can request a search for non-inventory items.
Payment: C, MO, V, MC, AE
Delivery: UPS, USPS

Returns: If item ordered is not as described, it may be returned for a refund within five days of receipt.

Eugenia's Place
1574 Cave Road NW
Atlanta, GA 30327
Phone: 404-261-0394 (weekdays)
404-458-0682 (weekends)
Specialties: Original *Gone With the Wind* perfume bottles.
Catalog: None. Stock is subject to prior sale. Collectors should notify Eugenia's Place of particular wants by sending a letter of inquiry with an SASE.
Payment: C, MO, V, MC
Delivery: UPS, USPS
Returns: Any item may be returned for store credit only.

Hake's Americana & Collectibles
PO Box 1444
York, PA 17405
Specialties: Original *Gone With the Wind* perfume bottles.
(See listing under AUCTIONS)

That's Entertainment
222 Blue Hills Road
North Haven, CT 06473
Phone: 203-872-9207
Specialties: *Gone With the Wind* ceramic figurines and powder jars.
Catalog: None. Stock is subject to prior sale. Collectors should contact That's Entertainment to check the current availability of *GWTW*–related items.
Payment: C, V, MC
Delivery: USPS
Returns: If item is not as described, telephone That's Entertainment on the day of receipt to arrange refund.

Clothing

SCARLETT'S exquisite costumes were designed by Walter Plunkett, a contract designer borrowed from Metro–Goldwyn–Mayer.

He had started out at RKO in 1926 and first worked with David O. Selznick in

GWTW scarf and hankies. *(The collection of John Wiley Jr.)*

1937's *Nothing Sacred.* In 1946 Plunkett began a twenty-year association with MGM. There his work as a designer of historical costumes earned him kudos.

After Selznick selected him to design the costumes for *Gone With the Wind,* Plunkett traveled to Atlanta to research the styles of clothing worn during the Civil War and Reconstruction periods. He also collected fabric swatches from dresses displayed in Southern museums. These swatches were sent to a Pennsylvania textile mill, which made all the cotton cloth used for the costumes.

When he returned to Selznick's studio, Plunkett was faced with designing gowns and petticoats for an unknown actress, since the role of Scarlett had not yet been cast. Additionally, Plunkett supervised the Civil War fashions industry that had sprung up on the studio lot. Seamstresses, weavers, hatmakers, and shoemakers created hundreds of dresses, uniforms, and accessories. A retired corset maker provided expertise

on antebellum foundation garments, and ironworkers forged hoops for skirts.

While Vivien Leigh could luxuriate in her Plunkett finery, the story was a bit different for Clark Gable. Gable was unhappy with the wardrobe made for him by Selznick's costume department. The shirt collars choked him, and the suits and cravats were ill-fitting.

He complained to Selznick, who fired off a memo to the wardrobe department: "I think it is very disappointing indeed to have the elegant Rhett Butler wandering around with clothes that look as though he had bought them at the Hart, Schaffner, and Marx of that period and walked right out of the store with them." Selznick urged his wardrobe staff to observe Gable's personal wardrobe: "Look at how well he looks in his own clothes generally, and compare the fit and the tailoring and the general attractiveness with what I regard as the awful costuming job we are doing with him."

To keep his star happy, Selznick ordered a

complete new wardrobe made for Rhett Butler by Gable's Beverly Hills tailor, Eddie Schmidt.

Alexander Gallery
980 Madison Avenue
New York, NY 10021
Phone: 212-472-1636
Specialties: Original *Gone With the Wind* costumes and accessories.

Clark Gable/Rhett's Suit is a three-piece gray wool suit designed by costume designer Walter Plunkett and worn by Clark Gable during the filming of *Gone With the Wind*. The suit is labeled with the actor's name, and a movie still of Gable wearing the suit is included. $12,500.

Vivien Leigh/Scarlett's Day Dress. Designed by Walter Plunkett and bearing a label "Scarlett," this two-piece cotton day dress is in very good condition. The blue-gray bolero jacket with matching full skirt, both trimmed in black cord, was worn during the scene in which Scarlett drove her carriage through Shantytown. Included with the dress are two movie stills of Vivien Leigh wearing the costume. $15,000.

Vivien Leigh/Scarlett's Straw Hat. This wide-brimmed straw hat with green velvet ties was worn by Vivien Leigh during the barbecue scene. Matching gloves and two movie stills of the actress accompany the hat. $15,000.

Vivien Leigh/Scarlett's Black Hat. The wide-rim straw hat, scalloped at the back, with a wide pink silk ribbon across the front, has a label with Vivien Leigh's name. $15,000.

Catalog: $50. Stock is subject to prior sale. Collectors should contact Alexander Gallery to check the current availability of *GWTW*–related items.
Payment: C, MO
Delivery: Arranged when order is placed
Returns: No returns.

Hake's Americana & Collectibles
PO Box 1444
York, PA 17405

Specialties: Original *Gone With the Wind* hankies.
(See listing under AUCTIONS)

Sotheby's
1334 York Avenue
New York, NY 10021
Phone: 212-606-7000
FAX: 212-606-7249
Specialties: Movie costumes.
(See listing under AUCTIONS)

That's Entertainment
222 Blue Hills Road
North Haven, CT 06473
Phone: 203-872-9207
Specialties: Original *Gone With the Wind* scarves and hankies.
Catalog: None. Stock is subject to prior sale. Collectors should contact That's Entertainment to check the current availability of *GWTW*–related items.
Payment: C, V, MC
Delivery: USPS
Returns: If item is not as described, telephone That's Entertainment on the day of receipt to arrange refund.

Dolls

BEATRICE ALEXANDER, founder of the Alexander Doll Company, was destined to create the world's most beautiful dolls. She was born in the family's New York City apartment, located above her father's doll hospital. At the hospital—the first of its kind in the United States—cracked and broken porcelain dolls were lovingly repaired, and Beatrice saw first hand the joy that pretty dolls could bring to little girls.

The bullets and bombs of World War I halted the supply of imported European dolls, so Beatrice fashioned her own, including the "Red Cross Nurse" rag dolls. As a result, her husband, Phillip Behrman, encouraged her to begin her own doll business.

In 1923 Beatrice founded the Alexander Doll Company in New York City and be-

Wendy Scarlett of 1972. *(Jan Lebow,* The Fashion History of Alexander Scarlett Dolls, 1937–1992*)*

Scarlett of 1939–43. *(Jan Lebow,* The Fashion History of Alexander Scarlett Dolls, 1937–1992*)*

came known in the doll world as Madame Alexander. Her early dolls were made of cloth with mask-type faces, and she painted the features of each one by hand.

Almost immediately the company was successful. Doll lovers recognized the quality and elegance that Madame brought to her Alexander dolls. Hand-painted faces from eyelash to smile; individually combed, curled, or braided hair styles; luxurious fabrics and trimmings for costumes; and perfect-touch accents such as shoes, hats, and parasols were the hallmarks of each Alexander creation.

In 1937 Madame Alexander obtained the trademark for Scarlett O'Hara dolls, based on Margaret Mitchell's best-selling novel. The first Scarlett O'Hara doll arrived that same year. The Tiny Betty Scarlett, a seven-inch, pre-movie composition doll, wore a simple yellow organdy dress with a matching ruffled-hem trim and an attached gauze petticoat. Her accessories included cotton pantaloons and a natural straw hat decorated with flowers. Her eyes, shoes, and socks were hand painted.

From that lovely beginning, Alexander Scarlett dolls have appeared through the years in a number of exquisite costumes. The series expanded to include other characters such as Melanie, Ashley, Rhett, Mrs. O'Hara, Bonnie Blue, Mammy, Prissy, Suellen, Carreen, Aunt Pittypat, and Belle Watling.

From 1950 to 1954 the fashion industry honored Madame Alexander with four consecutive Fashion Academy Awards, in recognition of her skill as a fashion designer. In 1986 Madame Alexander was honored with the first DOTY (Doll of the Year) Lifetime Achievement Award, presented by *Doll Reader* magazine. The award recognized her "skill, style and adherence to quality, detail and authenticity."

Madame Alexander died in October 1990 at the age of 95. However, she left behind a legacy of excellence and high standards that remain the guiding forces of the Alexander Doll Company today.

C. Dickens Fine, Rare, & Collectible Books
Lenox Square
3393 Peachtree Road NE
Atlanta, GA 30326
Phone: 404-231-3825
800-548-0376 (orders)
Specialties: Vivien Leigh doll, 11″ porce-
lain, 1983, by Ann Parker Dolls in En-
gland. $395. #AB6490.
Ashley doll, 21″ porcelain, by The
Franklin Mint. $250. #AC3310.
Rhett doll, 21″ porcelain, by The Frank-
lin Mint. $250. #AC3311.
Melanie doll, 21″ porcelain, by The
Franklin Mint. $250. #AC3312.
Catalog: None. Stock is subject to prior
sale. A list of items offered by C. Dickens
is available by sending a request and en-
closing a SASE. Collectors can request a
search for non-inventory items.
Payment: C, MO, V, MC, AE
Delivery: UPS, USPS
Returns: If item ordered is not as described,
it may be returned for a refund within
five days of receipt.

Scarlett of 1940–43. *(Jan Lebow,* The Fashion
History of Alexander Scarlett Dolls, 1937–1992*)*

Dollsville Dolls & Bearsville Bears
461 North Palm Canyon Drive
Palm Springs, CA 92262
Phone: 619-325-2241
800-225-2327 (orders)
FAX: 619-322-1691
Specialties: Dolls from the Alexander Doll
Company:
Scarlett, 8″, white lace, $69.95
Scarlett, 8″, 1990, $69.95
Scarlett At the Ball, 10″, $84.95
Scarlett, 14″, $195.00
Scarlett, 21″, $274.95
Scarlett Green Velvet, 21″, porcelain,
$795.00
Melanie, 21″, portrait, $295.00
Melanie, 8″, $52.95
Officer Ashley, 8″, $49.95
Ashley, 8″, $69.95
Carreen, 14″, $124.95
Prissy, 8″, $44.95
Mrs. O'Hara, 8″, $52.95
Belle Watling, 10″, $89.95

Coco Scarlett of 1966. *(Jan Lebow,* The Fashion
History of Alexander Scarlett Dolls, 1937–1992*)*

Scarlett at the Ball. *(Alexander Doll Company)*

Mammy. *(Alexander Doll Company)*

Aunt Pitty Pat. *(Alexander Doll Company)*

Mrs. O'Hara. *(Alexander Doll Company)*

Confederate Officer, 12", $74.95
Union Officer, 12", $74.95
Catalog: $1.00. Stock is subject to prior
sale. Collectors should contact Dollsville
to check the current availability of
GWTW–related items.
Payment: V, AE
Delivery: UPS
Returns: Items may be returned within three
days for in-store credit only.

Frasher's
Route l, Box 142
Oak Grove, MO 64075
Specialties: Antique and collectible dolls,
including *Gone With the Wind* dolls.
(See listing under AUCTIONS)

Hemetro
127 South Main Street
New Hope, PA 18938
Phone: 215-862-5629
800-362-5336 (orders)
Specialties: Gone With the Wind dolls.
Catalog: None. Stock is subject to prior
sale. Collectors should notify Hemetro of
particular wants by telephoning or send-
ing a letter of inquiry with a SASE.
Payment: C, MO, V, MC, D, AE
Delivery: UPS
Returns: No returns.

La Tours Antiques & Imports
16 Alva Street
East Greenbush, NY 12061
Phone: 518-477-5128
Specialties: Vintage *Gone With the Wind*
dolls.
Catalog: None. Stock is subject to prior
sale. Collectors should notify La Tours of
particular wants by telephoning or send-
ing a letter of inquiry with a SASE.
Payment: C, MO
Delivery: UPS
Returns: Items may be returned up to five
days after receipt.

Jan Lebow
504 South Independence Boulevard
Virginia Beach, VA 23452
Phone: 804-497-4338
804-486-1992

*Specialties: The Fashion History of Alexan-
der Scarlett O'Hara Dolls, 1937–1992,
Volume 2,* a comprehensive reference
book on Alexander Scarlett dolls, fully
illustrated with 4" by 6" color photo-
graphs.
Catalog: None. Write or call to order.
Payment: C, MO
Delivery: UPS
Returns: No returns.

Lots of Dolls
215 Garfield
Milford, OH 45150
Phone: 513-248-2151
800-755-6402 (orders)
Specialties: Dolls from the Alexander Doll
Company:
Scarlett, 8", 1989, $95
Scarlett, 8", 1990, $60
Mammy, 8", 1989, $65
Prissy, 8", 1990 (MIB), $60
Ashley, 8", 1990 (MIB), $50
Bonnie Blue, 14", $100
Catalog: None. Stock is subject to prior
sale. Collectors should contact Lots of
Dolls to check the current availability of
GWTW–related items.
Payment: V, MC, D
Delivery: UPS
Returns: Any item may be returned within
five days in the same condition as pur-
chased.

McMasters Productions, Inc.
PO Box 1755
Cambridge, OH 43725
Specialties: Antique and collectible dolls,
including *GWTW*–related dolls.
(See listing under AUCTIONS)

My Doll House of Hilltop, Inc.
1860 Laskin Road
Virginia Beach, VA 23454
Phone: 804-425-6900
FAX: 804-461-4669
Specialties: Dolls from the Alexander Doll
Company:
Scarlett, style #426; $49.95
Scarlett, style #626; $54.95
Melanie, style #627; $54.95

Prissy. *(Alexander Doll Company)*

Ashley as Officer. *(Alexander Doll Company)*

Ashley, style #628; $49.95
Prissy, style #630; $46.95
Scarlett, style #1100; $74.95
Melanie, style #1101; $69.95
Scarlett, style #1300; $99.95
Suellen, 12", style #1301; $84.95
Bonnie Blue, style #1305; $109.95
Scarlett, 14", style #1590; $119.95
Scarlett, style #1591; $89.95
Scarlett, style #2247; $259.95
Melanie, style #2254; $274.95

Catalog: Free. Stock is subject to prior sale. Collectors should contact My Doll House to check the current availability of *GWTW*–related items.

Payment: C, MO, V, MC, D, AE, layaways

Delivery: UPS, USPS, Federal Express

Returns: Defective items may be returned within seven days of purchase if accompanied by receipt.

Lia Sargent, Inc.
74 The Oaks
Roslyn Estates, NY 11576
Phone: 516-621-4883
Specialties: Gone With the Wind dolls that were manufactured by the Alexander Doll Company from 1936 to 1965.
Catalog: $5.00. Catalogs are issued twice a year, in March and October. Stock is subject to prior sale. Collectors should contact Lia Sargent, Inc. to check the current availability of *GWTW*–related items.
Payment: C, MO, V, MC, AE
Delivery: UPS
Returns: Items may be returned for any reason within three days of receipt.

That's Entertainment
222 Blue Hills Road
North Haven, CT 06473
Phone: 203-872-9207
Specialties: Vintage *Gone With the Wind* dolls.
Catalog: None. Stock is subject to prior sale. Collectors should contact That's Entertainment to check the current availability of *GWTW*–related items.
Payment: C, V, MC
Delivery: USPS

Returns: If item is not as described, telephone That's Entertainment on the day of receipt to arrange refund.

Jewelry

O NE of the most glittering names associated with *Gone With the Wind* was Joseff of Hollywood. Known as the Jeweler to the Stars, Joseff crafted the beautiful pieces that adorned Vivien Leigh and the other stars of *Gone With the Wind*.

Chicago-born Eugene Joseff was artistic from an early age, and an interest in metal work lead to an apprenticeship in a foundry. Since jewelry design appealed to him, he studied techniques, dismantled and reassembled pieces, and experimented with new jewelry-making methods.

He initially viewed his interest in jewelry design as a sideline while he pursued a career in advertising. As the Depression spread its tentacles of darkness and despair across the country, Joseff decided to leave Chicago for the brightness and hope promised by Los Angeles and Hollywood.

The entertainment industry welcomed those with exciting new ideas, and Joseff fit the bill. He also became friends with many of Hollywood's film professionals, including costume designer Walter Plunkett.

But Joseff soon realized that jewelry design was more satisfying to him than advertising. While continuing to work in the business, he began to supply jewelry and props to the film industry.

In 1934, while viewing *The Affairs of Cellini*, Joseff was struck by an enormous error right there on the screen. He saw Constance Bennett and her lady-in-waiting, played by Lucille Ball, dressed in historically accurate costumes representing sixteenth century Italian gowns. However, the baubles and bangles accenting the attire were clearly pieces of twentieth century jewelry.

Joseff just could not believe that designers who were so meticulous in re-creating authentic costumes could ruin the overall

Bonnie Blue. *(Alexander Doll Company)*

Belle Watling. *(Alexander Doll Company)*

impression by using inappropriate jewelry. He brought the anachronism to the attention of Walter Plunkett.

"Well, if you're so smart," Plunkett told him, "let's see what you can do."

What Joseff did was nothing short of miraculous. Armed with a number of designing projects promised by several films, Joseff sketched out his ideas and brought them to most of the area jewelry manufacturers. They declared his designs not only original and intriguing but impossible to produce. Undeterred, Joseff decided to manufacture the pieces himself. He converted his workshop into a small manufacturing center, hired assistants, and set about to prove the experts wrong. He succeeded magnificently.

Joseff was exacting in the jewelry design work he completed for films. When a costume designer or art director submitted sketches, Joseff conducted careful research to ensure historical accuracy. He collected a library of rare books and used the illustrations to help guide his designs. But he didn't stop there. He incorporated his own ideas so that the finished pieces not only reflected the historical period but the mood demanded by the film. As a result, the studios flocked to him, and costume designers expressed admiration of his work:

• "The execution of the design far exceeded my expectations." (designer at Twentieth Century Fox, 1938);

• "It will be simple to keep you advised on all new ideas and, whenever it is possible, to use some of your latest pieces . . . It may be to our mutual advantage to design a gown to accent the jewelry." (designer at Columbia Pictures, 1938);

• "The things you did for me on *Mary of Scotland* and all the others were so beautifully done that of course you know that you will be the only one I will consider to carry out my designs." (Walter Plunkett, Selznick International Pictures, 1939).

Plunkett selected Joseff to design the jewelry for use in *Gone With the Wind*. The memorable pieces include:

• the coral necklace Scarlett wears to the barbecue at Twelve Oaks

• the cigar case Rhett Butler donates on behalf of Scarlett and Melanie at the Atlanta bazaar

• the "earbobs" Scarlett offers to Rhett in the jailhouse in exchange for money to pay the taxes on Tara

• Scarlett's "vulgar" diamond engagement ring

• the amethyst-and-diamond necklace Scarlett wears on her New Orleans honeymoon

• the bell earrings Belle Watling wears when she convinces Rhett to return to Scarlett for the sake of Bonnie Blue.

Joseff, who was known simply by that single name, designed jewelry for more than ninety percent of all the films made in the 1930s and 1940s, including *Anna Karenina, Camille, Marie Antoinette, The Prisoner of Zenda, The Private Lives of Elizabeth and Essex, Lillian Russell,* and *That Hamilton Woman.*

Tragically, Joseff was killed in an airplane crash in September 1948, just one week short of his forty-third birthday. Fortunately, in the early years Joseff had decided to lease rather than sell his jewelry to movie studios. Many pieces have gone on to appear in other films and on television and have thus perpetuated the memory and the genius of Joseff, Jeweler to the Stars.

After the premiere of *Gone With the Wind,* fans bought items of jewelry with *GWTW* tie-ins. For example, a simulated cameo brooch, designed to resemble the one originated by Joseff and worn by Vivien Leigh, was offered for fifteen cents and three wrappers from Lux toilet soap. Will you be fortunate enough to locate one of the brooches to add to your *Gone With the Wind* collection?

Eugenia's Place
1574 Cave Road NW
Atlanta, GA 30327
Phone: 404-261-0394 (weekdays)
404-458-0682 (weekends)

Specialties: Gone With the Wind original premium brooches.

Catalog: None. Stock is subject to prior sale. Collectors should notify Eugenia's Place of particular wants by sending a letter of inquiry with a SASE.

Payment: C, MO, V, MC

Delivery: UPS, USPS

Returns: Any item may be returned for store credit only.

Hake's Americana & Collectibles
PO Box 1444
York, PA 17405

Specialties: Gone With the Wind original premium brooches.
  (See listing under AUCTIONS)

Hemetro
127 South Main Street
New Hope, PA 18938

Phone: 215-862-5629
800-362-5336 (orders)

Specialties: Original *Gone With the Wind* jewelry.

Catalog: None. Stock is subject to prior sale. Collectors should notify Hemetro of particular wants by telephoning or sending a letter of inquiry with a SASE.

Payment: C, MO, V, MC, D, AE

Delivery: UPS

Returns: No returns.

Matinee Idol
8650 Melrose Avenue
Los Angeles, CA 90069

Phone: 310-659-5569

Specialties: Gone With the Wind original premium brooches.

Catalog: None. Stock is subject to change. A list of items offered by Matinee Idol is available by sending a SASE.

Payment: C, MO, V, MC

Delivery: USPS

Returns: None.

That's Entertainment
222 Blue Hills Road
North Haven, CT 06473

Phone: 203-872-9207

Specialties: Original *Gone With the Wind* jewelry.

Catalog: None. Stock is subject to prior sale. Collectors should contact That's Entertainment to check the current availability of *GWTW*–related items.

Payment: C, V, MC

Delivery: USPS

Returns: If item is not as described, telephone That's Entertainment on the day of receipt to arrange refund.

Paper

PAPER is perishable. Because of its high acid content, paper made in the twentieth century will eventually yellow, turn brown, then crumble into dust.

Paper is also disposable. Items such as theater tickets were originally intended to be used once and then discarded. Other items, such as movie posters, were meant to be used for a longer period before being discarded.

Perishable, disposable paper products that were never meant to last are known as *ephemera*. And because of its transitory nature, ephemera is valued highly by collectors, especially motion picture ephemera.

Although film ephemera was destined to be discarded, many of the programs, posters, and lobby cards were saved through the years, and some of that original ephemera is available to collectors today. One of the most sought-after, hard-to-find items is the press book.

A press book is a publication detailing the publicity and advertising materials available to promote a specific film. From 1910 until the mid 1930s, a press book was referred to as a ballybook or bally, derived from the word "ballyhoo," meaning flamboyant, exaggerated, or sensational advertising.

The bally overflowed with highly imaginative suggestions to help theater managers attract crowds to the film. One popular idea was to parade an elephant through town, regaled in colorful flags, bunting, and banners which announced the opening of the new film.

By the mid 1930s the ballybook had become the press book, and it could range in scope from a multi-paged publication to a one-to-two-pound box of materials. Typical elements of a press book were:
• a vividly written synopsis of the story
• feature stories about the cast, crew, and the making of the movie
• biographies of every cast member
• excerpts from contracts the stars had signed with the movie studio
• articles on the fashion and beauty styles featured in the movie
• specific ideas for local promotional campaigns
• lists, descriptions, and photographs of advertising and promotional items available, including posters, lobby and window cards, press stills, banners, heralds, and giveaway items such as dishware, glasses, toys, hats, ties, handkerchiefs, games, and puzzles.

The theater manager reviewed the press book, decided what would be useful for promoting the film and ordered the materials from the regional movie exchange. From the mid 1920s to the mid 1950s, there were thirty movie exchanges across the United States which acted as local booking agents for films and distributed advertising and promotional materials.

After the run of the film, the materials which the theater manager bought were either stored, given away, or discarded. Since press books were no longer useful, they were usually thrown away. The rented items were usually returned to the movie exchange.

Once a film was taken out of circulation, the movie exchange sometimes offered the leftover promotional materials, including extra press books, to local collectors. But most often the items were bundled together, sold to a scrap-paper dealer, and shredded.

Press books were issued for *Gone With the Wind*'s premiere and subsequent reissues. In 1967, when the film returned in 70-millimeter splendor, the press book was just as spectacular.

The theater display materials, available from National Screen Service, featured the flaming-embrace pose of Rhett and Scarlett in half-sheets, one-sheets, three-sheets, six-sheets, window and insert cards, title display, banners, and valances.

A selection of full-length feature stories were included that the theater owner could submit to the entertainment editor of the local newspaper which carried the theater's advertising. The articles discussed Margaret Mitchell's writing of the novel, the selection of Vivien Leigh to play Scarlett, Leslie Howard's reluctance to play Ashley, Clark Gable's refusal to cry on camera.

The list of promotional ideas encouraged theater owners to:
• deploy to beaches and ball games groups of young men and women wearing tee-shirts bearing the message "Don't Miss *GWTW*" on the front and the name of the theater on the back
• request that the mayor officially proclaim *Gone With the Wind* "the greatest motion picture of all time" and display the proclamation in the lobby
• conduct a Vivien Leigh look-alike contest
• arrange for a horse-drawn carriage to ride through town with a couple dressed as Scarlett and Rhett
• locate children named Scarlett or Rhett and arrange media interviews with their parents
• sponsor a coloring contest, featuring drawings of Scarlett shooting the Yankee deserter, and Rhett carrying Scarlett upstairs
• hire models to wear *Gone With the Wind*–style gowns to the theater's premiere
• distribute Georgia peaches to patrons arriving for the opening performance.

In the merchandising arena:
• MGM Records offered the first official soundtrack album, which featured "13 selections in stereophonic sound from Max Steiner's memorable score" and offered a "32-page illustrated souvenir program of color photographs and text."
• RCA Victor reissued an album of mu-

Nunnally's Scarlett Chocolates box and enclosures. *(The collection of John Wiley Jr.)*

sic composed and conducted by Steiner.

• The Remick Music Corporation published sheet music featuring "Tara's Theme" and "My Own True Love" for piano, accordion, organ, orchestra, and choir.

• Macmillan released Margaret Mitchell's novel in paperback, hardcover, a deluxe edition, and a two-volume, large-print edition. Pocket Books issued a mass-market paperback edition.

The press book is just one type of *Gone With the Wind* ephemera for keen-eyed collectors to add to their collections. Other examples include advertisements of the novel's publication, newspaper clippings of reviews, magazine stories about the stars and the making of the film, tickets to the 1939 premiere, premiere programs, *Gone With the Wind* garment tags, and hundreds of other paper items. This ephemera should have been used then discarded, but the

items were saved and remain historical links to *Gone With the Wind*'s rich past.

A & S Book Company
304 West 40th Street
New York, NY 10018
Phone: 212-695-4897
Specialties: Back issues of film magazines and popular news periodicals.
Catalog: None. Stock is subject to prior sale. Collectors should contact A & S Book Company to check the current availability of *GWTW*–related items.
Payment: C, MO
Delivery: UPS, USPS
Returns: Issues may be returned for a refund as long as nothing has been clipped from the periodical.

Bluff Park Rare Books
2535 East Broadway
Long Beach, CA 90803

GWTW issues of *Life*.

Phone: 310-438-9830
Specialties: Original *Gone With the Wind* programs.
Catalog: None. Stock is subject to change. Collectors should notify Bluff Park Rare Books of particular wants by sending a letter of inquiry with a SASE.
Payment: C
Delivery: UPS, USPS, Federal Express
Returns: Any item may be returned within ten days for refund if not as described.

Cinemonde
1932 Polk Street
San Francisco, CA 94109
Phone: 415-776-9988
415-776-5270
Specialties: Original *Gone With the Wind* programs, first-release and reissue.
Catalog: $8.50. Stock is subject to prior sale. Collectors should contact Cinemonde to check the current availability of *GWTW*–related items.
Payment: MO, V, MC, AE, DC, CB
Delivery: UPS, Federal Express
Returns: Any item may be returned within seven days.

Clean Sheets
199 Tarrytown Road
Manchester, NH 03103
Phone: 603-668-5466
Specialties: Sheet music.
Catalog: None. Stock is subject to change. A list of items offered by Clean Sheets is available by sending a request and enclosing a SASE.
Payment: C
Delivery: USPS
Returns: Since material is clearly described, returns are not expected. If a return is desired, contact Clean Sheets immediately.

Dwight Cleveland
PO Box 10922
Chicago, IL 60610-0922
Phone: 312-266-9152
Specialties: Original *Gone With the Wind* programs.
Catalog: None. Stock is subject to prior sale. Collectors should notify Dwight Cleveland of particular wants by sending a letter of inquiry with a SASE.
Payment: C, MO
Delivery: UPS, USPS

Returns: Any item may be returned in the same condition within three days for full refund.

Cobweb Collectibles
9 Walnut Avenue
Cranford, NJ 07016
Phone: 908-272-5777 (11 A.M. to 5 P.M. Eastern Time, Monday through Saturday)
Specialties: Original *Gone With the Wind* programs, sheet music, and other paper collectibles.
Catalog: None. Stock is subject to prior sale. Collectors should notify Cobweb Collectibles of particular wants by sending a 3 " by 5 " postcard. Company maintains a "want card" system and will inform collectors of new material which meets collecting needs.
Payment: C, MO, V, MC, D
Delivery: UPS, USPS
Returns: All sales are final. No returns or exchanges.

Cohasco, Inc.
Postal 821
Yonkers, NY 10702
Specialties: Paper collectibles.
(See listing under AUCTIONS)

C. Dickens Fine, Rare, & Collectible Books
Lenox Square
3393 Peachtree Road NE
Atlanta, GA 30326
Phone: 404-231-3825
800-548-0376 (orders)
Specialties: Original *Gone With the Wind* programs, matchbook covers, and other *GWTW*–related paper collectibles.
Catalog: None. Stock is subject to prior sale. A list of items offered by C. Dickens is available by sending a request and enclosing a SASE. Collectors can request a search for non-inventory items.
Payment: C, MO, V, MC, AE
Delivery: UPS, USPS
Returns: If item ordered is not as described, it may be returned for a refund within five days of receipt.

Eugenia's Place
1574 Cave Road NW

Atlanta, GA 30327
Phone: 404-261-0394 (weekdays)
404-458-0682 (weekends)
Specialties: *Gone With the Wind* programs, paper dolls, cookbooks, original newspapers and magazines featuring *GWTW* articles.
Catalog: None. Stock is subject to prior sale. Collectors should notify Eugenia's Place of particular wants by sending a letter of inquiry with a SASE.
Payment: C, MO, V, MC
Delivery: UPS, USPS
Returns: Any item may be returned for store credit only.

Hake's Americana & Collectibles
PO Box 1444
York, PA 17405
Specialties: Original *Gone With the Wind* programs and other *GWTW*–related paper collectibles.
(See listing under AUCTIONS.)

Hemetro
127 South Main Street
New Hope, PA 18938
Phone: 215-862-5629
800-362-5336 (orders)
Specialties: Original *Gone With the Wind* paper dolls and newspaper items.
Catalog: None. Stock is subject to change. Collectors should notify Hemetro of particular wants by telephoning or sending a letter of inquiry with a SASE.
Payment: C, MO, V, MC, D, AE
Delivery: UPS
Returns: No returns.

The Lighter Side Gift Catalog
4514 19th Street Court East
Box 25600
Bradenton, FL 34206-5600
Phone: 813-747-2356
FAX: 813-746-7896
Specialties: Vintage magazines. Savor the memories of an important date in *GWTW*'s history with an original, circulated American magazine published that same week or month. Provide the month, day, and year between 1936 and 1980

GWTW theatre program from the British stage production.

and receive the most readily available popular magazine nearest that date. For dates between 1937 and 1972, the magazine will most likely be *Life.* (*Life* from December 25, 1939, carried the photographs and story of the Atlanta premiere.) Each magazine is packaged in a protective vinyl case with a certificate of authenticity. Allow four to five weeks for delivery; # T 861.
Catalog: Free. Stock is subject to change. Collectors should contact The Lighter Side to check the current availability of *GWTW*–related items.
Payment: C, MO, V, MC, AE, DC, D ($15 minimum credit card charge)
Delivery: UPS, USPS, Air Express delivery option

Returns: Return item for refund or item exchange.

Matinee Idol
8650 Melrose Avenue
Los Angeles, CA 90069
Phone: 310-659-5569
Specialties: Original *Gone With the Wind* programs, sheet music, and paper dolls.
Catalog: None. Stock is subject to change. A list of items offered by Matinee Idol is available by sending a request and enclosing a SASE.
Payment: C, MO, V, MC
Delivery: USPS
Returns: None.

Miscellaneous Man
Box 1776
New Freedom, PA 17349
Phone: 717-235-4766
Specialties: Original *Gone With the Wind* programs and other *GWTW*–related paper collectibles from the U.S. and Europe.
Catalog: None. Miscellaneous Man has a large inventory of items. Write or telephone with specific wants for a price quote.
Payment: C, V, MC
Delivery: USPS, Federal Express
Returns: Items may be returned three days after receipt.

Movie Poster Gallery
308½ South State Street #25
PO Box 2745
Ann Arbor, MI 48106
Phone: 313-665-3151 (11 A.M. to 8 P.M. Eastern Time, Monday through Friday)
Specialties: Original reissue press books.
Catalog: $3.00. Stock is subject to prior sale. Collectors should telephone Movie Poster Gallery to determine current availability of *GWTW*–related items.
Payment: C, MO, V, MC
Delivery: UPS, USPS
Returns: Exchanges only. No refund or credit of shipping charges.

Tickets and badge from 1939 Atlanta Junior League Ball and Premiere of *Gone With the Wind*. *(The collection of John Wiley Jr.)*

Movie Poster Place

PO Box 128
Lansdowne, PA 19050-0128
Phone: 215-622-6062
FAX: 215-622-6062
Specialties: Gone With the Wind 1973 reissue press book (ads only).
Gone With the Wind, 1974 reissue press book.
Catalog: $1.00, which can be deducted from first order. Stock is subject to prior sale. Collectors should contact Movie Poster Place to check the current availability of *GWTW*–related items.
Payment: C, MO, V, MC
Delivery: UPS, USPS, Federal Express
Returns: Any item may be returned for refund or exchange for any reason.

Paper Chase Antiques

PO Box 145
North Bridgton, ME 04057
Phone: 207-647-2230
Specialties: Original *Gone With the Wind*–related paper collectibles.
Catalog: None. Stock is subject to change. Collectors should notify Paper Chase Antiques of particular wants by sending a letter of inquiry with a SASE.
Payment: C, MO
Delivery: USPS
Returns: Items may be returned within two weeks of receipt with a reasonable explanation about why the item is not acceptable.

Howard and Gail Rogofsky

PO Box 107
Glen Oaks, NY 11004
Phone: 718-723-0954 (after 6 P.M. Eastern Time)
Specialties: TV Guides
Catalog: $3.00. Stock is subject to prior sale. Collectors should contact Howard and Gail Rogofsky to check the current availability of *GWTW*–related items.
Payment: C, MO
Delivery: USPS
Returns: No returns.

Ellen Roth Books

47 Truman Drive
Marlboro, NJ 07746
Phone: 908-536-0850
Specialties: Original *Gone With the Wind* programs and other paper collectibles.
Catalog: None. Stock is subject to prior sale. Collectors should inform Ellen Roth Books of particular wants by telephoning or sending a letter of inquiry with a SASE. Company maintains a want list and will inform collectors of new material which meets collecting interests.
Payment: C, MO
Delivery: UPS, USPS
Returns: Items may be returned if they are not as described.

TV Guide featuring *Gone With the Wind*.

Scarlett's
247 East Main Street
Ashland, OR 97520
Phone: 503-488-2745
Specialties: Original tobacco cards of Clark Gable, Vivien Leigh, Leslie Howard, and Olivia de Havilland.
Catalog: None. Scarlett's has a large inventory of items. Write or telephone with specific wants for a price quote.
Payment: C, MO, V, MC, D, AE
Delivery: UPS
Returns: Items may be returned for exchange or refund within thirty days of receipt.

Sheet Music Center
Box 367
Port Washington, NY 11050
Phone: 516-938-4905
Specialties: Original *Gone With the Wind* sheet music.
Catalog: For a copy of the current monthly catalog, send a written request and enclose ten first-class stamps. Stock is subject to prior sale. Collectors should contact Sheet Music Center to check the current availability of *GWTW*–related items.
Payment: C, MO
Delivery: UPS
Returns: If an item is not as described, a full refund is made.

Swann Galleries, Inc.
104 East 25th Street
New York, NY 10010
Specialties: Paper collectibles.
    (See listing under AUCTIONS)

Tattered Cover Book Shop
2023 Boston Pike
Richmond, IN 47374
Phone: 317-935-6293
Specialties: Original *Gone With the Wind* paper collectibles.
Catalog: None. Stock is subject to prior sale. Collectors should notify Tattered Cover Book Shop of particular wants by sending a letter of inquiry with a SASE. Company maintains an ongoing list of wants and will inform collectors of new material which meets collecting interests.
Payment: C
Delivery: UPS, USPS
Returns: Any item may be returned within fourteen days for refund.

That's Entertainment
222 Blue Hills Road
North Haven, CT 06473
Phone: 203-872-9207
Specialties: Magazine covers relating to *Gone With the Wind*.
Catalog: None. Stock is subject to prior sale. Collectors should contact That's Entertainment to check the current availability of *GWTW*–related items.
Payment: C, V, MC
Delivery: USPS
Returns: If item is not as described, telephone That's Entertainment on the day of receipt to arrange refund.

Harry A. Victor
1422 18th Avenue
San Francisco, CA 94122
Phone: 415-664-4286
Specialties: Original tobacco, food, and
  beverage cards featuring Vivien Leigh,
  Clark Gable, Olivia de Havilland, and
  Leslie Howard.
Catalog: $1.00 per star. Harry A. Victor
  will provide photocopies of available
  cards.
Payment: C, MO
Delivery: USPS
Returns: Any item may be returned within
  seven days for exchange or refund.

Yesterday
1143 West Addison Street
Chicago, IL 60613
Phone: 213-248-8087
Specialties: Original *Gone With the Wind*
  programs, newspaper and magazine ads,
  press books.
Catalog: None. Stock is subject to prior
  sale. Collectors should notify Yesterday
  of particular wants by sending a letter of
  inquiry with a SASE. Company maintains a "want card" system and will inform collectors of new material which
  meets collecting interests.
Payment: C, MO
Delivery: USPS
Returns: Any item may be returned for full
  refund if not satisfied.

Yesteryear Book Shop Inc.
3201 Maple Drive NE
Atlanta, GA 30305
Phone: 404-237-0163
Specialties: Original *Gone With the Wind*
  and Margaret Mitchell–related paper
  collectibles, including programs, magazines, premiere-ticket stubs, engraved
  Mitchell funeral passes, condolence
  thank-you cards.
Catalog: None. Stock is subject to prior
  sale. Collectors should notify Yesteryear
  Book Shop of particular wants by telephoning or sending a letter of inquiry
  with a SASE. Company will inform col-

lectors of new material which meets collecting interests.
Payment: C, MO
Delivery: UPS
Returns: Any item may be returned within
  five days as long as the merchandise is in
  the same condition as it was sent to the
  customer.

Posters

ONE look at the poster displayed outside your neighborhood movie house,
and you'll be tempted to plunk down
money for a ticket. After all, that is the
purpose of the poster—to entice patrons
into the theater.

One look at a *Gone With the Wind*
poster displayed in a dealer's catalog, and
you'll be tempted to pull out your wallet,
too. But you'll be paying more than the
price of a theater admission ticket. Acquiring original first-release or reissue *Gone
With the Wind* film advertising material is
one of the hottest and most expensive areas
of collecting today.

From the earliest days of movie making,
films were announced by some form of
advertising. Handbills and post bills—
simple, printed notices in various sizes—
used black ink and bold letters to spread
the news about a movie. Sometimes a line
drawing or a photograph was added.

As movies became more popular, the
handbills and post bills gave way to vividly
stunning color posters created by artists.
The posters captured the movie's theme,
illustrated the film's stars, and transcended
mere advertising to become art. In fact,
historians point to the twenty-year period
from 1920 to 1940 as a time during which
the finest movie posters were produced. The
golden age of Hollywood, 1930 to 1940,
was an extraordinarily rich decade for
movie posters. Some of the most beautifully
designed and most memorable posters were
created during that era.

The movie poster was just one item available to theaters for promoting a film. In

Original 1939 lobby cards. *(The collection of John Wiley Jr.)*

addition to the standard 27-inch by 41-inch poster—also called a one-sheet—there were:

- a half-sheet (a 22-inch by 28-inch poster)
- a two-sheet (a 45-inch by 59-inch poster)
- a three-sheet (a 41-inch by 81-inch poster)
- a six-sheet (an 81-inch by 81-inch poster)
- a twenty-four-sheet (109-inch by 236-inch billboard-size poster)
- a banner (24-inch by 82^1/$_2$-inch)
- insert (a 14-inch by 36-inch poster)
- lobby card (an 11-inch by 14-inch poster, which usually came in a set of eight—one title card and seven scene cards)
- window card, which came in three sizes—a regular size 14-inch by 22-inch poster, a mini-size 8-inch by 14-inch poster and an over-size 14-inch by 28-inch.

When a studio rereleased a movie, the advertising art changed. Generally collectors prefer to acquire the one-sheet and half-sheet posters, inserts, and lobby cards from the first-release only. *Gone With the Wind* is one of the few films for which collectors also desire reissue material.

Reissue material is identified by the letter R printed or stamped on the lower border of the poster. Beware if that part of the poster is trimmed or obliterated in any way. Reissue items are much more affordable than materials from the first release, depending, of course, upon condition.

Since few of these original first-release and reissue materials remain in mint condition, expect to find items that are pinholed, soiled, torn, taped, or even water damaged. The posters will probably bear signs of their original folded position. Some posters may have been mounted on linen as a preservation method, and this extends the longevity of the paper. Avoid the poster that is faded, brittle, trimmed, has pieces missing, or that has been glued to backing material.

Now you should be ready to take out that wallet.

Eddie Brandt's Saturday Matinee
6310 Colfax Avenue
North Hollywood, CA 91606
Phone: 818-506-4242
818-506-7722
Specialties: Original 1939–1940 and reissue

Gone With the Wind posters, lobby cards, and stills.

Catalog: Free. Stock is subject to prior sale. Collectors should contact Eddie Brandt's Saturday Matinee to check the current availability of *GWTW*–related items.

Payment: C, MO, V, MC, AE

Delivery: UPS, Federal Express

Returns: Contact Eddie Brandt's Saturday Matinee if dissatisfied with item.

Camden House Auctioneers, Inc.
427 North Canon Drive
Beverly Hills, CA 90210
Specialties: Posters.
 (See listing under AUCTIONS.)

Christie's East
219 East 67th Street
New York, NY 10021
Specialties: Posters.
 (See listing under AUCTIONS.)

Cinema City
Box 1012
Muskegon, MI 49443
Phone: 616-722-7760
FAX: 616-722-4537
Specialties: Original 1939–1940 and reissue *Gone With the Wind* posters, lobby cards, stills.

Catalog: $3.00. Catalog fee is refundable with order. Stock is subject to prior sale. Collectors should notify Cinema City of particular wants by telephoning or sending a letter of inquiry with an SASE.

Payment: C, CC, MO, V, MC

Delivery: UPS, USPS

Returns: Items to be returned must first be authorized by Cinema City within seven days of receipt. Returned material must be received in its original condition. If returned parcels are not adequately packaged and material is damaged, return will not be accepted. If you receive a package that was damaged in transit, contact Cinema City immediately for complete instructions.

Cinema Memories (formerly Memory Shop West of San Francisco)

1630 Laird Street
Key West, FL 30340
Phone: 305-292-0038
Specialties: Original black-and-white stills, 8″ by 10″; original color photos, 8″ by 10″, 11″ by 14″, 16″ by 20″; original posters and lobby cards.

Catalog: None. Cinema Memories supplies proof sheets of stills and photos; provides year, condition, and description of posters and lobby cards. Collectors should contact Cinema Memories to check the current availability of *GWTW*–related items.

Payment: C, MO, V, MC

Delivery: UPS, USPS

Returns: All sales are final.

Cinemonde
1932 Polk Street
San Francisco, CA 94109
Phone: 415-776-9988
415-776-5270
Specialties: Original 1939–1940 and reissue *Gone With the Wind* posters and lobby cards, which include the following:

First-release one-sheet, 27″ by 41″; #3794, $7000.

First-release stone lithograph from Argentina, linen-backed, 28″ by 43″; #3795, $2000.

Poster dated 1950, said to be first release in Italy, linen-backed, 39″ by 55″; #2687, $1500.

Lobby Cards: The Classic Films (1987), quality reproductions of 80 exceptional pieces (1919–1943) from the Michael Hawks collection. Hardcover, 176 pages, including advice on how to acquire well. #3736.

Hollywood Souvenirs (1986), 136-page hardcover book showing Belgian posters (165 in color) for American movies, 1925–1950. Imported. #3939.

Cinemonde Movie Poster Collection, fall 1985, catalog with over 300 photos (54 in full color), of highly desirable posters/lobby cards from 1929 to 1985. Features the *Gone With the*

Wind French poster on the cover. Very
limited copies. #3735.

The Movie Poster Book (1979), 100-page
book showing rare U.S. and foreign
posters (119 in full color), 1896 to
1965, 14 pages on the history of film
posters and collecting. Out of print.
#1855.

Catalog: $8.50. Stock is subject to prior
sale. Collectors should contact Cinemonde to check the current availability of
GWTW–related items.

Payment: MO, V, MC, AE, DC, CB

Delivery: UPS, Federal Express

Returns: Any item may be returned within
seven days.

Dwight Cleveland
PO Box 10922
Chicago, IL 60610-0922
Phone: 312-266-9152
Specialties: Original 1939–1940 and reissue
Gone With the Wind posters.
Catalog: None. Stock is subject to prior
sale. Collectors should notify Dwight
Cleveland of particular wants by sending
a letter of inquiry with a SASE.
Payment: C, MO
Delivery: UPS, USPS
Returns: Any item may be returned in the
same condition within three days for full
refund.

Collectors Book Store
1708 North Vine Street
Hollywood, CA 90028
Phone: 213-467-3296
FAX: 213-467-4536
Specialties: Original 1939–1940 and reissue
Gone With the Wind posters and lobby
cards.
Catalog: None. Stock is subject to prior
sale. Collectors should notify Collectors
Book Store of particular wants by tele-
phoning or sending a letter of inquiry
with a SASE.
Payment: C, MO, V, MC, D, AE
Delivery: UPS, USPS
Returns: Any item may be returned for full
refund or credit if returned in good con-
dition within fourteen days.

C. Dickens Fine, Rare, & Collectible Books
Lenox Square
3393 Peachtree Road NE
Atlanta, GA 30326
Phone: 404-231-3825
800-548-0376 (orders)
Specialties: Photographs and posters.
Catalog: None. Stock is subject to prior
sale. A list of items offered by C. Dickens
is available by sending a request and enclosing a SASE. Collectors can request a
search for non-inventory items.
Payment: C, MO, V, MC, AE
Delivery: UPS, USPS
Returns: If item ordered is not as described,
it may be returned for a refund within
five days of receipt.

Larry Edmunds Bookshop
6644 Hollywood Boulevard
Hollywood, CA 90028
Phone: 213-463-3273
Specialties: Reissue *Gone With the Wind*
posters and lobby cards.
Catalog: None. Stock is subject to prior
sale. Collectors should notify Larry Ed-
munds Bookshop of particular wants by
sending a letter of inquiry with a SASE.
Payment: C, MO, V, MC
Delivery: UPS
Returns: All sales final. No returns, credits
or exchanges.

Gone Hollywood
172 Bella Vista Avenue
Belvedere, CA 94920
Phone: 415-435-1929
Specialties: Original 1939–1940 and reissue
Gone With the Wind posters and lobby
cards.
Catalog: None. Stock is subject to prior
sale. Collectors should notify Gone Hol-
lywood of particular wants by telephon-
ing or sending a letter of inquiry with a
SASE.
Payment: C, MO, V, MC
Delivery: UPS, USPS, Federal Express
Returns: Any item may be returned within
five days in same condition as received
for refund or exchange.

Gryphon Bookshops
2246 Broadway
New York, NY 10024
Phone: 212-362-0706
Specialties: Gone With the Wind posters and photographs.
Catalog: None. Gryphon Bookshops has a large inventory of items. Write or telephone with specific wants for a price quote. Company maintains want lists and will inform collectors of new material which meets collecting interests.
Payment: C, MO, V, MC
Delivery: UPS
Returns: Any item may be returned within ten days for refund or exchange.

Hemetro
127 South Main Street
New Hope, PA 18938
Phone: 215-862-5629
800-362-5336 (orders)
Specialties: Original 1939–1940 and reissue *Gone With the Wind* posters.
Catalog: None. Stock is subject to prior sale. Collectors should notify Hemetro of particular wants by telephoning or sending a letter of inquiry with a SASE.
Payment: C, MO, V, MC, D, AE
Delivery: UPS
Returns: No returns.

Hollywood Poster Exchange
965 North La Cienega Boulevard
Los Angeles, CA 90069
Phone: 310-657-2461
Specialties: Original 1939–1940 and reissue *Gone With the Wind* posters and lobby cards.
Catalog: None. Stock is subject to prior sale. Collectors should contact Hollywood Poster Exchange to check the current availability of *GWTW*–related items.
Payment: C, MO
Delivery: USPS, Express Mail, Federal Express
Returns: Any item may be returned for full refund.

La Belle Epoque
11661 San Vicente Boulevard #211
Los Angeles, CA 90049
Phone: 310-442-0054
FAX: 310-393-2973
Specialties: Original 1939–1940 and reissue *Gone With the Wind* posters and lobby cards.
Catalog: None. Stock is subject to change. A list of items offered by La Belle Epoque is available by sending a request and enclosing a SASE.
Payment: C, MO, V, MC, AE
Delivery: UPS, USPS
Returns: Any item may be returned for refund or exchange.

La Tours Antiques & Imports
16 Alva Street
East Greenbush, NY 12061
Phone: 518-477-5128
Specialties: Original 1939–1940 and reissue *Gone With the Wind* posters and advertising items.
Catalog: None. Stock is subject to change. Collectors should notify La Tours Antiques of particular wants by telephoning or sending a letter of inquiry with a SASE.
Payment: C, MO
Delivery: UPS
Returns: Items may be returned up to five days after receipt.

The Last Moving Picture Company
2044 Euclid Avenue
Cleveland, OH 44115
Phone: 216-781-1821
Specialties: Original 1939–1940 and reissue *Gone With the Wind* posters, lobby cards, stills.
Catalog: None. Stock is subject to prior sale. Collectors should contact The Last Moving Picture Company to check the current availability of *GWTW*–related items.
Payment: C, MO, V, MC
Delivery: UPS, USPS, Federal Express, Air Express
Returns: Only if item has been incorrectly described.

The Last Moving Picture Company
6307 Hollywood Boulevard
Hollywood, CA 90028
Phone: 213-467-0838
Specialties: Original 1939–1940 and reissue *Gone With the Wind* posters, lobby cards, stills.
Catalog: None. Stock is subject to prior sale. Collectors should contact The Last Moving Picture Company to check the current availability of *GWTW*–related items.
Payment: C, MO, V, MC
Delivery: UPS, USPS, Federal Express, Air Express
Returns: Only if item has been incorrectly described.

Matinee Idol
8650 Melrose Avenue
Los Angeles, CA 90069
Phone: 310-659-5569
Specialties: Original 1939–1940 and reissue *Gone With the Wind* posters.
Catalog: None. Stock is subject to change. A list of items offered by Matinee Idol is available by sending a request and enclosing a SASE.
Payment: C, MO, V, MC
Delivery: USPS
Returns: None.

Miscellaneous Man
Box 1776
New Freedom, PA 17349
Phone: 717-235-4766
Specialties: Original 1939–1940 and reissue *Gone With the Wind* posters.
Catalog: None. Miscellaneous Man has a large inventory of items. Write or telephone with specific wants for a price quote.
Payment: C, V, MC
Delivery: USPS, Federal Express
Returns: Items may be returned three days after receipt.

MovieArt
PO Box 164291
Austin, TX 78716-4291
Phone: 512-479-6680

Specialties: Original 1939–1940 and reissue *Gone With the Wind* posters, lobby cards, and stills, including the following:
Original six-sheet, 81″ by 81″, a full stone lithograph depicting Rhett and Scarlett in the wagon riding through a burning Atlanta. The poster is linen-backed. $12,500.
Catalog: None. MovieArt has an in-house computerized database which has complete inventory on line. MovieArt can search by artist, actor, title, etc. Stock is subject to prior sale.
Payment: C, MO, V, MC, AE
Delivery: UPS, USPS, Federal Express
Returns: Any poster may be returned for any reason provided that the buyer seeks prior permission, that the piece be returned within three days of receipt and that the poster be returned in the same condition as it was originally shipped.

Movie Art of Santa Rosa
2411 Jenes Lane
Santa Rosa, CA 95403
Phone: 707-526-1283
Specialties: Original 1939–1940 and reissue *Gone With the Wind* posters and lobby cards.
Catalog: None. Stock is subject to change. Collectors should notify Movie Art of Santa Rosa of particular wants by telephoning or sending a letter of inquiry with a SASE.
Payment: C, MO, V, MC
Delivery: USPS
Returns: Any item may be returned within seven days for refund or exchange.

Movie Poster Gallery
308½ South State Street #25
PO Box 2745
Ann Arbor, MI 48106
Phone: 313-665-3151 (11 A.M. to 8 P.M. Eastern Time, Monday through Friday)
Specialties: Original 1939–1940 and reissue *Gone With the Wind* posters, U.S. and foreign.
Catalog: $3.00. Stock is subject to prior sale. Collectors should telephone Movie

Original *GWTW* six-sheet poster. *(MovieArt, Austin/Cinemonde, San Francisco)*

Poster Gallery to determine current availability of *GWTW*–related items.
Payment: C, MO, V, MC
Delivery: UPS, USPS
Returns: Exchanges only. No refund or credit of shipping charges.

Movie Poster Place
PO Box 128
Lansdowne, PA 19050-0128
Phone: 215-622-6062
FAX: 215-622-6062
Specialties: Gone With the Wind reissue Benton Company window cards.
  Gone With the Wind 1980 reissue one-sheet, 27″ by 41″.
  Gone With the Wind fiftieth-anniversary one-sheet, 27″ by 41″.
  Gone With the Wind French poster, 48″ by 60″.
Catalog: $1.00 which can be deducted from first order. Stock is subject to prior sale. Collectors should contact Movie Poster

Place to check the current availability of *GWTW*–related items.
Payment: C, MO, V, MC
Delivery: UPS, USPS, Federal Express
Returns: Any item may be returned for refund or exchange for any reason.

Phillips West Two
10 Salem Road
Bayswater
London W2 4DL
Specialties: Posters.
   (See listing under AUCTIONS)

Sotheby's
1334 York Avenue
New York, NY 10021
Phone: 212-606-7000
FAX: 212-606-7249
Specialties: Posters.
   (See listing under AUCTIONS)

That's Entertainment
222 Blue Hills Road

North Haven, CT 06473
Phone: 203-872-9207
Specialties: Original 1939–1940 and reissue *Gone With the Wind* posters, lobby cards, and stills.
Catalog: None. Stock is subject to prior sale. Collectors should contact That's Entertainment to check the current availability of *GWTW*–related items.
Payment: C, V, MC
Delivery: USPS
Returns: If item is not as described, telephone That's Entertainment on the day of receipt to arrange refund.

Yesterday
1143 West Addison Street
Chicago, IL 60613
Phone: 213-248-8087
Specialties: Original 1939–1940 and reissue *Gone With the Wind* posters, lobby cards, and stills.
Catalog: None. Stock is subject to prior sale. Collectors should notify Yesterday of particular wants by sending a letter of inquiry with a SASE. Company maintains a "want card" system and will inform collectors of new material which meets collecting interests.
Payment: C, MO
Delivery: USPS
Returns: Any item may be returned for full refund if not satisfied.

Yesteryear Book Shop Inc.
3201 Maple Drive NE
Atlanta, GA 30305
Phone: 404-237-0163
Specialties: *Gone With the Wind* photographs and foreign posters.
Catalog: None. Stock is subject to prior sale. Collectors should notify Yesteryear Book Shop of particular wants by telephoning or sending a letter of inquiry with a SASE. Company will inform collectors of new material which meets collecting interests.
Payment: C, MO
Delivery: UPS
Returns: Any item may be returned within

five days as long as the merchandise is in the same condition as it was sent to the customer.

Records

IN October 1939 David O. Selznick selected Warner Bros. composer Max Steiner to compose the score for *Gone With the Wind*. Vienna-born Steiner, who was the godson of composer Richard Strauss, was well known for his work on *Jezebel, A Star Is Born, Garden of Allah,* and *King Kong.* Selznick told Steiner he wanted "instead of two or three hours of original music, little original music and a score based on the great music of the world, and of the South in particular."

Steiner ignored Selznick's request. The score he composed contained mostly original music, but he did use some Southern favorites such as "Dixie" and "The Bonnie Blue Flag" as well as military and patriotic tunes. Steiner wrote separate themes for Tara and for the leading characters. He also included love themes for the relationships between Melanie and Ashley, Scarlett and Ashley, and Scarlett and Rhett.

Since Selznick feared that Steiner would not be able to meet the short deadline he had been given, Selznick hired composer and conductor Franz Waxman to write an "insurance score." Selznick wasn't pleased with Waxman's work. The producer discreetly talked to Herbert Stothard, MGM's musical director and composer, about taking over the score. Unfortunately, Stothard blabbed that he was taking over for Steiner. This got back to Steiner, and all hell broke loose.

But as a result, Steiner increased his output, and this in turn pleased Selznick, who advised the composer to "just go mad with schmaltz in the last three reels." Steiner ignored this piece of advice, too, and as a result the lushly orchestrated, richly textured score that Steiner produced for *Gone With the Wind* was a movie masterpiece.

Selznick suggested to record companies

GWTW long-playing record albums. *(The collection of John Wiley Jr.)*

the idea of recording an album of *Gone With the Wind*'s music from Steiner's soundtracks. Unbelievably, the record companies turned down the idea.

In 1954 RCA Victor released a ten-inch, long-playing album of *Gone With the Wind* music written and conducted by Max Steiner. But this wasn't a soundtrack. Steiner composed a special arrangement of *Gone With the Wind*'s individual themes. The music was interpreted by a thirty-piece orchestra under Steiner's direction.

The best-known of *Gone With the Wind*'s themes, "Tara's Theme," also acquired a lyric by Mack David in 1954. Titled "My Own True Love," the song was a successful recording for several vocalists.

In 1970 a long-playing album was released, celebrating the Japanese musical production of *Scarlett*. Two years later, when the musical, renamed *Gone With the Wind,* arrived on the British stage, two albums were released: a cast album and one by Harold Rome. The album cover of the latter proclaimed

Here It Is!
The Superb Rather Exciting
Revolutionary Score of

that new EPIC musical
Gone With the Wind
modestly sung and played by
the creator of its words and music
HAROLD ROME
accompanied by the Et Tu Brutus
Ensemble.

Broadway–Hollywood Recording
Box 496
Georgetown, CT 06829
Phone: 203-438-2663
Specialties: Gone With the Wind record albums of Max Steiner, Harold Rome, and Japanese musical *Scarlett.*
Catalog: $1.50. Stock is subject to prior sale. Collectors should contact Broadway-Hollywood Recording to check the current availability of GWTW-related items.
Payment: C, MO, D
Delivery: USPS
Returns: Return items within thirty days.

C. Dickens Fine, Rare, & Collectible Books
Lenox Square
3393 Peachtree Road NE
Atlanta, GA 30326
Phone: 404-231-3825
800-548-0376

Sheet music and record albums from the British musical. *(The collection of John Wiley Jr.)*

Specialties: Gone With the Wind record albums.

Catalog: None. Stock is subject to prior sale. A list of items offered by C. Dickens is available by sending a request and enclosing a SASE. Collectors can request a search for non-inventory items.

Payment: C, MO, V, MC, AE

Delivery: UPS, USPS

Returns: If item ordered is not as described, it may be returned for a refund within five days of receipt.

House of Oldies
35 Carmine Street
New York, NY 10014
Phone: 212-243-0500
FAX: 212-989-1697
Specialties: Gone With the Wind record albums, 45s and extended-play 45s.
Catalog: $50.00. Stock is subject to change. Collectors should notify House of Oldies of particular wants by telephoning or sending a letter of inquiry with a SASE.
Payment: C, MO, V, MC, AE
Delivery: UPS, USPS, Federal Express
Returns: Return defective item for exchange.

Movie Poster Place
PO Box 128
Lansdowne, PA 19050-0128
Phone: 215-622-6062
FAX: 215-622-6062
Specialties: Gone With the Wind soundtrack album featuring the music of Max Steiner.
Gone With the Wind radio spots.
Catalog: $1.00, which can be deducted from first order. Stock is subject to prior sale. Collectors should contact Movie Poster Place to check the current availability of GWTW–related items.
Payment: C, MO, V, MC
Delivery: UPS, USPS, Federal Express
Returns: Any item may be returned for refund or exchange for any reason.

Spin Dizzy
PO Box 20708
Milwaukee, WI 53220
Phone: 414-321-7746 (answering service)
FAX: 414-321-7921
Specialties: Gone With the Wind records, including albums of Max Steiner, Harold Rome, and Japanese musical *Scarlett*.

Items from the Japanese musical. *(The collection of John Wiley Jr.)*

Catalog: Free. Items in catalog represent only a small percentage of inventory, and stock is subject to prior sale. Collectors should notify Spin Dizzy in writing about particular wants and the price they are willing to pay for the item. Company maintains a "want list" system and will inform collectors of new material which meets collecting interests. All want lists are kept on file about three months.
Payment: C, MO, V, MC
Delivery: UPS, USPS
Returns: If defective merchandise is received, write to customer service department to explain the problem. Company assigns a return authorization number which must be written on the mailing label of the returned item. Exchanges or in-store credit only; no refunds.

This and That

You'll never know what vintage *Gone With the Wind* collectibles you're bound to find. Here are samples:

C. Dickens Fine, Rare, & Collectible Books
Lenox Square
3393 Peachtree Road NE
Atlanta, GA 30326
Phone: 404-231-3825
800-548-0376 (orders)
Specialties: Gone With the Wind leather luggage tag with identification card; #AB7391, $30.
Catalog: None. Stock is subject to prior sale. A list of items offered by C. Dickens is available by sending a request and enclosing a SASE.
   Collectors can request a search for non-inventory items.
Payment: C, MO, V, MC, AE
Delivery: UPS, USPS
Returns: If item ordered is not as described, it may be returned for a refund within five days of receipt.

Hake's Americana & Collectibles
PO Box 1444
York, PA 17405
Specialties: Gone With the Wind original marble games.
   (See listings under AUCTIONS)

GWTW presidential campaign buttons. *(The collection of John Wiley Jr.)*

GWTW puzzles. *(The collection of John Wiley Jr.)*

Searching for GWTW Collectibles

What a Search Service Can Offer to the Collector

ARE you trying to find a set of lobby cards from *Gone With the Wind*'s 1954 reissue? Perhaps you are hoping to locate a fine copy of Kathleen Gable's book *Clark Gable: A Personal Portrait*. If you have had little success on your own, consider the benefits of using a search service.

Search services are companies comprised of one or several individuals, possessing a knowledge of collectibles and a desire to find that elusive piece of memorabilia. Frequently, access to elaborate search networks permits a company to locate a collectible faster than a collector can.

All of the companies appearing in this section will search for *Gone With the Wind* memorabilia. Many will search for books, including first editions of *Gone with the Wind* as well as books about Margaret Mitchell, the making of the film, biographies of its stars, and so forth. Some specialize in searching for other kinds of *Gone With the Wind* collectibles, including posters, press kits, and lobby cards. Each listing provides details on how to contact the company and the type of information needed to begin a search. Many companies offer free searches; others charge for their services.

If you wish to try a search service, compile a want list and contact one of the companies. However, avoid sending your list simultaneously to every service listed. Since the networks of many search services overlap, multiple appeals for the same items can create a false surge of interest in those specific collectibles. The likely result will be an abnormal rise in prices.

Let one company work on your list for a few weeks or months before sending it to one of the other services. Most search services will be able to locate a few of your items in a reasonable length of time unless, of course, all of the collectibles listed are the highly desirable ones. Those need more time to appear.

When the search service locates an item on your list, the company will contact you by mail or by telephone with a price quote and information on the item's condition. There is no obligation to accept the item if the reported condition is less than what you expected or if the price is too high. Simply request that the company continue searching.

Avonlea Books
Box 74, Main Station
White Plains, NY 10602
Phone: 914-946-5923
800-423-0622 (orders)

FAX: 914-946-5924

Specialties: Rare, out-of-print, and used-book search service.

What to Do: Send the title, author, and date of publication along with your name and address. The search takes three to four weeks. Avonlea Books will contact you with a price quote and information on the condition of the book. The total cost per book will be at least $20.00. Prices are determined by supply, demand, and condition.

The Better Book Getter
Richard Chalfin's
Book Search Service
310 Riverside Drive, Apt. 301
New York, NY 10025
Phone: 212-316-5634
Specialties: Rare and out-of-print book-search service.

What to Do: 1. Send the title, author, and date of publication along with your name and address or phone number. The search takes one day to two weeks. If the book is found, The Better Book Getter will contact you with a price quote and information on the condition of the book.

2. If the initial search is unsuccessful, contact The Better Book Getter about advertising in a national bookdealers's trade paper. The charge for this service is $1.00 per title, and it takes three to four weeks for results.

3. Request that the desired book be listed on a nationwide computer book-search file. The charge for this service is $3.00 per title and can yield immediate response. The ad stays active for one year.

Bluff Park Rare Books
2535 East Broadway
Long Beach, CA 90803
Phone: 310-438-9830
Specialties: International search service for rare, out-of-print, and used books, and *GWTW*–related collectibles of all kinds.
What to Do: For books, send the title, au-

thor, publisher, and date of publication along with your name, address, and telephone number. Bluff Park Rare Books will contact you with a price quote and information on the condition of the book. There is a $4.50 charge for this service.

For collectible items, send a complete description of each wanted item. Bluff Park Rare Books will contact you with a price quote and information on the condition of the item. There is a $4.50 charge for this service.

Art Carduner's Booksearch
6228 Greene Street
Philadelphia, PA 19144
Phone: 215-843-6071
Specialties: Out-of-print and used book-search service.

What to Do: Send the title, author, publisher, and publication date along with your name, address, and telephone number. Art Carduner's Booksearch will contact you with a price quote and information on the condition of the book.

Cinema City
Box 1012
Muskegon, MI 49443
Phone: 616-722-7760
FAX: 616-722-4537
Specialties: Original 1939–1940 and reissue *Gone With the Wind* posters, lobby cards, stills.

What to Do: Send a complete description of the wanted item along with your name, address, and telephone number plus a SASE. Cinema City will contact you with a price quote and information on the condition of the item.

C. Dickens Fine, Rare, & Collectible Books
Lenox Square
3393 Peachtree Road NE
Atlanta, GA 30326
Phone: 404-231-3825
800-548-0376 (orders)
Specialties: Original *Gone With the Wind*

autographs, books, posters, lobby cards, photographs, records, ceramics, dolls, ephemera, and more.

What to Do: Contact C. Dickens with a complete description of each wanted item. C. Dickens will contact you with a price quote and information on the condition of the item. There is a $3.00-per-item charge for this service.

Gryphon Bookshops
2246 Broadway
New York, NY 10024
Phone: 212-362-0706
Specialties: Rare and out-of-print book search service.
What to Do: Send the title, author, and date of publication along with your name and address. Gryphon Bookshops will contact you with a price quote and information on the condition of the book.

MovieArt
PO Box 164291
Austin, TX 78716-4291
Phone: 512-479-6680
Specialties: Search service for original movie material, including posters, press kits, lobby cards, books, and advertising art.
What to Do: Contact MovieArt with a complete description of each wanted item. MovieArt will contact you with a price quote and information on the condition of the item. There is a charge for this service.

Out-of-State Book Service
Box 3253
San Clemente, CA 92674-3253
Phone: 714-492-2976
Specialties: Hard-to-find, out-of-print book search service.
What to Do: Send the title, author, and date of publication along with your name, address, and phone number.

Out-of-State Book Service will contact you with a price quote and information on the condition of the book.

Reading Room Books
264 South Wabash Street

Wabash, IN 46992
Phone: 219-563-6421
FAX: 219-563-4558
Specialties: Hard-to-find, out-of-print, and used book search service.
What to Do: Send the title, author, and date of publication along with your name and address. The search usually takes a minimum of three weeks or longer. Reading Room Books will contact you with a price quote and information on the condition of the book.

Ellen Roth Books
47 Truman Drive
Marlboro, NJ 07746
Phone: 908-536-0850
Specialties: Search service for rare, out-of-print, and used books and paper collectibles.
What to Do: For books, send the title, author, and date of publication along with your name and address. Ellen Roth Books will contact you with a price quote and information on the condition of the book.

For paper collectibles, send a complete description of each wanted item along with your name and address. Ellen Roth Books will contact you with a price quote and information on the condition of the item.

Tattered Cover Book Shop
2023 Boston Pike
Richmond, IN 47374
Phone: 317-935-6293
Specialties: Rare, out-of-print, and used book search service.
What to Do: Send the title, author, and date of publication along with your name and address. Tattered Cover Book Shop will contact you with a price quote and information on the condition of the book.

A Glossary of Book Terms

WHEN a book search service responds to your request, the company will describe the book and its condition. The description may contain some of the following terms:

-ana – a suffix that refers to any kind of material about an author or subject. For example, Mitchellana means any book or item about Margaret Mitchell.

Advance copy – a first-edition copy of a book released by the publisher before publication, for review purposes.

Association copy – a book inscribed and signed by the author for a famous person or someone important in the author's life or work.

Author's copy – a book belonging to the author which is so inscribed or bears the author's bookplate.

Autographed copy – a book signed by its author.

Backstrip – the covering over the spine of a book. This part is visible when the book is standing between two other books on a shelf.

Binding – the cover of the book.

Bookplate – a printed, decorative label pasted in a book to indicate ownership.

Chipped – a term which indicates that the edges of a dust jacket have small pieces missing.

Copyright page – the page bearing the copyright notice.

Dampstained – discoloration or staining caused by excessive moisture.

Dedication copy – the copy of the book inscribed by the author to the individual to whom the book is dedicated.

Dust jacket – the printed or pictorial cover used to protect a book's binding. Also referred to as dustwrapper.

End papers – usually-blank pages pasted to the inside covers of a book.

Fly leaves – usually-blank pages not pasted down to the inside covers of a book.

Ex-library or *Ex libris* – a book that bears marks of having once belonged to a library. The book may have a library stamp, a card pocket, a call number, and so forth. Such books have little value to collectors because of the worse-than-normal wear the book probably has endured.

First edition – copies of a book produced during the first press run.

Foxing – Yellowish-brown spots or stains. Foxing can occur if books are stored for a long time in a humid climate.

Hinge – the part of the binding where the book's covers join the backstrip. This part bends when the book is opened and receives the most wear and tear. The terms "hinge cracking" and "hinges weak" mean that the cover is starting to separate from the body of the book.

In print – a book which is available from a publisher.

Inscribed – a term which describes a book bearing an inscription to a specific person and the author's signature.

Limited edition – a special edition of a book with a specific number of copies and characteristics that distinguish it from other editions, including better paper, more expensive binding, a slipcase. A limited edition is usually numbered and may be signed by the author or illustrator.

Original cloth – the original publisher's cloth binding.

Out of print – a book that is no longer available from any publisher.

Pirated edition – an unauthorized edition of a book.

Plates – pictures in a book that are sometimes printed on different paper than the text.

Point – an identifying characteristic that helps determine the edition of a book, such as typographical errors or misspellings that were corrected later, changes in bindings, deletions, additions, and so forth. For example, the point that distinguishes a first edition of *Gone with the Wind* from subsequent editions is the notation "Published May, 1936" on the copyright page.

Presentation copy – a copy of the book owned by the author and given to a family member or friend, bearing an inscription.

Rebound – replacement of the original binding.

Recto – the right-hand page of a book.

Rubbed – a book's binding that is scuffed or shows wear and fraying.

Signed – bearing only the signature of the author.

Slip case – a book's protective case, made of materials such as cardboard, pasteboard, or leather.

Sunned – a book that has become faded from exposure to direct sunlight.

Title page – the page at the front of the book containing the title, author's name, publisher's name, date, and place of publication.

Verso – the left-hand page of a book.

Water stained – discoloration and possible shrinkage of the pages or binding caused by water.

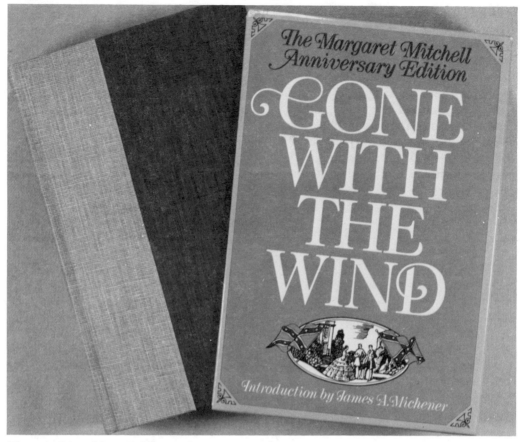

Slipcased edition of *Gone With the Wind*.

Caring for Your GWTW Collection

How to Display Your Collection

I know a *Gone With the Wind* collector who loves collector plates. She began with the Knowles series in 1978, worked her way through the Golden Anniversary series, Critic's Choice, and The Passions of Scarlett series.

Her collection must be stunning. I say "must be" because I've never seen it in its entirety and neither has anyone else.

When a new plate arrives, my friend opens the package to make sure the plate is undamaged, secures the box once again, and places the parcel in the closet in the guest bedroom. This collector's concern that her plates remain safe blinds her to the fact that collections deserve to be enjoyed.

You don't have to keep your collectibles hidden away. Proper display methods will safeguard your *Gone With the Wind* items and allow you to delight in your collectibles at the same time.

Plates. If your collection of plates is modest in number, you might consider creating a shelf or table display using plate stands or adjustable easels.

A plate stand has a base upon which the plate rests and a back support that keeps the plate in position. Stands are available in many materials, including metal, wood, and

Lucite. If you select a wooden stand, make sure that there are no structural defects such as loose joints or uneven bases. Avoid the ones that are Oriental in design, with a hinged side that opens to accommodate the plate. Those stands tend to be flimsily made and do not offer the protection you want for your plates.

The stand should hold the plate sturdily at an eye-pleasing angle. The angle will vary depending upon the size of the plate and that of the plate stand. Bypass stands that are top-heavy and those that position the plate at a dangerous angle or at an angle that distorts the view of the plate.

Adjustable easels offer the collector much more flexibility in displaying plates. Made of metal or Lucite, easels cradle plates, and the adjustable rear supports can position the plate at any angle. Easels are much less costly than plate stands and offer much more protection.

When your plate collection has grown, you can create striking wall arrangements using plate frames or hang-ups, shadow boxes or plate rails.

Plate frames are constructed of wood and are finished in a variety of natural wood tones. Most feature swing clips made of steel to hold the plates securely and a cut-out back for easy viewing of the backstamp. Some frame styles offer an inside gilded rim, which beautifully sets off the displayed plates.

Plate hang-ups are circles of metal that feature polished grippers with non-scratch tips to hold plates in place. Hang-ups are an economical way to display large plate collections so that nothing but the beauty of the plates can be seen.

Wooden shadow boxes comes in various shapes—round, square or octagonal—and can have an open front or a glass front. Deep and much wider than the plate, the box is usually lined in a rich velvet material so that the plate appears to float in the display. Shadow boxes can accommodate one, two or up to four plates.

Solid hardwood plate rails offer a cluster or gallery arrangement for plates. Each rail features deep, polished grooves that hold the plate and provide an ideal viewing angle. Rails are available to display four, six, eight, twelve plates, or more.

As your collection increases in worth, you may decide to move some of the more valuable plates to the ultimate safety and security of a glass-fronted cabinet. Cabinets range from the simple to the ornate, and some even include recessed lights for showcasing the collectibles.

Figurines. Some *Gone With the Wind* figurines, such as the ones issued by the Franklin Mint, have their own display cabinet. Other figurines can be accented by domes. A dome consists of two parts: a hand-blown glass cover with a round or oval diameter, and a similarly shaped wood or wood veneer base. The base has a groove into which the glass cover fits tightly.

Figurines can also be shown in Lucite or glass cases. Cases are available in various sizes and shapes. As with domes, traditional cases have grooved, wood bases which ensure a close fit. Some cases eliminate the wood base in favor of a mirrored bottom. Larger cases come with or without shelves. Lucite tends to scratch easily and attract dust more readily than glass, but either type of case will nicely set off your *Gone With the Wind* figurines.

Ornaments. Beautifully crafted *Gone With the Wind* ornaments grace your tree during the holidays. Ornament stands allow you to enjoy them during the rest of the year, too. The hardwood base of an ornament stand supports a curved wire hanger. The ornament is suspended from the hanger for a permanent display. For fragile or expensive ornaments, you can add the protection of a glass or Lucite dome.

Music Boxes. Music boxes can be featured prominently in a number of ways. Arrange them flat or on easels in a display cabinet or on a display rail. Place each box on a decorative pedestal and display on a tabletop. For a more dramatic look, cover each music box with an oval or round glass dome or enclose each box in a hexagon-shaped glass or Lucite case.

Dolls. Doll experts recommend that a new doll should be removed from its box (put your hand underneath the dress on the doll's waist and pick her up gently), fluffed up, put in a display case and admired from afar. This will protect the doll from dust, the quick hands of small children and your own desire to handle the doll more than is necessary. Be cautious of lighting, both natural and artificial, because light can spot or fade the doll.

Books. The best place to display your collection of books is in a glass-fronted bookcase placed out of the range of sunlight, heating ducts, and the possibility of dampness. Avoid packing the volumes too tightly or loosely on the shelves.

As long as similar precautions are taken, open shelves can also be used to display books. If you use metal bookends, be especially careful. Insert a thickness of cardboard or a book dummy next to each bookend. This will prevent placing a book accidentally onto the bookend instead of next to it and damaging the book.

For valuable *Gone with the Wind* first editions, consider wrapping each book in a sheet of plastic, available from library supply or document preservation companies. The plastic serves as a second, transparent dust jacket.

Since the condition of a book is such a crucial factor, handle first editions as little as possible. Never use a first edition for reading; instead, buy an inexpensive hardcover or paperback copy for that purpose.

Paper. Paper collectibles are so fragile that you might think they cannot be displayed at all. Wrong! Custom-made hardbound display albums constructed with acid-free materials are available at reasonable prices from document preservation companies. The albums provide easy access to collectibles while preserving and protecting the ephemera. Paper collectibles such as *Gone With the Wind* sheet music or significant newspaper articles can also be framed.

Posters, Lobby Cards, Photographs. Framing is the best option for displaying posters, lobby cards, and photographs. Use the services of a professional framer for original one-sheets. Reproduction posters can be encased in Lucite box-type poster frames. You can obtain inexpensive wood or metal frames and use acid-free backing materials for showcasing lobby cards and photographs.

Artfully arranged *Gone With the Wind* collectibles can lead to breathtaking displays. But breathtaking can turn to boring if the arrangement of collectibles becomes permanently ensconced.Experiment with different methods of displaying your items to freshen the look. Rotate the objects you have on display. For example, if you have a shadow box of four collector plates, display a selection from the Knowles series for six months then replace those with representatives from the Critic's Choice series. Variety is the spice of life not only in displaying your collectibles but in enjoying them as well.

(Information on mail-order display products can be found in the "Resources for Collectors" section.)

Caring for Your Collectibles

While gazing at your display of *Gone With the Wind* Critic's Choice collector plates one afternoon, you notice that a layer of fine dust has accumulated on the various poses of Scarlett and Rhett.

You look at your *Gone With the Wind* teddy bears and they, too, look a bit dingy. Well, you think, there's nothing else to do but gather up the plates and bears and march right to the kitchen sink for an impromptu washing.

Don't touch those collectibles! Don't turn on that faucet!

Dust, grime, and other air pollutants do invade our air and settle onto our collectibles. But collectibles are made of different materials, and a cleaning method that might be safe for one could destroy another.

Collectible experts agree that conservation is the key to caring for your collectibles. The guiding principle of conservation is this: *do nothing to a collectible that cannot be undone.* Once a collectible has been permanently altered, its value as a collectible decreases.

Maintain the value of your *Gone With the Wind* items by properly displaying the collectibles and thus reducing the need for cleaning. When cleaning is absolutely necessary, do so with care, following the manufacturer's instructions. In the absence of specific directions, use these general guidelines.

Ceramics. Collectible ceramics include those items made of porcelain (sometimes called china), stoneware, and earthenware. There are also so-called non-ceramic ceramics, known as cold-cast objects.

Porcelain. If the porcelain figurine is solid, without fragile extrusions such as arms or fingers, hold the figurine at its largest torso point (never the head or arms) and carefully use a feather duster or lint-free dusting cloth.

For figurines with delicate extrusions, avoid cleaning with a feather duster or a lint-free dusting cloth. You run the risk of having a loose feather or a frayed area of the cloth catch on the fragile extrusions. The more delicate figurines are best cleaned using the brush-and-blow method.

Grip the figurine firmly and blow off the overall layer of dust. Apply a very-soft-bristled brush ($1/2$-inch to $3/4$-inch soft artist's brush with camel or sable bristles) to all the crevices of the figurine. Begin at the top and move to the bottom, blowing away the released dust as you work. Have several brushes on hand so that as each becomes soiled, you can switch to another.

To care for a porcelain collector plate or music box, hold the item firmly while dusting lightly with a feather duster or lint-free dusting cloth. Never dust a plate or music box while it rests on a stand or rack. Overenthusiastic dusting could cause the object to topple and crash to the floor.

That should be all the care your porcelain collectibles require unless the accumulation of dust and grime is impenetrable. In that case, there are ways to restore the lustrous beauty of your collectibles, including cleaning with a wet brush, wiping with a damp cloth, and submerging your objects in a memorabilia bath.

Some figurines and plates should never be placed into water, including those signed by the artist (the signature may run) and any figurine attached to a wooden base. Never immerse porcelain music boxes in water.

For signed objects, clean them with a brush dipped into soapy water. Use a second brush dipped into clear water to rinse the object. Make sure none of the water drips into the signature area of the object. Use the same two-brush technique to clean the figurine mounted on a wooden base. However, be sure to protect the base before you begin the cleaning. Wrap the base in plastic and seal it tightly with a rubber band. Apply a small amount of furniture polish to restore the rich texture of the wooden base.

For porcelain music boxes, gently wipe the top and sides with a damp, lint-free cloth. Dry with a soft towel.

For collectibles that are immersible, you might consider the memorabilia bath. Unfortunately, the bath also puts your collectibles at their greatest risk. Any damage likely to occur will happen while you are up to your elbows in soap suds.

Experts recommend creating the proper environment for bathing your collectibles. This means using a sink, two plastic pans, a supply of thick, thirsty towels, and soft-bristled brushes and a paper cup. Line the sink and the pans with towels, then fill each with warm water. Add a squirt of baby shampoo or other mild detergent to the water in the sink. Add nothing to the water in one of the plastic pans. To the second pan, add white distilled vinegar ($1/2$ cup per gallon of water). Spread the remaining towels onto the countertop and drain area. As a precaution, move the faucet out of the way, and, as extra insurance, wrap the faucet with a soft towel. You would hate to take such extreme care of your figurine only to whack its head off accidentally on the faucet.

While wearing rubber gloves, submerge one collectible at a time into the sink and wash the item thoroughly using one of the brushes. Fill the paper cup with some water from the pan of clear water and use this to rinse off most of the soap suds. Then place the collectible into the pan of water for a more thorough rinsing. Last, dip the collectible into the pan with the vinegar and water. This solution removes any lingering soap film and makes the object sparkle. Place the collectible onto a towel to air dry.

Stoneware. Clean stoneware collector plates as you would porcelain plates. Again, keep in mind that light dusting is always the preferable method. The memorabilia bath should only be the method of last resort.

Certain stoneware figurines should not be placed into water. The manufacturer's care instructions will indicate this. Instead, clean the figurine with a damp cloth and dry the object with a soft towel.

Earthenware. Light dusting will keep earthenware collector plates and figurines attractive. Avoid immersing collectible earthenware in water. Wipe gently with a damp cloth and dry the plate with a soft towel. Follow any specific cleaning directions packed with the collectible.

Cold-Cast Objects. To create cold-cast

objects, the artist combines polyester resin with specific fillers to create a clear-surfaced collectible with extraordinary strength. For example, cold-cast porcelain is a combination of polyester resin and porcelain dust. Most cold-cast collectibles cannot be submerged in water.

In the absence of specific cleaning instructions from the manufacturer, the blow-and-brush cleaning method for cold-cast collectibles is fine. If washing becomes necessary, apply a soft-bristled brush dipped into soapy water to remove the grime. Use a dry brush to absorb the moisture then immediately dry the object with a soft towel.

Posters and Prints. Since you've framed your *Gone With the Wind* posters and prints, you probably figure you have nothing to worry about. After all, what possible care could a framed collectible need?

Framed graphics require regular light dusting with a feather duster or a lint-free dusting cloth. If such care has been neglected and there is an accumulation of dust, take the print from the wall, hold the frame at an angle and apply the duster or cloth so that the dust falls away from the frame. Avoid cleaning a very dusty framed collectible while it hangs on the wall. You could force some of the dust particles inside the frame and onto the print.

If there are smudges on the glass, dampen a lint-free cloth with a mild glass-cleaning solution and lightly wipe the glass. Avoid using a spray cleaner on the glass or on the frame molding. Some of the liquid could seep inside the frame and cause damage to the poster.

Experts recommend that you examine your graphics regularly because framing does not protect the artwork forever. In rooms with high humidity (75 percent plus), fungus molds or yellowish-brown stains called foxing can develop. Humidity and temperature changes can also cause cockling, which is a common puckering or wrinkling of the print. Small insects can work their way into the frame package and leave marks on the poster. At the first sign

of any of these problems, bring the graphic to a framing specialist for an evaluation.

Records. Dusty phonograph records can be cleaned using a soft, dry, lint-free cloth. If a record is grimy, you can wash it. Fill a plastic dishpan with warm water and a squirt of mild dish detergent. Dip one section of the record at a time into the suds, making sure you do not wet the record label. Wipe the dirt from the disk with a soft cloth, rinse with tap water, and dry with a soft towel.

Wood. Generally, the collectibles made of wood are music boxes and figurines. Figurines need little care except occasional dusting. In addition to dusting, music boxes require care to protect their finish.

The finish of a music box is sealed usually with lacquer, shellac, or varnish. To maintain the bright patina, waxing or polishing several times a year is recommended. Polish music boxes using a good paste wax and pieces of an old cotton sheet, and rub the wood to a mirror-like shine. Avoid too-frequent polishings because excessive coats of wax will dull the music box's finish.

Metals. Collectible medallions and figurines can be made of or plated with gold, silver, bronze, copper, pewter, or other metals. With a soft-bristled brush, remove surface dust from the crevices with the brush-and-blow cleaning method. If more extensive cleaning is necessary, apply a soft-bristled brush dipped into soapy water. Rinse with a clean brush and dry with a soft cloth.

Check the manufacturer's guidelines before you attempt to submerge a metal collectible into a pan of soapy water. Some strong detergents may eat into the metal, pitting the surface; and some metals, pewter for example, may begin to melt in very hot water.

Stuffed Bears. If your Scarlett and Rhett bears are looking a bit bedraggled, spruce them up. But don't toss them into the washing machine or into a basin to soak because they may never look their pristine best again. Bears that are washed can become stiff, limp or misshapen; their fur texture can change; their metal eyes can rust and cause stains.

The safest way to clean a stuffed bear is with a hand-held vacuum cleaner and a pair of pantyhose. Place the pantyhose over the bear to guard against loose trim, fur or eyes disappearing into the vacuum bag. Light strokes of the vacuum will remove any surface dust.

Dolls. Doll experts suggest leaving the cleaning of composition dolls to the experts. However, if your doll's eyes have turned a yellowish color, lightly apply sewing-machine oil with a cotton swab several times, and a more natural color should emerge.

For more current dolls, some experts recommend dusting with a soft-bristled artist's brush or covering the doll with pantyhose and applying a hand-held vacuum. Other experts cringe at those suggestions because they believe that dusting forces microscopic debris into the doll's clothing. They do not recommend cleaning the doll in any way. While the authorities debate about dusting, they do agree that you should never wash doll clothing. Washing is an irreversible and potentially damaging procedure for textiles.

If a doll made of porcelain requires attention, you can spot clean. Fill a pan with a quart of warm water and add one teaspoon of ammonia or rubbing alcohol. Dampen a soft cloth in the solution and rub the doll gently. Pat dry with a soft towel.

Reduce the need for cleaning your *Gone With the Wind* collectibles by properly displaying them. If you must clean collectibles, follow the manufacturer's guidelines or the above suggestions. And follow the conservation principle to do nothing to a collectible that cannot be undone.

Preparing an Inventory

A written record of your collection not only provides information for insurance purposes but is also an ideal way to keep track of the items you own. Experienced collectors recommend preparing an inventory and updating the record as collectibles are added or as information changes.

You can compile your inventory using either index cards, a loose-leaf notebook, or a computer data base. Categorize the listings by collectible type (plates, posters, dolls, autographs, etc.) and include the following information, as appropriate:

Type of Collectible and Description:
Collection Number:
Condition:
Title:
Artist:
Producer:
Series / Year:
Number:
Issue Price:
Purchased / Received From:
Purchase Price:
Date:
Sold / Given To:
Selling Price:
Date:
Market / Appraisal Value:
Notes / Comments:

(A facsimile inventory sheet for your use can be found in the "Resources for Collectors" section.)

In addition to the written information, you'll want to include a visual record of the collection. Take photographs of collectibles such as figurines, books, and posters and make photocopies of flat items such as stills, autographed letters, and other ephemera. Assign a collection number to each item in the written record and mark this number on the back of each photograph or photocopy for identification purposes. The visual record can be organized into albums or filed in accordian-style expanding envelopes.

Collectors frequently prepare two sets of such written and visual records. The second set is kept offsite with a friend or relative or, if the collection is especially valuable, with the insurance agent. If you choose to keep a second set of records, make sure that second set is updated as frequently as the set you keep at home.

Insuring Your Collection

NO one likes to think about losing any part of a collection. But fire, theft, and other disasters often force collectors to confront this painful issue. In the event of a loss, those with small collections of currently available items would have no trouble replacing their collectibles. However, those with large collections of more-valuable, difficult-to-replace items have a good deal more at risk and should consider the protection that insurance affords.

Check with several insurance companies about the specific policies and riders available to you for your collection. Obtain rate quotations from each company and decide which gives you the most protection for the most affordable price. Here is information on insurance that will help you get started.

Usually, a comprehensive homeowner's or renter's policy provides coverage for personal property, including memorabilia collections. However, under those policies, the personal property is grouped together, not listed individually, and there may not be full-value coverage. The coverage is usually limited to the "actual cash value," which means the cost of the item new less depreciation. If you have a collectible that has appreciated substantially, this could be a problem. Additionally, there is no coverage for breakage or accidental damage.

This type of protection may be adequate for your needs if your collection is modest. For expensive collections, you might consider adding a fine-arts rider to your policy. Under a fine-arts rider, each collectible is listed—or scheduled—individually, and for an additional fee, insurance is offered against breakage. Other companies offer blanket coverage up to $5,000, $10,000, or $20,000, so a collector of vintage items would not have to contact the insurance agent with every new acquisition.

Some insurance companies require a certified appraisal of scheduled items to determine the assigned or replacement value of each item. Obtaining a professional appraisal of vintage collectibles can be time consuming and expensive, and finding an expert who can appraise in various collectible areas can be challenging. Start with the dealer from whom you regularly purchase collectibles to determine if he or she can provide an appraisal. You might also look under "Appraisers" in your telephone book's yellow pages or contact one of the following organizations to locate an appropriate professional in your area:

Appraiser's Association of America
60 East 42nd Street, Suite 2505
New York, NY 10165
212-867-9755

American Society of Appraisers
Box 17265
Washington, DC 20041

Those who collect limited-edition items can often bypass the formal appraisal process. The market values of limited-edition collectibles are available from a variety of sources, including the current list prices supplied to dealers by manufacturers, listings from sources such as The Bradford Exchange and price guides included in collector's reference books. Many insurance companies will accept this type of documentation in lieu of a certified appraisal.

Once you have arranged for insurance protection, keep in mind that the market values of collectibles change as time goes by. Review your policy with your agent every year to make sure you have adequate protection, and regularly update the written and photographic inventory of your collection. If you suffer a loss, the inventory will be invaluable in establishing ownership and proving the current value of the scheduled items—both of which are the responsibilities of the collector.

Losing items you have lovingly collected over the years is difficult to think about. Replacing those collectibles without the benefit of insurance is even worse to contemplate. Investigate your options and decide what is best for you and your collection. Insurance may turn out to be a small price to pay for peace of mind.

Restoration

OOOPS! Crash! The Clark Gable mug in which you enjoyed your morning coffee is now in pieces on your kitchen floor. You're sorry to see it go, but the mug is an inexpensive, easy-to-obtain collectible, and you'll just buy another one. You sweep up the debris and toss them into the trash.

Now picture a similarly shattering experience occurring with "Scarlett," the first collector plate issued by the Edwin M. Knowles China Company. You're heartbroken. That's because you know the plate will be expensive to replace *if* you are able to find it on the secondary market. You gather the pieces into a towel and think about repairing it yourself. Now where's that miracle glue?

Stop right there. Do-it-yourself home fix-its often cause further damage to and destroy the value of original pieces of memorabilia. Avoid gluing, taping, rebinding, repainting, laminating, or altering in any way original *Gone With the Wind* collectibles. Such pieces should never be tampered with unless taking no action will lead to further damage. For example, one-sheets are frequently mounted on linen to keep the paper from disintegrating. Some books are rebound to keep the pages from falling out. However, restoration is best left to professionals who can often not only restore the collectible but recover at least 50 percent of its market value.

Choose a restoration expert or conservator carefully. A conservator should bring a holistic approach to the care of collectibles. This approach focuses on long-term preservation and well-being, not just on the aesthetic appearance of an object.

A conservator follows a strict code of ethics in the treatment of objects which states that the original material must not be compromised in any way. Cosmetic restoration entails restoring the aesthetic integrity of an object by, for example, replacing missing parts. Restoration can be done to a high ethical standard which does not damage or alter the original character of the object in any way. Conservators accomplish this by using reversible materials which have good aging properties.

An irreversible restoration, such as the re-firing of a broken ceramic piece to make it appear undamaged would not be an example of conservation. It would be considered unethical restoration because the process alters the original nature of the piece by hiding original material under restoration material which cannot be removed.

Conservators use the most benign, least harmful methods to stabilize, repair, and restore the appearance of objects. They have backgrounds in chemistry, art history, and fine arts. Most of them have participated in extensive apprenticeships.

Look for a restorer who has expertise in the area appropriate to your collectible. For example, an expert who restores composition dolls may not be qualified to restore your original one-sheet. Check with your local historical society or state library for referrals to experts, or contact the Foundation of the American Institute for Conservation of Historic and Artistic Works (FAIC).

FAIC provides a Conservation Services Referral System, listing professional conservation services related to the following specializations: books and paper, objects, paintings, architecture, photographic materials, wooden artifacts, and textiles. In response to inquiries, a computer-generated list of conservators will be compiled and grouped geographically, by specialization, and by type of service provided. Every conservator in the Referral System is a member of the American Institute for Conservation of Historic and Artistic Works, the national professional organization committed to promoting knowledge of the conservation of our cultural heritage. Contact the FAIC at:

The Foundation of the American Institute for Conservation of Historic and Artistic Works
1400 16th Street, NW
Suite 340
Washington, DC 20036
Telephone: 202-232-6636
FAX: 202-232-6630

When you contact a restoration expert, explain the extent of the damage to the collectible and request an estimate of how much the work will cost. Ask the conservator about his/her training, length of professional experience, experience in working with the kind of object for which you seek help, availability, references, and previous clients. Avoid working with conservators who seem reluctant to discuss these issues. A professional is always glad to provide background information and to answer questions. Check references and then make your decision about whom to entrust your collectible.

Once you have selected a restoration expert, you will probably be asked to leave the collectible with the expert for examination. The restorer will issue an examination report and a treatment proposal which outlines the defects that require correction, an outline of the recommended treatment, and a cost estimate. Generally, your written authorization is required to begin restoration work.

When the work is completed, the conservator should provide a written examination report that describes the object's condition, the treatment proposal, and the treatment report recording what was done, with full disclosure of all the materials used. All treatments should aspire to the principle of reversibility: Materials used must have good aging properties, and procedures used should be able to be undone without damage to the object. The conservator will also be able to provide you with recommendations for safe storage and display of your collectible. Before-and-after photographs of the collectible are usually included with the report. If the report inspires any questions, bring those concerns to the restoration expert.

A damaged or deteriorating collectible can devastate a collector. Happily, many memorabilia items can be saved. Don't undertake the work yourself; leave it to the experts—qualified restoration professionals.

Storing a Collection

A collector, proud of the British editions of *Gone with the Wind* he had gathered over the years, stored the volumes side by side in a bookcase in his apartment. The bookcase was opposite the room's only window, and he kept the drapes drawn at all times.

One day he scanned the bookcase, looking for the edition with the red dust jacket. In the place he thought the book should be was a book whose spine was yellow. That can't be it, he thought, but he pulled the book from the shelf anyway. With horror, he discovered that it was indeed the volume. The front and back of the book were brilliant red, while the spine—which had received indirect light through the closed drapes—was faded from its original splendor.

Unfortunately, heartbreaking yet painfully true stories such as this are not unusual. But you can spare yourself anguish and your collection destruction by keeping your collectibles away from the elements that will nibble away at their longevity and their value: heat, sunlight, humidity, dust, and dampness.

For home storage of collectibles that you do not wish to display, keep in mind these general guidelines:

1. Store collectibles in basements only if the rooms are safe from dampness. Use a dehumidifier if possible.

2. Avoid placing collectibles in attics that are extremely hot during the summer.

3. Never store collectibles on the floor where they can be kicked and broken or damaged by water or rodents.

4. Pack collectibles in wooden or plastic crates or cardboard boxes. Cardboard boxes are suitable for some collectibles but are not recommended for paper items. Cardboard boxes are made with unstable, high-acid paper. As the paper disintegrates, acidifiers are released that can harm paper collectibles with which they come into contact. If cardboard boxes are used, make sure each stored paper item is individually wrapped in acid-free plastic. Acid-free storage boxes can be purchased from library supply or document preservation companies.

Here are specific suggestions for home storage of the major categories of collectibles:

Books. Books can be stored in protective cases. There are several styles, including the slipcase and the clam-shell design.

The inexpensive slipcase is a popular case, but it leaves the spine of the book exposed and can cause excessive wear and tear on the dust jacket. The best protection comes from the clam-shell case, a double-hinged case that lies flat when opened. This case allows the book to be lifted out with no possibility of damage to the dust jacket. The cases can be stored in wood or plastic crates or on out-of-the way shelves. Avoid storing books on low shelves where young children can reach them. Valuable first editions can be stored in a fireproof safe or file cabinet.

Do not store newspaper clippings in books. The cheaper newsprint deteriorates more quickly than the paper used in the book and can damage the book's pages.

Plates. Plates can be stored in their boxes and stacked one on top of the other, within reason. If the boxes are all the exact same size, the weight should be distributed evenly, but stack no more than six plates in this manner. For plate boxes of unequal sizes, the best storage method is packing them in a cardboard carton and storing the carton sideways so that each plate stands on its end.

Each plate box must be stored firmly within the carton. If the carton is too large,

either cut it down or stuff it with packing material. Packing chips or mailing peanuts are the best materials, so save the ones that come to you in the packages you order. If you don't have a sufficient supply of such chips, use folded or tightly rolled corrugated cardboard or newspapers packed together in tight bundles. Remember that newspaper ink sometimes rubs off. If the boxes you are storing are elaborate presentation boxes, wrap them in plastic first and then secure with the newspaper wads. This will prevent the boxes from being damaged by the ink from the newspaper.

Secure the packing carton with strong plastic packing tape, label the outside with a list of the carton's contents, and store.

Figurines, Wood, and Ceramic Objects. The best storage for figurines, wood, and ceramic objects is a tightly packed cardboard box. A ceramic mug, for example, can be placed in a plastic bag then placed into the cardboard box filled with packing chips. Delicate figurines and music boxes need extra-special protection.

Wrap layers of tissue paper carefully and firmly around the figurine or music box then wrap the object in a thick towel, a diaper, or paper towels. Nestle the collectible in a box filled with packing chips then place that box into a larger storage carton packed with chips or tight bundles of newspaper. Secure the carton with strong plastic packing tape, label the outside with the carton's contents, and store upright rather than on its side.

Paper Collectibles. Paper collectibles run the gamut from autographs, magazines, newspapers, and posters to photographs, prints, sheet music, and everything in between. Unfortunately, paper made in the twentieth century does not age gracefully. The high-acid content of paper fairly guarantees that eventually colors will fade, and pages will turn brown and crumble into dust.

To stave off the damaging effects, keep small and medium-sized paper collectibles in plastic bags with acid-free cardboard backings. Library supply or document pres-

Proposal-embrace tote bag. *(The Turner Store)*

ervation companies can furnish acid-free storage materials. Store plastic-wrapped items flat in strong, good-sized boxes. More valuable paper collectibles such as autographs can be stored in individual, acid-free folders in a fireproof safe or filing cabinet. The folders can also be punched for use in a three-ring storage binder. Never glue a paper item to cardboard or have a collectible laminated; the value will be ruined.

Large paper items such as unframed posters and prints can be covered with large sheets of plastic then sandwiched between two pieces of poster board or cardboard cut to fit the poster size. Loosely tape the poster board or cardboard pieces together and store flat on the floor underneath a bed.

Phonograph Records. Store vinyl 45s and LPs vertically in individual jackets or album covers. Placing the records in an old metal record rack is fine as long as the rack is kept away from sunlight and all other sources of heat.

Dolls. Dolls should not be stored in their boxes. Over time, dyes from the tissue paper can leak into the doll's clothing. Store the doll upright under glass in a cool place away from excessive temperatures, bright lights, or dampness. Place the doll's box

and tissue paper in plastic and store in a large box filled with packing chips. Always save doll boxes and tissue paper for possible resale. Never remove wrist or clothing tags from your dolls.

Collectors with large collections and small living spaces may elect to move some of their collectibles to locations outside the home. Two ideal locations are safe-deposit boxes and self-storage warehouses.

Metal safe-deposit boxes, available in various sizes, are rented from banks and kept in temperature- and humidity-controlled vaults. More valuable items such as first editions and autographs would be protected and secure since thieves rarely violate safe-deposit boxes. On occasions when the boxes are disturbed, robbers generally bypass collectibles in favor of cash and jewelry.

Self-storage warehouses are popping up across the landscape as quickly as dandelions. The warehouses rent individual stalls that are both roomy and secure. For an additional charge, most warehouses offer insurance. Before renting a storage stall, find out about any possible problems with excessive temperature, dampness, and rodents. Check with those who currently rent at the facility for any problems they have experienced.

(Information on mail-order storage products can be found in the "Resources for Collectors" section.)

Selling Your Collectibles

SOME day you may decide to sell one piece, several items, or your entire collection of *Gone With the Wind* memorabilia. Sell the smart way by knowing the value of the items and the best ways to liquidate them. Only then will you be able to sell your collectibles at a profit or at the very least at prices near their original cost.

Know the Value. If you've had the collectible for a number of years, the value has no doubt appreciated. Determine the current market value of the piece by checking prices in memorabilia catalogs and periodicals, talking to dealers and collectors, and visiting collectible shows to see the prices for which similar items are selling. Gather as much information as you can so that you will be able to set a realistic price for your items. Setting your price too low guarantees that you'll be giving the item away. Setting your price too high means you may scare away potential buyers who may know what a realistic price range should be.

Choose the Right Way to Sell. There are various ways for you to sell your collectibles. Not every way will be appropriate, and will depend upon the number of collectibles, their value, how much you want to sell them for, and how quickly you want to make a sale. Consider the following avenues for selling your memorabilia, and think carefully before you make a decision.

Flea Markets. Since customers are looking for bargains, flea markets are good for selling inexpensive items such as postcards, movie stills, and star photographs. But do you have enough inventory to make flea market selling worthwhile?

You will have expenses in renting the booth or table, transportation to and from the site, plus costs for food and beverages during the day. Most likely you will be responsible for collecting sales tax, which can be a headache. You'll also be tying up at least a full day of your time with no guarantee that your collectibles will sell or that you will sell enough to recoup your upfront expenses.

If you are determined to pursue the flea market route, consider combining forces with other collectors. Two or three collectors split expenses to rent a single booth, take turns working the table, and keep track of sales for each collector.

It's preferable to choose partners whose collecting interests are different from yours. For example, team up with a *Wizard of Oz* collector and someone who collects comic books. A good mix of collecting areas should attract more potential buyers, and you'll avoid problems when you close up shop. At the end of the day, each collector removes his or her own merchandise—thus

averting collectible confusion — and proceeds are distributed according to each collector's sales.

Garage Sales. As with flea markets, garage sales are best reserved for selling inexpensive collectibles. You can expand the garage sale by offering other items (clothing, dishes, glassware, toys, for instance) in addition to your *Gone With the Wind* collectibles. A variety of items will attract more potential customers.

Your expenses will probably be minimal. You can place a newspaper advertisement announcing the date and time of the sale or just put up posters around the neighborhood. The largest investment will be your time, but you may be able to share garage-sale duties with friends or members of your family.

Auctions. Despite the glitz and glamour associated with prestigious auctions, an auction will most likely net only a wholesale price for your memorabilia unless your *Gone With the Wind* collectible is highly prized or extremely rare. (Auction houses can provide an unofficial appraisal of an item's probable selling price before you submit it for auction.) Factor in the fees you will be charged for consigning your items plus the time you have to wait to receive your settlement check, and you will see readily the disadvantages of disposing of a modest collection through an auction.

Large houses usually require that collectibles be consigned at least one month before the sale. You, the consignor, may be charged for storage, insurance, photography for the auction catalog, and other services, plus a special fee if the item fails to sell. Houses also assess seller's charges, a percentage of the total price for which the lot sold. You have no guarantee that the auction will be successful, and generally, after all the auction excitement dies down, it takes anywhere from two to six weeks for the settlement check to arrive.

Collectible Stores/Antique Shops. A better selling approach is offering your memorabilia to collectible stores or antique shops. Keep in mind, though, that the price you realize from the sale may be less than you had anticipated, depending upon the dealer's ability to resell the items.

Most dealers maintain a file of customers and their particular wants. If your *Gone With the Wind* collectible meets the needs of one of the dealer's customers, you may be offered up to 90 percent of the item's market value. However, if there is no waiting customer, the dealer may not be inclined to offer you more than 50 percent of the collectible's value. The dealer has to weigh the cash outlay with the length of time it may take to find a buyer for the item. If you aren't satisfied with the price you are offered for your collectible, negotiate.

If negotiation doesn't significantly increase the dealer's offer, there are other options you can explore:

1. Suggest that the dealer accept the collectible on a consignment basis. You leave the item with the dealer until it sells, then pay the dealer a percentage of the selling price.

2. Retain the collectible but register it for sale with the dealer and possibly with other shops. When one dealer has a buyer for the item, the sale is negotiated, and the dealer receives a modest fee for the transaction.

3. Trade the collectible for an item or items of equivalent value offered by the dealer.

If you are liquidating an entire collection that contains various elements such as dolls, limited-edition plates, ephemera, and first editions of Margaret Mitchell's novel, you may be better served by approaching several dealers specializing in those collectible areas. Your profit margin will often be greater by negotiating individually than it would be if you offered the whole collection to one dealer.

Collectible Shows. Attending a collectible show and offering your collectibles to the dealers in attendance is another good approach for you to consider. Dealers welcome the opportunity to add to their inventories but usually balk at paying the full market value for collectibles. They need to keep their profit margins in mind. Because they hope to resell at full market value, they are likely to offer only between 20 and 80 percent of the item's worth, depending upon the desirability of the collectible, how long the item is likely to be in inventory, and other factors. But that doesn't mean you can't negotiate a price that is fair to both of you.

You can approach selling to show dealers in three ways:

1. If you are offering collectibles of the same quality, price each item individually. In that way each dealer can select the items he or she wants.

2. If you are offering a mix of items—a few fine pieces along with items of lesser quality and value—establish a set price for the entire lot. Approach each dealer until you make a sale. In this way, you avoid the problem of dealers buying the prized items and leaving you with the less-desirable ones.

3. If you are unsure about how much you can obtain for your collectibles, consider a walk-around auction. Approach each dealer, asking each to bid on the lot of items and indicating that you will accept the highest bid. You'll have to circulate the floor a number of times, giving dealers a chance to increase their bids, but soon the field of bidders will be whittled down. The highest bidder will emerge from that select group.

Caution: At no time should you attend a collectible show and attempt to sell your memorabilia to other collectors unless you are registered at the show as a dealer. As Aunt Pittypat would say, "It simply isn't done."

Some collectible shows do offer swap-meets or let's-make-a-deal sessions for collectors in areas off the selling floor. The only ones selling on the floor are the registered dealers, who have incurred some expense in renting their booths and getting to the show. If you—a non-dealer—are caught offering your items on the selling floor, the dealers will have your head!

Selling through the Bradford Trading

Floor. Limited-edition plate collectors have an advantage in the selling arena with the Bradford Trading Floor, part of The Bradford Exchange. Bradford brokers can help collectors sell back-issues via the telephone or through the mail. Once the Exchange has confirmed a match, that transaction is guaranteed for both parties. Collectors selling through the Exchange are charged a 30 percent commission. For information, contact the Bradford Trading Floor at 800-323-8078 or in Illinois at 708-966-1900.

Selling through the Mail. Your most profitable approach to selling memorabilia is a one-to-one deal between you and another *Gone With the Wind* collector who recognizes the value of your collectible and is willing to pay close to full market value. An easy way to achieve this goal is by selling directly to collectors through the mail.

Most collector periodicals accept classified advertisements to buy and sell memorabilia. You can approach direct sales to *Gone With the Wind* collectors in two ways:

1. Read the classified ad section to find collectors wanting to buy what you are selling.

2. Place a classified ad offering your memorabilia.

Addresses for publications that are outlets for selling *Gone With the Wind* collectibles are listed in this book. For a modest price, single issue copies are often available as samples so you can decide before you subscribe if the publication will meet your selling needs.

If you find an appropriate want-to-buy ad, you can usually contact the collector by telephone or by mail. Describe the collectible you are selling as accurately as possible and state the price at which you are offering the item. Expect the buyer to dicker a bit. Once you have settled on a price, close the deal by agreeing on the method of payment and the means of shipment.

Accepting a money order or a certified check is probably the safest way to conduct business at a distance. Discourage the buyer from sending cash through the mail. If you accept a personal check, wait until the

check has cleared at the bank before you ship the collectible.

Package the item carefully, especially if there is a chance it will break during transit. Insure the parcel and ship it either through the United States Postal Service (USPS) or United Parcel Service (UPS).

If you decide to place a for-sale ad, you'll find that advertisement rates in collector periodicals are generally low, and discounts are often given if you run the ad in more than one issue. Check the periodical for its section on classified advertising information. This section will tell you the ad rates, applicable discounts, deadline for receipt of ad copy, and how to prepare your advertisement.

Scanning the periodical's for-sale section will give you an idea of the style your ad should take. Write your ad carefully and clearly in as few words as possible. Indicate exactly what collectibles you are offering. Here are some examples of for-sale ads:

FOR SALE: Autographed copy of *Scarlett O'Hara's Younger Sister,* by Evelyn Keyes, $100.

FOR SALE: Original *Gone With the Wind* movie program, $500. Call 914-452-5555.

FOR SALE: *Gone with the Wind* Motion Picture Edition, paperback, back cover missing, $30; 1967 *GWTW* press book, $50; and plate #4 in W. S. George "Critic's Choice" series, "The Paris Hat," in box with papers, $25.

For highly desirable *Gone With the Wind* collectibles, you can offer an item for sale through a mail auction. In your advertisement, state that the sale is by auction to the highest bidder and indicate the time frame during which you will accept mail bids. Request that all participants include their telephone numbers with their bids. Consider all the bids that arrive by your deadline and notify the successful high bidder by telephone. While you are on the phone, you can nail down the pertinent details about payment and shipment.

In addition to selling to collectors through the mail, you may also be able to offer *Gone With the Wind* collectibles to dealers you locate through collecting periodicals. Frequently, full-page, half-page, or quarter-page display advertisements placed by dealers mention that they not only sell collectibles but are looking for memorabilia. For example,

WANTED
GWTW Premiere Programs
$CASH REWARDS$
for these and many other examples of
GWTW ephemera.
Seeking collectible *GWTW* paper in
very good or better condition.
TOP PRICES PAID!
No collection is too large or small.
Send us a list of what you have for a
quick reply or give us a call.

Of course, the price you will realize from a dealer will be less than what you could expect from a collector.

Networking. Another profitable approach to selling memorabilia is through networking. Contact collectors you know and have them spread the word about your for-sale items to the collectors they know.

Never underestimate the power of this informal grapevine. Word of mouth is the best advertising and may enable you to locate a prospective buyer who knows of you (through his or her contact), has confidence in the collectible you offer, and will, therefore, pay the full market price.

Estate Disposal of Collectibles

THOSE who collect *Gone With the Wind* items, or their heirs, are eventually faced with the disposal of that collection. If your collection is large or prestigious, you might direct that items be parceled out for sale to auctions houses, dealers, or other collectors. On the other hand, you may prefer that the collection remain intact. If so, you may wish to consider donating or selling your collection to an institution.

Selecting the Institution. Choosing the institution is a vital first step. It is essential that you discuss with your institution of choice whether it is interested in acquiring your collection. Some institutions may not have the space to exhibit the collection, and for other institutions, the collection may not be appropriate. For example, a library may not be interested in acquiring your vintage Madame Alexander Scarlett dolls.

Agree on Treatment of Collection. Once you have decided upon the institution, you need to discuss the treatment of the collection. The institution may have a policy of extracting needed items and disposing of unwanted or duplicate pieces. If your goal is to keep the collection intact, you need to make this absolutely clear before you donate, sell, or will the collection to the institution.

Negotiate the Transfer. Collections can be transferred through sale or donation either before or after your death. In either case, experts recommend having a professional appraisal conducted.

The appraisal should consist of a written, itemized, descriptive list of every item in the collection, along with the total value. The institution can use this appraisal not only to determine their interest in acquiring the collection but also to make a presentation to the board that governs funding appropriations.

Before you conclude the transfer of your collection, be certain to check with your accountant about the tax situation resulting from capital gains. Consult with your accountant even if you make a gift of your collection. Donating your collectibles can earn a tax deduction of which you may be able to take advantage. If the transfer of your collection will take place after your death, contact your attorney to have an appropriate clause written into your will.

Your *Gone With the Wind* collection of items, lovingly collected throughout your lifetime, is a wonderful legacy you can leave for others to enjoy.

Resources for GWTW Collectors

Books

THE following books—most in print but some out of print—provide information on Margaret Mitchell, her novel, the film, the stage version, *Gone With the Wind* collectibles, David O. Selznick, George Cukor, Sidney Howard, Vivien Leigh, Clark Gable, Olivia de Havilland, Leslie Howard, Hattie McDaniel, and Evelyn Keyes. And some are just for fun.

Bakewell, William. *Hollywood Be Thy Name*. Metuchen, NJ: The Scarecrow Press, 1991.

Barker, Felix. *The Oliviers*. Philadelphia: J.P. Lippincott, 1953.

Bartel, Pauline. *The Complete GONE WITH THE WIND Trivia Book*. Dallas: Taylor Publishing Co., 1989.

Beard, Henry, Christopher Cerf, Sarah Durkee, and Sean Kelly, comps. *The Book of Sequels*. New York: Random House, 1990.

Behlmer, Rudy, ed. *Memo from David O. Selznick*. New York: The Viking Press, 1971.

Bernardoni, James. *George Cukor: A Critical Study and Filmography*. Jefferson, NC: McFarland & Co., 1985.

Bowers, Ronald. *The Selznick Players*. Cranbury, NJ: A.S. Barnes and Co., 1976.

Bridges, Herb. *The Filming of GONE WITH THE WIND*. Macon, GA: Mercer University Press, 1984.

——— *"Frankly, My Dear . . .": GONE WITH THE WIND Memorabilia*. Macon, GA: Mercer University Press, 1986.

———and Terryl C. Boodman. *GONE WITH THE WIND: The Definitive Illustrated History of the Book, the Movie, and the Legend*. New York: Simon & Schuster/Fireside, 1989.

Cameron, Judy, and Paul J. Christman. *The Art of GONE WITH THE WIND: The Making of a Legend*. New York: Prentice–Hall, 1989.

D'Urberville, Missy. *Today Is Another Tomorrow: The Epic GONE WITH THE WIND Parody*. New York: St. Martin's Press, 1992.

Edwards, Anne. *Vivien Leigh*. New York: Simon & Schuster, 1977.

———*Road to Tara: The Life of Margaret Mitchell*. New Haven, CT: Ticknor & Fields, 1983.

Essoe, Gabe. *The Complete Films of Clark Gable*. New York: Carol Publishing Group, 1992.

Farr, Finis. *Margaret Mitchell of Atlanta.* New York: William Morrow, 1965.

Flamini, Roland. *Scarlett, Rhett and a Cast of Thousands: The Filming of GONE WITH THE WIND.* New York: Macmillan, 1975.

Gable, Kathleen. *Clark Gable: A Personal Portrait.* Englewood Cliffs, NJ: Prentice–Hall, 1961.

Garceau, Jean. *Dear Mr. G—.* Boston: Little, Brown and Co., 1961.

Gardner, Gerald, and Harriet Model Gardner. *The Tara Treasury: A Pictorial History of GONE WITH THE WIND.* Westport, CT: Arlington House, 1980.

Gwin, Yolande, ed. *I Remember Margaret Mitchell.* Lakemont, GA: Copple House Books, 1987.

Hanson, Elizabeth I. *Margaret Mitchell.* Boston: G. K. Hall & Co. / Twayne Publishers, 1990.

Harwell, Richard, ed. *GONE WITH THE WIND as Book and Film.* Columbia, SC: University of South Carolina Press, 1983, 1992.

———*Margaret Mitchell's GONE WITH THE WIND Letters, 1936–1949,* second edition. New York: Macmillan, 1986.

Haver, Ronald. *David O. Selznick's GONE WITH THE WIND.* New York: Bonanza Books, 1986.

———*David O. Selznick's Hollywood.* New York: Alfred A. Knopf, 1980.

Higham, Charles. *Sisters: The Story of Olivia de Havilland and Joan Fontaine.* New York: Coward–McCann, 1984.

Howard, Leslie Ruth. *A Quite Remarkable Father.* New York: Harcourt, Brace and Co., 1959.

Howard, Ronald. *In Search of My Father: A Portrait of Leslie Howard.* New York: St. Martin's Press, 1981.

Howard, Sidney. *GONE WITH THE WIND: The Screenplay.* Edited by Herb Bridges and Terryl C. Boodman. New York: Dell Publishing, 1989.

———*GWTW: The Screenplay.* Edited by Richard Harwell. New York: Macmillan, 1980.

Jackson, Carlton. *The Life of Hattie McDaniel.* Lanham, MD: Madison Books, 1989.

Keyes, Evelyn. *I'll Think about That Tomorrow.* New York: NAL–Dutton, 1991.

———*Scarlett O'Hara's Younger Sister: My Lively Life in and out of Hollywood.* New York: Carol Publishing Group, 1977.

Lambert, Gavin. *GWTW: The Making of GONE WITH THE WIND.* Boston: Little, Brown & Co., 1973.

———*On Cukor.* New York: G. P. Putnam's Sons, 1972.

Lebow, Jan. *Fiddle-Dee-Dee . . . Fifty Years of Me: Scarlett Dolls by Madame Alexander.* Virginia Beach, VA: Jan Lebow, 1989.

———*The Fashion History of Alexander Scarlett O'Hara Dolls, 1937–1992, Volume 2.* Virginia Beach, VA: Jan Lebow, 1992.

McBean, Angus. *Vivien Leigh: A Love Affair in Camera.* Oxford: Phaidon, 1989.

McGilligan, Patrick. *George Cukor: A Double Life.* New York: St. Martin's Press, 1991.

Mitchell, Margaret. *Margaret Mitchell: A Dynamo Going to Waste—Letters to Allen Edee, 1919–1921.* Edited by Jane Bonner Peacock. Atlanta: Peachtree, 1985.

———*Margaret Mitchell's GONE WITH THE WIND Letters, 1936–1949.* Edited by Richard Harwell. New York: Macmillan, 1976.

Molt, Cynthia Marylee. *GONE WITH THE WIND on Film: A Complete Reference.* Jefferson, NC: McFarland & Co., 1990.

Myrick, Susan. *White Columns in Hollywood: Reports from the GWTW Sets.* Edited by Richard Harwell. Macon, GA: Mercer University Press, 1982.

Pfeifer, Diane. *Gone With the Grits: Gourmet Cookbook.* Atlanta: Strawberry Patch, 1992.

Pratt, William. *Scarlett Fever: The Ultimate Pictorial Treasury of GONE WITH THE WIND.* New York: Macmillan, 1977.

Pyron, Darden Asbury. *Southern Daughter: The Life of Margaret Mitchell.* New York: Oxford University Press, 1991.

————*Recasting: GONE WITH THE WIND in American Culture.* Gainesville, FL: University Presses of Florida, 1983.

Rome, Florence. *The Scarlett Letters.* New York: Random House, 1971.

Samuels, Charles. *The King.* New York: Coward–McCann, 1962.

Shavin, Norman and Austin McDermott. *Strange Tales of GONE WITH THE WIND.* Atlanta: Capricorn, 1980.

Shavin, Norman and Martin Sharter. *The Million Dollar Legends: Margaret Mitchell and GONE WITH THE WIND.* Atlanta: Capricorn, 1985.

Smith, Patricia. *The Collector's Encyclopedia of Madame Alexander Dolls, 1965–1990.* Paducah, KY: Collector Books, 1991.

Taylor, Helen. *Scarlett's Women: GONE WITH THE WIND and Its Female Fans.* New Brunswick, NJ: Rutgers University Press, 1989.

Taylor, John Russell. *Vivien Leigh.* New York: St. Martin's Press, 1984.

Thomas, Bob. *Selznick.* New York: Garland, 1985.

Thomas, Tony. *The Films of Olivia de Havilland.* New York: Carol Publishing Group, 1983.

Thomson, David. *Showman: The Life of David O. Selznick.* New York: Alfred A. Knopf, 1992.

Tornabene, Lyn. *Long Live the King: A Biography of Clark Gable.* New York: G. P. Putnam's Sons, 1976.

Turner, Adrian. *A Celebration of GONE WITH THE WIND.* New York: Smithmark, 1990.

Vance, Malcolm. *Tara Revisited.* New York: Universal–Award House, 1976.

Vickers, Hugo. *Vivien Leigh: A Biography.* Boston: Little, Brown and Co., Inc., 1989.

White, Sydney H. *Sidney Howard.* New York: Irvington, 1977.

Periodicals

The following periodicals can help collectors keep current with the changing field of collectibles.

The American Collectors Journal
PO Box 407
Kewanee, IL 61443
Phone: 308-852-2602
Bimonthly tabloid covering antiques and collectibles.

The Antique Trader Weekly
PO Box 1050
Dubuque, IA 52001
Phone: 319-588-2073
FAX: 319-588-0888
Weekly tabloid for collectors and dealers in antiques and collectibles featuring classified ads.

Antiques & Collecting Hobbies
Lightner Publishing Company
1006 South Michigan Avenue
Chicago, IL 60605
Phone: 312-939-4767
Monthly magazine featuring articles on collecting plus classified ads.

The Big Reel
3130 U.S. 220
Madison, NC 27025
Phone: 919-427-5850
FAX: 919-427-7372
Monthly tabloid featuring articles and reviews, information on auctions, plus classified ads for collectors of movie and television memorabilia. Specializes in 16-millimeter films.

Classic Images
PO Box 809
Muscatine, IA 52761
Phone: 319-263-2331
Monthly magazine featuring articles, news and photos about classic films plus classified ad section.

Collector Editions
Collector Communications Corp.
170 Fifth Avenue
New York, NY 10010
Phone: 212-989-8700
Bimonthly magazine containing features, secondary-market reports, new products, and a classified ad section for porcelain and glass collectibles.

Collectors News & The Antique Reporter
506 Second Street
Box 156
Grundy Center, IA 50638
Phone: 319-824-6981
FAX: 319-824-3414
A monthly tabloid covering antiques, collectibles, and nostalgic memorabilia.

Collectors' Showcase, America's Premier Collecting Magazine
Sports Magazines of America
#210
7130 South Lewis
Tulsa, OK 74136
Phone: 918-496-7405
FAX: 918-496-7485
Monthly magazine covering antique dolls, toys, advertising, and Americana.

Collectors United
PO Box 1160
Chatsworth, GA 30705
Phone: 706-695-8242
Monthly tabloid containing classified ads for collector dolls. Subscriptions and single copies available.

Doll Reader Magazine
Hobby House Press
900 Frederick Street
Cumberland, MD 21502
Phone: 301-759-3770
800-435-9610 (subscriptions)
Magazine published nine times a year, featuring articles, features, news, calendars of collectible shows, new products, classified ads, question-and-answer columns.

Dolls, The Collector's Magazine
Collector Communications Corp.
170 Fifth Avenue
New York, NY 10010
Phone: 212-989-8700
800-347-6969 (subscriptions)
Magazine published nine times a year, covering doll collecting for collectors of antique, contemporary, and reproduction dolls.

GONE WITH THE WIND Collector's Newsletter
PO Box 2072
Dublin, GA 31040-2072
Quarterly publication containing news and articles related to the book and film plus classified ads for a wide variety of collectibles. For information about placing an ad, contact John Wiley Jr., 1347 Greenmoss Drive, Richmond, VA 23225 and include a SASE.

The Illustrator Collector's News
PO Box 1958
Sequim, WA 98382
Phone: 206-683-2559
FAX: 206-683-9708
Bimonthly publication containing feature articles on collecting, news and reviews, information on auctions, plus classified ads for a wide variety of paper collectibles.

International Doll World, The Doll Lover's Magazine
House of White Birches
306 East Parr Road
Berne, IN 46711
Phone: 219-589-8741
FAX: 219-589-8093
Bimonthly magazine covering doll collecting and restoration.

Movie Collector World
PO Box 309
Fraser, MI 48026
Phone: 313-774-4311

FAX: 313-774-5450
Biweekly tabloid featuring articles and reviews, information on auctions, plus classified ads for collectors of movie and television memorabilia.

Nostalgia World for Collectors & Fans
PO Box 231
North Haven, CT 06473
Phone: 203-235-8072
Bimonthly magazine featuring profiles of collectors, and articles on collections and various collectibles, including movie and television memorabilia.

Paper Collectors Marketplace
Watson Graphic Designs, Inc.
470 Main Street
PO Box 128
Scandinavia, WI 54977-0128
Phone: 715-467-2379
Monthly magazine featuring articles on paper collectibles plus classified ads for collectors of ephemera.

Teddy Bear Review
Collector Communications Corp.
170 Fifth Avenue
New York, NY 10010
Phone: 212-989-8700
Quarterly magazine on teddy bears.

Treasure Chest
253 West 72nd Street, #211A
New York, NY 10023
Phone: 212-496-2234
Monthly magazine featuring articles on collectibles plus classified ads.

Yesteryear
Yesteryear Publications
PO Box 2
Princeton, WI 54968
Phone: 414-787-4808
Monthly tabloid for antique dealers and collectors, nostalgia buffs, people interested in collecting just about anything.

Organizations

These organizations help collectors keep in touch with those having similar interests.

Clark Gable Foundation
PO Box 65
Cadiz, OH 43907
(614-942-GWTW)
The organization, dedicated to keeping Clark Gable's spirit alive throughout the United States, publishes four newsletters a year and sponsors get-togethers in Clark Gable's hometown during the year.

Crescent Avenue Yacht Club
c/o Michael Motes
282 Kennesaw Avenue NW
Marietta, GA 30060-1636
404-429-8262
This organization meets regularly in the Atlanta area for discussions about Margaret Mitchell, *Gone With the Wind,* and collecting.

The Madame Alexander Doll Club
PO Box 330
Mundelein, IL 60060-0330
The Club encourages research and preservation of Madame Alexander dolls, sponsors symposia and an annual convention, publishes four newsletters a year and six shoppers (listing classified ads for dolls).

Universal Autograph Collectors Club
PO Box 6181
Washington, DC 20044-6181
UACC is the largest organization in the world for autograph collectors. Members receive a 48-page, bimonthly journal, *The Pen and Quill,* containing articles about autograph collecting and free classified ads from members.

Suppliers

The following companies specialize in "collection protection" and offer catalogs of their products.

All Wood Products
171 East Payson Street
Azusa, CA 91702
Phone: 818-334-1766
Specialties: Oak, cherry, or maple frames to hold one, two, five, eight, nine, or thirteen collector plates. Glass-front option for some models is available.

Bags Unlimited, Inc.
7 Canal Street
Rochester, NY 14608
Phone: 716-436-9006
800-767-BAGS (orders)
FAX: 716-328-8526
Specialties: Acid-free bags, backings, and boxes for protection and preservation of a wide variety of collectibles.

Briant & Sons
7821 South Highway 97
Redmond, OR 97756
Phone: 503-923-1473
Specialties: Springless-stretcher plate hangers available in leaf or fleur-de-lis pattern with brilliant-brass, antique-brass, or silver-nickel finishes.

Brodart Company
500 Arch Street
Williamsport, PA 17705
Phone: 717-326-2461
800-233-8467 (orders)
Specialties: Acid-free products for document preservation, including storage boxes, files, envelopes, sheet protectors, folders, binders, photo and slide storage, and more.

DEMCO, INC.
PO Box 7488
Madison, WI 53707-7488
Phone: 608-241-1201
800-356-1200 (orders)
FAX: 800-245-1329
Specialties: Acid-free products for document preservation, including storage boxes, cases, files, envelopes, sheet protectors, folders, binders, photo and slide storage, record sleeves, and more.

Document Preservation Center
Postal 821
Yonkers, NY 10702
Phone: 914-476-8500
Specialties: Acid-free products for document preservation, including print protectors, polyethylene bags, ring binders, photo binders, garment and document briefcases, envelopes, boxes, folders, and more.

Easels by Amron
PO Box 9338
San Rafael, CA 94912-9338
Phone: 800-553-4438
Specialties: Wall-mounted, wood-veneer display cases with Plexiglas fronts, plus metal-plate easels and wall hangers.

The Enchanted Doll House
Operations Center
PO Box 1617
Manchester, CT 06045-1617
Phone: 203-646-5008
800-243-9110 (orders)
FAX: 203-645-0504
Specialties: Accessories for dolls, including stands, dust covers, glass domes on fruitwood bases.

Larry E. Krein Company
3725 Portland Avenue South
PO Box 7126
Minneapolis, MN 55407
Phone: 612-824-9422
Specialties: Polyethylene open-ended and reclosable bags, backing boards, custom-made display albums with bound-in pages, acid-free paper inserts for albums.

Lynette Decor
1559 West Embassy Street
Anaheim, CA 92802
Phone: 714-956-2161
Specialties: Decorative square plate frames

in gold, walnut, or walnut with gold trim; holds 7^1/$_2$" to 8^1/$_2$" plates.

Oak Originals
14534 Lowe
Riverdale, IL 60627
Phone: 708-849-6068
Specialties: Handcrafted oak plate racks and shelves. Racks are available in horizontal and vertical designs. Finishes available: light, dark, unfinished. Doll cases with oak base and mirrored back.

Pack & Wrap
466 Derby Avenue
West Haven, CT 06516
Phone: 203-389-1983
800-541-9782 (orders)
FAX: 203-389-9416
Specialties: Polyethylene open-end and re-closable bags in a wide range of sizes, packaging and shipping supplies.

Plate Racks International, Inc.
4819 NE 12th Avenue
Fort Lauderdale, FL 33334
Phone: 305-491-2411
Specialties: Vertical brass plate racks and holders.

Putnam Distributors
PO Box 477
Westfield, NJ 07091
Phone: 908-232-9200
Specialties: Plate frames, two sizes available, fitting 7" to 9" plates or 9" to 11" plates. Finishes available: antique gold, oak, walnut with gold.

Sapir Studios
1215 West Devon
Chicago, IL 60660
Phone: 312-465-0066
FAX: 312-465-3465
Specialties: Clear-acrylic, single-piece construction plate stands.

Show-Plate Designs
5025-B Swenson Road
Deer Park, WA 99006
Phone: 509-276-5498
Specialties: Solid-oak plate frames and rails:

two-plate horizontal safety rail, four-plate vertical or horizontal frame, one-plate full frame, one-plate expandable frame. Patented spring mechanism expands to fit plates from 4" to 10^1/$_2$" in diameter.

Talsco of Florida
5427 Crafts Street
New Port Richey, FL 34652
Phone: 813-847-6370
Specialties: Modular, hexagon-shaped plate cases in oak, walnut, pecan, or antique gold finish with velvet liner, various sizes. Glass display cases in various sizes with wood frame in oak, walnut, or cherry finish; mirrored back available.

Through the Looking Glass
Division of Mechanical Mirror Works, Inc.
27-02 First Street
Long Island City, NY 11102
Phone: 718-204-0200
Specialties: Glass étagère, 20" by 10" by 68", with mirror and brass accents.

Under the Lilac
10101 Balsamwood Drive
Laurel, MD 20708-3153
Phone: 301-725-3655
Specialties: Adjustable doll and bear stands.

Universal Traders
4014 Birch Haven Drive
Kingwood, TX 77339
Phone: 713-360-3937
Specialties: Invisible plate hanger, an adhesive disc that sticks to the back of a glazed or unglazed plate. Holds plate flat to the wall. Each pack contains five different sizes: 1^1/$_4$", 2", 3", 4", and 5^1/$_2$" discs.

Van Hygan & Smythe
1735 South Marshall Drive
Des Plaines, IL 60018
Phone: 708-966-2325
Specialties: Limited-edition plate frames, shadow boxes, rails, hang-ups, storage boxes. Display cabinets for limited-edition plates and music boxes. Museum-edition doll cases.

Woodlore Craftsman
6837 SE Cottrell Road
Gresham, OR 97080
Phone: 503-663-2096
Specialties: Knotty pine or oak plate rails
and shelves. Finishes available: Danish
walnut stain on oak or pine, wheat stain
on oak, unfinished.

Worldwide Collectibles & Gifts
2 Lakeside Avenue
Berwyn, PA 19312-0158
Phone: 215-644-2442

800-222-1613 (orders)
Specialties: Fruitwood plate frames with
gold pin stripe for a range of plate sizes
from 4″ to 10¹/₂″.

Xenium
263 Riverside Drive
Northfield, IL 60093
Phone: 708-446-4830
800-888-4654 (orders)
Specialties: Collectible floor lamp, 21″ by
22″ by 60″, made of beveled, tempered
glass with fruitwood base.

Inventory Sheet

Type of Collectible and Description: _____

_____

Collection Number: _____

Condition: _____

Title: _____

Artist: _____

Producer: _____

Series/Year: _____

Number: _____

Issue Price: _____

Purchased/Received From: _____

Purchase Price: _____

Date: _____

Sold/Given To: _____

Selling Price: _____

Date: _____

Market/Appraisal Value: _____

Notes/Comments: _____

_____

_____

_____

VIII

The Ins and Outs of Buying by Mail

SHOPPING by mail can be a fun and convenient way of adding items to your collection. Keep in mind, though, that occasional hassles do occur. If you're new to mail-order buying, take a few minutes to read this section. You may save yourself time and money.

Catalogs—Frequency and Cost

Most mail-order companies publish written materials describing their merchandise. The materials can be simple photocopied single-sheet price lists, modest leaflets, and brochures or sophisticated, multicolor catalogs. Some companies update their materials every few months, every year, or every few years. Usually materials are dated, so you will know if you have a current catalog.

Many companies offer free catalogs. A few request that you send a business-sized (#10) self-addressed, stamped envelope (SASE) to receive their information. Still others charge a catalog fee. Some firms that charge a fee allow you to apply the cost of the catalog to your order, and this has been indicated in the section on sources.

To order a free catalog, write or telephone the company with your request. If you telephone, please *do not* use the company's toll-free number. This number is strictly for merchandise orders. If you

write, send a letter indicating the catalog you want (in case the firm offers several) and remember to print or type your complete return address. Enclose a SASE if the company requests one.

Requests for catalogs that require a fee must be in writing and prepaid. Send a check—never cash or stamps—along with your letter and be sure that your name and address are legible.

Getting a Price Quote

Many companies listed in this book have thousands of items in their inventories. Catalog items sometimes represent only a small percentage of the inventory, and stock can change frequently, especially with one-of-a-kind items. To offer customers up-to-the-minute information on available items, these companies quote prices to those who call or write.

Maybe you are interested in getting a price quote on an original 1967 reissue *Gone With the Wind* poster. Just call or write the company, give the specifics of the item, and they'll tell you if they have it and how much they are selling it for. If you write, remember to include a SASE to make it easy for the company to respond.

Some companies even maintain a "want" system. If the company doesn't have the desired item, they will keep a record of your request. When the item becomes available, they will notify you with a price quote.

Comparison Shopping

Your prime consideration should be the bottom-line price of an item. Compare your price quotes and/or catalog prices to determine the delivered cost of the product (including shipping, handling, taxes). Also factor in the various return policies, warranties, or guarantees made by the companies. Once you've compared the costs and the variables, you'll be able to decide which company gives you the best deal.

Ways to Pay

The acceptable methods of payment are indicated in each company's listing in this book. The key to the symbols is as follows:

AE – American Express
AEO – American Express/Optima
C – personal check (The company may wait several days for the check to clear before shipping your order.)
CC – cashier's check/certified check (Your bank may charge a nominal fee for such checks.)
CB – Carte Blanche
COD – cash on delivery
D – Discover
DC – Diner's Club
MC – Mastercard
MO – money order (Money orders are available at banks and post offices for a nominal fee.)
V – Visa

Shipping

Most of the items offered by companies in this book will be shipped either by United Parcel Service (UPS) or by the United States Postal Service (USPS). The USPS can ship via First Class, Registered Mail, or Parcel Post. If your address is a post office box, the only way packages can be sent to you is by Parcel Post. Make sure you mark your order "Deliver by Parcel Post Only."

Depending upon the value of the ordered item, some companies send packages via Registered Mail. This is more costly than Parcel Post delivery, but because you sign for the package, the company knows that the item was received.

If you are in a hurry to receive your order, you may wish to pay extra for Federal Express Delivery or Express Mail through USPS. Many companies offer these delivery alternatives.

Return Policies

Each listing in this book provides information about the company's return policy. Return policies can vary from "Absolutely no returns" to "Return at any time for the life of the product." Most companies fall somewhere in between, offering the customer the opportunity to return an item for refund or exchange up to thirty days after receipt. Make sure you understand the company's specific policy before you order.

Tips for Successful Buying
By Mail

1. Find the order blank in the company's catalog.

2. Use the self-sticking address label if one is provided on the catalog. If a label is not provided, print your name and address clearly.

3. Copy onto the order form all the pertinent information: catalog number, name of the item, number of items ordered, unit price, extension price, tax, shipping, handling charges. Keep in mind any minimum-order requirements.

4. Indicate method of payment. If you are sending a check or money order, be sure it is made out correctly and signed as appropriate. If you are authorizing a charge to your credit card, make sure the card number is transcribed correctly and that you include the expiration date and your signature.

5. Make a copy of the order before you mail it and keep the copy with the catalog. Indicate on the copy, the number of the check or money order that was used in payment.

By Telephone

1. Complete the order form as indicated in #3 above.

2. Have in front of you a credit card that is accepted by the company. Make sure the card is current and has a sufficient line of credit for the purchase.

3. Have the catalog handy in case the operator asks for page numbers of ordered items or encoded information on the address label.

4. After placing the order, ask for the grand total that will be charged to your credit account and compare this to the figure you calculated. Note on the order form the operator's name and the date you placed the order.

Second Choices and Substitutions

Some companies often recommend that you indicate a second choice when you order. If you've ordered a red *Gone With the Wind* mug, for example, and the company has sold out of all the red mugs, they will send the green mug you indicated as a second choice. The product is the same, but the color is different.

Other companies, especially those dealing with one-of-a-kind items, recommend that you indicate a second choice in case a substitution is necessary. In your order, you might indicate that your first choice is an autographed photograph of Vivien Leigh in the burgundy velvet dress. But by the time your order arrives, that item has been sold. The company can then fill your order with your second choice—a lobby card autographed by Vivien Leigh. If the company considers the lobby card comparable to the photograph, they can make this substitution but only if you have given your permission.

If you don't want a green mug when you ordered a red mug, or a lobby card when you ordered a photograph, write on the order form or tell the operator that no second choices or substitutions will be accepted.

How to Resolve Problems

Although most companies strive to get your complete order to you quickly, some-times problems occur. Here are the most common and what you can do about them:

1. The item you ordered sold out, and the company needs time to restock the merchandise.

The Federal Trade Commission established the Mail Order Rule in 1975 to help consumers with this problem. The rule states that a company must ship your merchandise within thirty days after receiving your order or advise you that there will be a delay. The company is bound by this rule unless the catalog specifically states that the shipment of goods, for example, custom-made clothing, will take longer. If the company cannot ship your order within thirty days, they must send you an option notice.

The option notice indicates the revised shipping date and offers you the choice of accepting the delay or canceling the order and receiving a refund. If the delay is fine, you don't have to do anything. If the delay is a problem and you decide to cancel the order, you must notify the company. The company is required to provide you with a cost-free method to do this, either a prepaid postcard, business-reply envelope, collect call, or an 800-telephone number.

Once you've canceled the order, the Rule states that you are entitled to a prompt refund. If you sent a check with your order, the company must send to you by first-class mail a refund check within seven business days. If you charged the order to your credit card, the company must credit your account within one billing cycle.

Please note that many states and counties have passed laws similar to the FTC Mail Order Rule. If those laws offer the consumer more protection, the state or local laws take precedence.

2. The package arrived damaged.

Check the contents immediately to determine if the merchandise is damaged. Most parcels can take a beating while still protecting the valuable contents. If the merchandise is damaged, see the steps outlined in #3 below.

3. The package was fine, but the collector's plate you ordered was in pieces.

Call the company right away to report the condition in which the item arrived and follow the instructions you are given about returning the merchandise. Most companies will ask you to enclose a note in the package describing the problem, rewrap the parcel, and mail it back to the company by insured or registered mail. Some companies assign a return-authorization number that must appear on the parcel before they will accept a return. Ask the company if you will be reimbursed for the return postage.

4. The merchandise is unsatisfactory.

You could be disappointed with your order for other reasons: the tee-shirt just isn't you; the doll is different than pictured in the catalog; the custom-made Confederate uniform is a perfect fit, but the company forgot to make the buttonholes. Check the company's return policy to determine your next step. Most companies want you to be satisfied and will allow you to return or to exchange unsatisfactory items. If there is the possibility that you will return items, keep the packaging materials and any receipts that accompanied the order.

5. Your check was cashed, but the order never arrived.

Notify the company by telephone and follow up the conversation with a letter and *copies* of both your order and the canceled check. Reputable companies will replace orders that have gone astray or offer you a refund. If the company does not send the merchandise or the refund, you can take action. File a complaint with your local postmaster, the Postmaster General, or the Better Business Bureau. Your state attorney general's office or the Federal Trade Commission may be able to help, too.

Bibliography

Ahearn, Allen. *Book Collecting: A Comprehensive Guide.* New York: G. P. Putnam's Sons, 1989.

Ball, Joanne Dubbs. *Jewelry of the Stars: Creations from Joseff of Hollywood.* West Chester, PA: Schiffer Publishing, 1991.

Bartel, Pauline. *The Complete GONE WITH THE WIND Trivia Book.* Dallas: Taylor Publishing Co., 1989.

Chaneles, Sol. *Collecting Movie Memorabilia.* New York: Arco Publishing Co., 1977.

Crittenden, Alan, ed. *Hidden Treasures.* Novato, CA: Union Square Books, 1985.

De Thuin, Richard. *Movie Memorabilia.* New York: House of Collectibles, 1990.

Fendelman, Helaine, and Jeri Schwartz in collaboration with Beverly Jacobson. *Money in Your Attic.* New York: Monarch Press, 1985.

Frankel, Betsy, ed. *The Encyclopedia of Collectibles.* Alexandria, VA: Time–Life Books, 1978.

Gottlieb, Richard, ed. *Directory of Mail Order Catalogs IV,* 4th revised edition. Sharon, CT: Grey House Publishing, 1989.

Hechtlinger, Adelaide, and Wilbur Cross. *The Complete Book of Paper Antiques.* New York: Coward, McCann & Geoghegan, 1972.

Hughes, Stephen. *Pop Culture Mania.* New York: McGraw Hill, 1984.

Ketchum, William C., Jr., *Auction!* New York: Sterling Publishing, 1980.

Lebow, Jan. *The Fashion History of Alexander Scarlett O'Hara Dolls 1937–1992, Volume 2.* Virginia Beach, VA: Jan Lebow, 1992.

LeFontaine, Joseph Raymond. *Turning Paper to Gold.* White Hall, VA: Betterway Publications, 1988.

Liman, Ellen. *The Collecting Book.* New York: Penguin, 1980.

Matthews, Jack. *Collecting Rare Books for Pleasure and Profit.* New York: G. P. Putnam's Sons, 1977.

Miller, Lowell, and Prudence McCullough. *The Wholesale-by-Mail Catalog,* 13th revised and updated edition. New York: HarperCollins, 1991.

Morella, Joe, Edward Z. Epstein, Eleanor Clark. *Those Great Movie Ads.* New Rochelle, NY: Arlington House, 1972.

The National Directory of Catalogs. New York: Oxbridge Comm., 1991.

Palder, Edward L. *Catalog of Catalogs II: The Complete Mail Order Directory.* Rockville, MD: Woodbine House, 1990.

Roberts, Ralph. *Auction Action!* Blue Ridge Summit, PA: Tab Books, 1986.

Sanders, George, Helen Sanders, Ralph Roberts. *The Price Guide to Autographs.* Radnor, PA: Wallace–Homestead, 1988.

Stark, Paul. *Limited Edition Collectibles: Everything You May Ever Need to Know.* Wilkes Barre, PA: New Gallery Press, 1988.

Tannen, Jack. *How to Identify and Collect American First Editions.* New York: Arco Publishing, 1976.

Wilson, Robert A. *Modern Book Collecting.* New York: Alfred A. Knopf, 1980.

Order Form

I would like to order the following books by Pauline Bartel:

The Complete GONE WITH THE WIND Trivia Book
$9.95 + $2.00 shipping. _____

The Complete GONE WITH THE WIND Sourcebook
$14.95 + $2.00 shipping. _____

Please make your check payable and mail to:
Taylor Publishing Co.
Attn: Order Dept.
1550 W. Mockingbird Ln.
Dallas, TX 75235

Name: _____

Address: _____

_____

_____